Peter Beckford

Thoughts Upon Hare and Fox Hunting

In a Series of Letters to a Friend

Peter Beckford

Thoughts Upon Hare and Fox Hunting
In a Series of Letters to a Friend

ISBN/EAN: 9783337169695

Printed in Europe, USA, Canada, Australia, Japan

Cover: Foto ©Andreas Hilbeck / pixelio.de

More available books at **www.hansebooks.com**

THOUGHTS

UPON

HARE AND FOX

HUNTING,

IN A

SERIES OF LETTERS TO A FRIEND,

IN WHICH ARE GIVEN

AMPLE DIRECTIONS FOR ERECTING A KENNEL, THE
MANAGEMENT OF HOUNDS, AND THE DUTIES
AND QUALIFICATIONS NECESSARY FOR
THE HUNTSMAN AND WHIPPER-IN.

ALSO

AN ACCOUNT

OF THE

Most Celebrated Dog Kennels in the Kingdom.

Illustrated with twenty beautiful Engravings.

By PETER BECKFORD, Esq.

———————— Si quid novisti rectius istis,
Candidus imperti : si non, his utere mecum.　　Hor.

A NEW EDITION.

LONDON:

PRINTED FOR VERNOR AND HOOD, BIRCHIN LANE,
CORNHILL. 1796.

THE Publifhers of the prefent Edition of this much-admired *Treatife upon Hunting* feel themfelves impelled to ftate candidly, but briefly, the motives which induced them to undertake it.

That moft fportfmen who were not already poffeffed of the former editions of this valuable *library of fporting knowledge*, have been defirous of procuring it, but fought for it in vain, is a fact well known to every frequenter of the chace; the book, therefore, meets the public eye in its prefent embellifhed ftate, in confequence of repeated folicitations from gentlemen in almoft every quarter of the kingdom, accompanied with well-grounded affurances from many of them, that it would by no means be difagreeable to Mr. Beckford.

Confcious of not being able to add to the literary fame which the writer has acquired by this publication, they have confined themfelves merely to the decorative, inferting only fuch explanatory defcriptions of the plates as appeared neceffary.

On the whole, they truft, that without giving any offence to the ingenious author, (the idea of which would be painful to them) they have contributed not a little to the gratification of every admirer of the cheerful and manly amufements of the field.

PREFACE.

AS the author of the following letters hath been charged with inhumanity, and yet conjectured to be a clergyman, it is now become neceſſary to publiſh his name; and though it may not be uſual to anſwer an anonymous writer, yet, as it is not impoſſible that ſome readers may have adopted his ſentiments, this conſideration, and this alone, induces the author to anſwer the objections which the critic hath ſo wantonly made. Whatever may be the imperfection of theſe letters, the author is deſirous that it ſhould fall, as it ought, upon himſelf only. The objections, which he thinks were unneceſſarily made, he has endeavoured to remove. All intentional cruelty

he

he entirely difclaims. His appeal from that accufation lies to thofe whom he addreffes as his judges; not (as the critic may think) becaufe they are equally barbarous with himfelf, but becaufe fportfmen only are competent to decide.

CONTENTS.

LETTER IV.   Page 37.

LETTER V.   Page 53.

LETTER VI.   Page 76.

LETTER VII.   Page 86.

LET-

LETTER VIII. Page 107.

Of difeafes and their remedies—A curious prefcription for the cure of the mange, either in man or beaft—Obfervations on madnefs.

LETTER IX. Page 122.

Of the huntfman and whipper-in—Obfervations on fcent.

LETTER X. Page 133.

Hare-hunting defcribed in all its parts—Of hounds beft fuited to that diverfion—Of the beft method of hunting them—-Sportfmen not intentionally cruel—Of the trial in a morning—Of hare finders—-A particular method of hare-hunting related—Curious advice about dreffing a hare.

LETTER XI. Page 145.

Hare-hunting continued—The many fhifts which a hare makes defcribed—A hint to fuch fportfmen as continue talking when their hounds are at fault—Chopping hares cenfured; directions how to prevent it—Of the harmony of a pack—A hint to fuch fportfmen as ride over their hounds.

LET-

LETTER XVI. Page 191.

LETTER XVII. Page 199.

LETTER XVIII. Page 209.

LET-

LETTER XXI. Page 266.

LETTER XXII. Page 278.

LETTER XXIII. Page 295.

LET-

LETTER XXIV.   Page 309.

DIREC-

DIRECTIONS to the BINDER,

FOR PLACING THE

C U T S.

THOUGHTS

UPON

HUNTING.

———

LETTER I.

Briftol Hot-Wells, March 20, 1779.

YOU could not have chofen, my friend, a better feafon than the prefent, to remind me of fending you my Thoughts upon Hunting; for the accident that brought me hither is likely to detain me fome time: befides, I have no longer a plea for not obeying your commands. Hitherto, indeed, I had excufed myfelf, in hopes that fome publication on the fubject might have rendered thefe letters needlefs; but fince nothing of the kind, although fo much wanted, has appeared, as I am now fufficiently unoccupied to undertake the tafk, I fhall not think it a tri-

B   fling

fling fubject, if you think it a neceffary one; and I wifh my own experience of the diverfion may enable me to anfwer the many queftions which you are pleafed to propofe concerning it. ·

Knowing your partiality to rhyme, I could wifh to fend you my thoughts in verfe; but as this would take up more time, without anfwering your purpofe better, I muft beg you to accept them in humble profe, which, in my opinion, is better fuited to the fubject. Didactic effays fhould be as little clogged as poffible; they fhould proceed regularly and clearly; fhould be eafily written, and as eafily underftood, having lefs to do with words than things. The game of *crambo* is out of fafhion, to the no fmall prejudice of the rhyming tribe; and before I could find a rhyme to *porringer*, I fhould hope to finifh a great part of thefe letters: I fhall therefore, without farther delay, proceed upon them: this, however, I muft defire to be firft underftood between us; that when, to fave trouble to us both, I fay a thing *is*, without tacking a falvo to the tail of it, fuch as, *in my opinion—to the beft of my judgment*, &c. &c.—you fhall not call my humility in queftion, as the affertion is not meant to be mathematically certain. When I have any better authority than my own, fuch as Somervile, for inftance, (who, by the bye, is the only one that has written intelligibly on this fubject) I

fhall

fhall take the liberty of giving it you in his own words, to fave you the trouble of turning to him.

You may remember, perhaps, that when we were hunting together at Turin, the hounds having loft the ftag, and the piqueurs (ftill more in fault than they) being ignorant which way to try, the king bid them afk *Milord Anglois.* Nor is it to be wondered at, if an Englifhman fhould be thought to underftand the art of hunting, as the hounds which this country produces are univerfally allowed to be the beft in the world: from whence I think this inference may be drawn, that although every man who follows this diverfion may not underftand it, yet it is extraordinary of the many who do, that one only of any note fhould have written on the fubject. It is rather unfortunate for me that this ingenious fportfman fhould have preferred writing an elegant poem to an ufeful leffon; fince, if it had pleafed him, he might eafily have faved me the trouble of writing thefe letters. Is it not ftrange in a country where the prefs is in one continued labour with opinions of almoft every kind, from the moft ferious and inftructive to the moft ridiculous and trifling; a country befides, fo famous for the beft hounds, and the beft horfes to follow them, whofe authors fometimes hunt, and whofe fportf-men fometimes write, that only the practical part

of

of hunting fhould be known? There is, however, no doubt that the practical part of it would
be improved, were it to be accompanied by
theory.

France, Germany, and Italy, are alfo filent,
I believe, on this fubject, though each of thefe
countries has had its fportfmen. Foxes, it is
true, they never hunt, and hares but feldom;
yet the ftag and wild boar, both in France and in
Germany, are ftill purfued with the utmoft fplen-
dour and magnificence. In Italy there has been
no hunting fince the death of the Duke of Par-
ma: he was very fond of it, and I apprehend all
hunting in that country ceafed with him. The
only fportfmen now remaining are gentlemen in
green coats, who taking their *couteaux de chaffe*
along with them, walk into the fields to catch
fmall birds, which they call *andar a la caccia*, or,
in plain Englifh, *going a hunting*; yet it has not
been fo with horfemanfhip; *that* has been treated
fcientifically by all—in Italy by Pignatelli—in
Germany by Ifenbourg—and in France by La
Gueriniere: nor are the ufeful leffons of the
Duke of Newcaftle confined to this country only;
they are both read and practifed every where;
nor is *he* the *only* noble lord who has written on
the fubject. While upon hunting, all are filent,
and were it not for the mufe of Somervile, who
has fo judicioufly and fo fweetly fung, the dog,

that

that ufeful, that honeft, that faithful, that difin-
tereſted, that entertaining animal, would be
fuffered to pafs unnoticed and undiftinguiſhed.

A northern court once, indeed, did honour
this animal with a particular mark of approbation and refpeſt; but the fidelity of the dog has
fince given place to the fagacity of the ele-
phant.* Naturalifts, it is true, have included
dogs in the fpecific defcriptions they have given
us of animals. Authors may have written on
hunting, and bookſellers may know many that
to fportfinen are unknown; but I again repeat,
that I know not any writer, ancient or modern,
from the time of Nimrod to the prefent day (one
only excepted) who has given any ufeful information to a fportfman.†

It may be objeſted, that the hunting of a
pack of hounds depends upon the huntfman, and
that the huntfman, generally fpeaking, is an il-
literate fellow, who feldom can either read or
write: this cannot well be denied. I muft,
therefore, obferve, that it is impoffible for the
bufinefs of a kennel to go on as it ought, unlefs

* Vide Mr. Pope's Letter to Mr. Cromwell.

† Many French authors have given rules for hunting the
hare, and ftag; to make this paffage lefs exceptionable, therefore, it may be better perhaps, inftead of *fportfman*, to read
fox-hunter.

B 3

the

the master himself knows something of it. There must be an understanding somewhere, and without it no gentleman can enjoy in perfection this noble diversion.

It was the opinion of a great sportsman, that it is not less difficult to find a perfect huntsman, than a good prime minister. Without taking upon me to determine what requisites may be necessary to form a good prime minister, I will describe some of those which are essentially necessary towards forming a perfect huntsman; qualities which, I will venture to say, would not disgrace more brilliant situations: such as a clear head, nice observation, quick apprehension, undaunted courage, strength of constitution, activity of body, a good ear, and a good voice.

There is not any one branch of knowledge, commonly dignified with the title of art, which has not such rudiments or principles, as may lead to a competent degree of skill, if not to perfection, in it: whilst hunting, the sole business of some, and the amusement of most of the youth in this kingdom, seems left entirely to chance. Its pursuit puts us, both to greater expence, and also, to greater inconvenience than any other; yet, notwithstanding this, we trust our diversion in it to the sole guidance of a huntsman: we follow just as he shall chuse to conduct us; and

we

we fuffer the fuccefs, or difappointment of the chace to depend folely on the judgment of a fellow, who is frequently a greater brute than the creature on which he rides. I would not be underftood to mean by this, that a huntfman fhould be a fcholar, or that every gentleman fhould hunt his own hounds: it is not neceffary a huntfman fhould be a man of letters; but give me leave to obferve, that had he the beft underfianding, he would frequently find opportunities of exercifing it, and intricacies which might put it to the teft. You will fay, perhaps, there is fomething too laborious in the occupation of a huntfman for a gentleman to take it upon himfelf; you may alfo think it is beneath him; I agree with you in both—yet I hope that he may have leave to underftand it. If he follow the diverfion, it is a fign of his liking it; and if he like it, furely it is fome difgrace to him to be ignorant of the means moft conducive to obtain it.

I find there will be no neceffity to fay much in commendation of a diverfion to you, which you fo profeffedly admire;* it would be needlefs,

there-

---

* Since the above was written, hunting has undergone a fevere cenfure, (vide Monthly Review for September, 1781) nor will any thing fatisfy the critic lefs than its total abolition. He recommends feats of agility to be practifed and exhibited inftead of it. Whether the amendment propofed by the learned

B 4 gentle-

therefore, to enumerate the heroes of antiquity who were taught the art of hunting; or the many great men (among whom was the famous Galen) who have united in recommending it. I shall, however, remind you, that your beloved hero, Henry the Fourth of France, made it his chief amufement, and his very love letters, ftrange as it may appear, are full of little elfe: and that one of the greateft minifters which our own country ever produced, was fo fond of this diverfion, that the firft letter he opened, as I have been told, was generally that of his huntfman.—In moft countries, from the earlieft times, hunting has been a principal occupation of the people, either for ufe or amufement; and many princes have made it their chief delight: a circumftance which occafioned the following *bon mot*.—Louis the Fifteenth was fo paffionately fond of this diverfion, that it occupied him entirely; the King of Pruffia, who never hunts, gives up a great deal of his time to mufic, and himfelf plays on the flute: a German, laft war meeting a French-

gentleman be defirable or not, I fhall forbear to determine; taking the liberty, however, to remind him, that as hunting hath ftood its ground from the earlieft times, been encouraged and approved by the beft authorities, and practifed by the greateft men, it cannot now be fuppofed to dread criticifm, or to need fupport. Hunting originates in nature itfelf, and it is in perfect correfpondence to this law of nature, that the feveral animals are provided with neceffary means of attack and defence.

man,

man, afked him very impertinently, "*Si fon maitre*
"*chaffoit toujours?*" "*Oui, oui*," replied the other
—"*il ne joue jamais de la flute.*"—The reply was
excellent, but it would have been as well, perhaps, for mankind, if that great man had never
been otherwife employed.—Hunting is the foul
of a country life; it gives health to the body,
and contentment to the mind; and is one of the
few pleafures we can enjoy in fociety, without
prejudice either to ourfelves, or our friends.

The Spectator has drawn with infinite humour
the character of a man who paffes his whole life
in purfuit of trifles; and it is probable, other
Will Wimbles might ftill be found. I hope,
however, that he did not think they were confined to the country only. Triflers there are of
every denomination. Are we not all triflers?
and are we not told that all is vanity?—The
Spectator, without doubt, felt great compaffion
for Mr. Wimble; yet Mr. Wimble might not
have been a proper object of it; fince it is more
than probable he was a happy man, if the employment of his time in obliging others, and
pleafing himfelf, can be thought to have made
him fo.—Whether vanity miflead us or not in the
choice of our purfuits, the pleafures or advantages which refult from them, will beft determine.
—I fear the occupation of few gentlemen will
admit of nice fcrutiny; occupations, therefore,
that

that amufe, and are at the fame time innocent;
that promote exercife and conduce to health;
though they may appear trifles in the eyes of
others, certainly are not fo to thofe who enjoy
them. Of this number I think I may reckon
hunting, and I am particularly glad the fame
author furnifhes a quotation in fupport of it;
" for my own part," fays this elegant writer, " I
" intend to hunt twice a week during my ftay
" with Sir Roger; and fhall prefcribe the mo-
" derate ufe of this exercife to all my country
" friends, as the beft phyfic for mending a bad
" conftitution, and preferving a good one."—
The inimitable Cervantes alfo honourably men-
tions this diverfion: he makes Sancho fay —
" Mercy on me, what pleafure can you find, any
" of ye all, in killing a poor beaft that never
" meant any harm!" that the Duke may reply,
" —You are miftaken, Sancho; hunting wild
" beafts is the moft proper exercife for knights
" and princes; for in the chace of a ftout noble
" beaft, may be reprefented the whole art of
" war, ftratagems, policy, and ambufcades, with
" all other devices ufually practifed to overcome
" an enemy with fafety. Here we are expofed
" to the extremities of heat and cold; cafe and
" lazinefs can have no room in this diverfion;
" by this we are inured to toil and hardfhip, our
" limbs are ftrengthened, our joints made fupple,
" and our whole body hale and active: in fhort,

" it

" it is an exercise that may be beneficial to many,
" and can be prejudicial to none."—Small, indeed, is the number of those, who in the course
of 5000 years have employed themselves in the
advancement of useful knowledge. Mankind
have been bleft with but one Titus, that we
know of; and, it is to be feared, he has had but
few imitators. Days and years fly away, nor is
any account taken of them, and how many may
reasonably be suppofed to pass without affording
even amusement to others, or fatisfaction to ourselves. Much more, I think, might be faid in
favour of the Wimbles; but it muft be confeffed,
that the man who fpends his whole time in trifles,
paffes it contemptibly, compared with thofe who
are employed in refearches after knowledge ufeful
to mankind, or in profeffions ufeful to the ftate.

I am glad to find that you approve of the plan
I propofe to obferve in the courfe of thefe letters,
wherein it fhall be my endeavour not to omit
any thing which it may be neceffary for you to
know; at leaft, as far as my own obfervation
and experience will give me leave. The experience I have had may be of ufe to you at prefent; others, perhaps, hereafter may write more
judicioufly and more fully on the fubject: you
know it is my intereft to wifh they would. The
few who have written on hunting, refer you to
their predeceffors for great part of the information
tion

tion you might expect from them; and who their predeceffors were I have yet to learn. Even Somervile is lefs copious than I could wifh, and has purpofely omitted what is not to be found elfewhere; I mean receipts for the cure of fuch difeafes as hounds are fubject to. He holds fuch information cheap, and beneath his lofty mufe. Profe has no excufe, and you may depend on every information that I can give. The familiar manner in which my thoughts will be conveyed to you in thefe letters, may fufficiently evince the intention of the author. They are written with no other defign than to be of ufe to fportf-men. Were my aim to amufe, I would not endeavour to inftruct. A fong might fuit the purpofe better than an effay. To improve health by promoting exercife; to excite gentlemen who are fond of hunting to obtain the knowledge neceffary to enjoy it in perfection; and to leffen the punifhments which are too often inflicted on an animal fo friendly to man, are the chief ends intended by the following letters.

I fhall not pretend to lay down rules which are to be equally good in every country; I fhall think myfelf fufficiently juftified in recommending fuch as have been tried with fuccefs in the countries where I have generally hunted. As almoft every country has a different dialect, you will alfo excufe, I hope, any terms that may not

be

be current with *you:* I will take the beſt care I can that the number ſhall be ſmall. I need not, I think, adviſe you not to adopt too eaſily the opinions of other men. You will hear a tall man ſay it is folly to ride any but large horſes; and every little man in company will immediately ſell his little horſes, buy ſuch as he can hardly mount, and ride them in hilly countries, for which they are totally unfit. Pride induces ſome men to dictate; indolence makes others like to be dictated to; ſo both parties find their account in it. You will not let this miſlead you. You will dare to think for yourſelf.—Nor will you believe every man who pretends to know what you like better than you do yourſelf. There is a degree of coxcombry, I believe, in every thing: you have heard, I make no doubt, that greyhounds are either black, or white, or black and white; and if you have any faith in thoſe who ſay they know beſt, they will tell you that there are no others.* Prejudice, however, is by far too blind a guide to be depended on.

I have read ſomewhere, that there is no book ſo bad, but a judicious reader may derive ſome advantage from the reading of it; I hope theſe

---

* There is a faſhion in greyhounds: ſome courſers even pretend that *all* not being of the faſhionable colour are curs, and not greyhounds. Greyhound ſeems to be a corruption from ſome other word—moſt probably from gaze-hound.

letters will not prove the only exception. Should
they fall into the hands of fuch as are not fportfmen, I need not, I think, make any excufes to
them for the contents, fince the title fufficiently
fhews for whom they were defigned. Nor are
they meant for fuch fportfmen as need not inftruction, but for thofe that do; to whom, I
prefume, in fome parts at leaft, they may be
found of ufe. Since a great book has been long
looked upon as a great evil, I fhall take care not
to fin that way at leaft, and fhall endeavour to
make thefe letters as fhort as the extent of my
fubject will admit.

I fhall now take my leave of you for the prefent; in my next letter I fhall proceed according
to your defire, till I have anfwered all your queftions. Remember you are not to expect enter-
tainment; I wifh that you may find fome inftruction: the drynefs of the fubject may excufe
your want of the one, and I cannot doubt of your
indulgence, whilft I am obeying your commands,
though *I* fhould fail in the other.

L E T-

LETTER II.

SINCE you intend to make hunting your chief amufement in the country, you are certainly in the right to give it fome confideration before you begin, and not like Mafter Stephen in the play, firft buy a hawk, and then hunt after a book to keep it by. I am glad to find that you intend to build a new kennel, and I flatter my-felf the experience I have had may be of fome ufe to you in building it : it is not only the firft thing that you fhould do, but it is alfo the moft important. As often as your mind may alter, fo often may you eafily change from one kind of hound to another; but your kennel will ftill re-main the fame; will ftill keep its original im-perfections, unlefs altered at a great expence; and be lefs perfect at laft than it might have been made at firft, had you purfued a proper plan. It is true, hounds may be kept in barns and fta-bles; but thofe who keep them in fuch places can beft inform you whether their hounds are capable of anfwering the purpofes for which they were defigned. The fenfe of fmelling, the *odora canum vis*, as Virgil calls it, is fo exquifite in a hound, that I cannot but fuppofe every ftench is hurtful to it. It is that faculty on which all our hopes depend :

depend; it is *that* which muſt lead us o'er greaſy fallows, where the feet of the game we purſue being clogged leave little ſcent behind, as well as o'er ſtony roads, through watery meads, and where ſheep have ſtained the ground.

Cleanlineſs is not only abſolutely neceſſary to the noſe of the hound, but alſo to the preſervation of his health. Dogs are naturally cleanly animals; they ſeldom, when they can help it, dung where they lie; air and freſh ſtraw are neceſſary to keep them healthy. They are ſubject to the mange; a diſorder to which poverty and naſtineſs will very much contribute. *This*, though eaſily ſtopped at its firſt appearance, if ſuffered to continue long may leſſen the powers of the animal; and the remedies which are then to be uſed, being in themſelves violent, muſt injure his conſtitution: it had better be prevented: let the kennel, therefore, be an object of your particular care.

> " Upon ſome little eminence erect,
> And fronting to the ruddy dawn ; its courts
> On either hand wide opening to receive
> The ſun's all-cheering beams, when mild he ſhines,
> And gilds the mountain tops."————

Let ſuch as Somervile directs be the ſituation; its ſize muſt be ſuited to the number of its inhabitants; the architecture of it may be conformable

to

to your own tafte. Ufelefs expence I fhould not recommend; yet, as I fuppofe you will often make it a vifit, at leaft in the hunting feafon, I could wifh it might have neatnefs without, as well as cleanlinefs within, the more to allure you to it; I fhould for the fame reafon wifh it to be as near to your houfe as you will give it leave. I know there are many objections to its being very near; I forefee ftill more to its being at a diftance: there is a vulgar faying, that it is the mafter's eye that makes the horfe fat; I can affure you it is even more neceffary in the kennel, where cleanlinefs is not lefs effential than food.

There are, I make no doubt, many better kennels than mine, fome of which you fhould fee before you begin to build; you can but make ufe of my plan in cafe that you like no other better. If, in the mean time, I am to give you my opinion what a kennel ought to be, I muft fend you a defcription of my own, for I have not feen many others.

I would advife you to make it large enough at firft, as any addition afterwards muft fpoil the appearance of it. I have been obliged to add to mine, which was built from a plan of my own, and intended, at firft, for a pack of beagles. My feeding-yard being too fmall, I will endeavour to remedy that defect in the defcription I fend you,

C which

which may be ftill enlarged or leffened, as you think fit, or as your occafions may require. The feeding troughs fhould be wide at the bottom, and muft have wooden covers.

I think two kennels abfolutely neceffary to the well-being of the hounds; when there is but one, it is feldom fweet; and when cleaned out, the hounds, particularly in winter, fuffer both whilft it is cleaning, and as long as it remains wet afterwards. To be more clearly underftood by you, I fhall call one of thefe the *hunting-kennel*, by which I mean that kennel into which the hounds, intended to hunt the next day, are drafted. Ufed always to the fame kennel, they will be drafted with little trouble; they will an-fwer to their names more readily, and you may count your hounds into the kennel with as much eafe as a fhepherd counts his fheep out of the fold.

When the feeder firft comes to the kennel in a morning, he fhould let out the hounds into the outer court; and in bad weather he fhould open the door of the hunting-kennel, left want of reft fhould incline them to go into it. The lodging-room fhould then be cleaned out, the doors and windows of it opened, the litter fhaken up, and the kennel made fweet and clean before the hounds return to it again. The great court and
the

the other kennels are not lefs to be attended to, nor fhould you pafs over in filence any omiffion that is hurtful to your hounds.

The floor of each lodging-room fhould be bricked, and floped on both fides to run to the centre, with a gutter left to carry off the water, that when they are wafhed they may be foon dry. If water fhould remain through any fault in the floor, it fhould be carefully mopped up; for as warmth is in the greateft degree neceffary to hounds after work, fo damps are equally prejudicial. You will think me, perhaps, too particular in thefe directions; yet there can be no harm in your knowing what your fervants ought to do; as it is not impoffible it may be fometimes neceffary for you to fee that it is done. In your military profeffion you are perfectly acquainted with the duty of a common foldier, and though you have no further bufinefs with the minutiæ of it, without doubt you ftill find the knowledge of them ufeful to you: believe me, they may be ufeful *here*; and you will pardon me, I hope, if I wifh to fee you a Martinet in the kennel as well as in the field. Orders given without fkill are feldom well obeyed, and where the mafter is either ignorant, or inattentive, the fervant will be idle.

C 2

I alfo

I alfo wifh that, contrary to the ufual practice
in building kennels, you would have three doors;
two in the front, and one in the back; the laft to
have a lattice-window in it, with a wooden fhut-
ter, which is conftantly to be kept clofed when
the hounds are in, except in fummer, when it
fhould be left open all the day. This door anfwers two very neceflary purpofes: it gives an
opportunity of carrying out the ftraw when the
lodging-room is cleaned, and as it is oppofite to
the window, will be a means to let in a thorough air, which will greatly contribute to keep
it fweet and wholefome. The other doors will
be of ufe in drying the room, when the hounds
are out; and as one is to be kept fhut, and the
other hooked back, (allowing juft room for a dog
to pafs) they are not liable to any objection.
The great window in the centre fhould have a
folding-fhutter; half, or the whole of which,
may be fhut at nights, according to the weather;
and your kennels by that means may be kept
warm or cool, juft as you pleafe to have them.
The two great lodging-rooms are exactly alike,
and as each has a court belonging to it, are diftinct kennels, fituated at the oppofite ends of the
building; in the centre of which is the boiling-
houfe and feeding-yard; and on each fide a leffer
kennel, either for hounds that are drafted off,
hounds that are fick or lame, or for any other
purpofe, as occafion may require. At the back

of

of which, as they are but half the depth of the two great kennels, are places for coals, &c. for the use of the kennel. There is also a small building in the rear for hot bitches. The floors of the inner courts, like those of the lodging-rooms, are bricked and sloped towards the centre: and a channel of water, brought in by a leaden pipe, runs through the middle of them. In the centre of each court is a well, large enough to dip a bucket to clean the kennels; this must be faced with stone, or it will be often out of repair. In the feeding-yard it should have a wooden cover.

The benches, which must be open to let the urine through, should have hinges and hooks in the wall, that they may fold up, for the greater convenience in washing out the kennel; they should also be made as low as possible, that a hound, when he is tired, may have no difficulty in jumping up; and at no time may be able to creep under:* let me add, that the boiler should be of cast iron.

* Benches cannot be too low :—If, owing to the smallness of the hound, it should be difficult to render them low enough, a projecting ledge will answer the same purpose, and the benches may be boarded at bottom to prevent the hound from creeping under.

C 3

The

The reft of the kennel confifts of a large court in front, which is alfo bricked, having a grafs-court adjoining, and a little brook running through the middle of it. The earth that was taken out of it is thrown up into a mount, where the hounds in fummer delight to fit. This court is planted round with trees, and has, befides, a lime tree, and fome horfe chefnut trees near the middle of it, for the fake of fhade. A high pale inclofes the whole; part of which, to the height of about four feet, is clofe; the other open; the interftices are about two inches wide. The grafs-court is pitched near the pale, to prevent the hounds from fcratching out. If you cannot guefs the intention of the pofts which you fee in the courts, there is fcarcely an inn window on any road, where the following line will not let you into the fecret:

" So dogs will p— where dogs have p—d before."

This is done to fave the trees, to which the urinary falts are prejudicial. If they be at firft backward in coming to them, bind fome ftraw round the bottom, and rub it with galbanum. The brook in the grafs-court may ferve as a ftew: your fifh will be very fafe.*

* It may alfo be ufed as a cold bath for fuch hounds as ftand in need of it. For lamenefs in the ftifle, and for ftrains, it will be found of fervice.

At

At the back of the kennel is a houfe, thatched and furzed up on the fides, big enough to contain at leaft a load of ftraw. Here fhould be a pit ready to receive the dung, and a gallows for the flefh. The gallows fhould have a thatched roof, and a circular board at the pofts of it, to prevent vermin from climbing up. If you can inclofe a piece of ground adjoining to your kennel, for fuch dog horfes as may be brought to you alive, it will be of great ufe, as it might be dangerous to turn them out where other horfes go; for you may not always be able to difcover their diforders. *Hither* you may alfo bring your hounds, after they have been fed, to empty themfelves; *here* you will have more opportunities of feeing them than in the kennel, and will be enabled, therefore, to make your draft for the next day with greater accuracy.

A ftove, I believe, is made ufe of in fome kennels; but where the feeder is a good one, a mop, properly ufed, will render it unneceffary. I have a little hay-rick in the grafs-yard, which, I think, is of ufe to keep the hounds clean and fine in their coats; you will find them frequently rubbing themfelves againft it: the fhade of it alfo is ufeful to them in fummer. If ticks at any time be troublefome in your kennel, let the walls of it be well wafhed; if that fhould

not

not deftroy them, the walls muft then be white-
wafhed.

In the fummer when you do not hunt, one
kennel will be fufficient ; the other then may be
fet apart for the young hounds, which fhould alfo
have the grafs-court adjoining to it.   It is beft at
that time of the year to keep them feparate, and
it prevents many accidents which otherwife might
happen ; nor fhould they be put together till the
hunting feafon begins.*   If your hounds be very
quarrelfome, the feeder may fleep in a cot, in the
kennel adjoining ; and if they be well chaftifed
at the firft quarrel, his voice will be fufficient to
fettle all their differences afterwards.†   Clofe to
the door of the kennel, let there be always a
quantity of little fwitches, which three narrow
boards, nailed to one of the pofts, will eafily
contain.‡

* The dogs and the bitches may alfo be kept feparate from
each other during the fummer months, where there are conveniences for it.

† In a kennel in Oxfordfhire the feeder pulls a bell, which
the hounds underftand the meaning of ; it filences them immediately, and faves him the trouble of getting out of his bed.

‡ When hounds are perfectly obedient, whips are no longer
neceffary ; fwitches, in my opinion, are preferable. The whips
I ufe are coach whips three feet long, the thong half the length
of the crop. They are more handy than horfe whips, correct
the hounds as well, and hurt them lefs,

My

My kennel is clofe to the road-fide, but it was
unavoidable. This is the reafon why my front
pale is clofe, and only the fide ones open; it is
a great fault : avoid it if you can, and your
hounds will be the quieter.

Upon looking over my letter, I find I begin
recommending, with Mr. Somervile, a high fituation for the kennel, and afterwards talk of a
brook running through the middle of it; I am
afraid that you will not be able to unite thefe two
advantages; in which cafe, without doubt, water fhould be preferred : the mount I have mentioned will anfwer all the purpofes of an emi-
nence : befides, there fhould be moveable ftages
on wheels for the hounds to lie upon; at any
rate, however, let your foil be a dry one.

You will think, perhaps, my lodging-rooms
higher than is neceffary. I know they are confiderably higher than is ufual; the intention of
which is, to give more air to the hounds; and
I have not the leaft doubt that they are the
better for it.—I will no longer perfecute you
with this unentertaining fubject, but take my
leave.

[Mr. Beckford has here pointed out with much
exactnefs the method of erecting a KENNEL.—
                                          The

The editor of the prefent edition, by way of further illuftration, concludes the work with a defcription of thofe of the greateft celebrity in the kingdom, accompanied with four beautiful and picturefque views of them.]

LETTER III.

I BEGIN this letter with affuring you that I have done with the *kennel:* without doubt, you will think I had need. If I have made even the name frightful to you, comfort yourfelf with the thoughts that it will not appear again.

Your criticifm on my fwitches I think unjuft. You tell me felf-defence would of courfe make you take that precaution—do you always walk with a whip in your hand, or do you think that a walking ftick, which may be a good thing to knock a dog on the head with, would be equally proper to correct him fhould he be too familiar? You forget, however, to **put a better fubftitute** in the room of them.—

You defire to know, what kind of hound I would recommend: As you mention not for any particular chace, or country, I underftand you generally; and fhall anfwer, that I moft approve of hounds of the middle fize. I believe all animals of that defcription are ftrongeft, and beft able to endure fatigue. In the height, as well as the colour of hounds, moft fportfmen have their pre-judices; but in their fhape at leaft, I think they muft all agree. I know fportfmen, who boldly

affirm,

affirm, that a ſmall hound will oftentimes beat a large one; that he will climb hills better, and go through cover quicker;—whilſt others are not leſs ready to aſſert, that a large hound will make his way in any country, will get better through the dirt than a ſmall one; and that no fence, however high, can ſtop him.—You have now three opinions; and I adviſe you to adopt that which ſuits your country beſt: there is, however, a certain ſize, beſt adapted for buſineſs; which I take to be that between the two extremes; and I will venture to ſay, that ſuch hounds will not ſuffer themſelves to be diſgraced in any country. Somervile, I find, is of the ſame opinion.——

> ——— ——— ——— " But here a mean
> Obſerve, nor the large hound prefer, of ſize
> Gigantic; he in the thick-woven covert
> Painfully tugs, or in the thorny brake
> Torn and embarraſs'd bleeds: but if too ſmall,
> The pigmy brood in every furrow ſwims;
> Moil'd in clogging clay, panting they lag
> Behind inglorious; or elſe ſhivering creep,
> Benumb'd and faint, beneath the ſhelt'ring thorn.
> For hounds of middle ſize, active and ſtrong,
> Will better anſwer all thy various ends,
> And crown thy pleaſing labours with ſucceſs."

I perfectly agree with you, that to look well, they ſhould be all nearly of a ſize; and, I even think, they ſhould all look of the ſame family.—

> " Facies non omnibus una,
> Nec diverſa tamen, qualem decet eſſe ſororum."

If

If handfome withall, they are then perfect. With
regard to their being fizeable, what Somervile
fays, is fo much in your own way, that I fhall
fend it you.—

> " As fome brave captain, curious and exact,
> By his fix'd ftandard forms in equal ranks
> His gay battalion, as one man they move
> Step after ftep, their fize the fame, their arms
> Far-gleaming, dart the fame united blaze :
> Reviewing generals his merit own ;
> How regular ! how juft ! and all his cares
> Are well repaid, if mighty GEORGE approve.
> So model thou thy pack, if honour touch
> Thy generous foul, and the world's juft applaufe."

There are neceffary points in the fhape of a
hound, which ought always to be attended to by
a fportfman ; for, if he be not of a perfect fymmetry, he will neither run-faft, nor bear much
work : he has much to undergo, and fhould have
firength proportioned to it.—Let his legs be
ftraight as arrows ; his feet round, and not too
large ; his fhoulders back ; his breaft rather wide
than narrow ; his cheft deep ; his back broad ;
his head fmall ; his neck thin ; his tail thick and
brufhy ; if he carry it well, fo much the better :
This laft point, however trifling it may appear to
you, gave rife to a very odd queftion : A gentleman, (not much acquainted with hounds) as we
were hunting together the other day, faid, " I

I

" obferve,

" obferve, Sir, that fome of your dogs tails ftand
" up, and fome hang down ; pray which do you
" reckon *the beft hounds?*"—Such young hounds
as are out at the elbows, and fuch as are weak
from the knee to the foot, fhould never be taken
into the pack.

I find that I have mentioned a fmall head, as
one of the neceffary requifites of a hound ; but
you will underftand it as relative to *beauty only* ;
for as to *goodnefs*, I believe large-headed hounds
are in no wife inferior. Somervile, in his defcription of a perfect hound, makes no mention of the
head, leaving the fize of it to Phidias to determine ; he therefore muft have thought it of little
confequence.   I fend you his words.—

  — — — " See there with countenance blythe,
And with a courtly grin, the fawning hound
Salutes thee cow'ring, his wide-op'ning nofe
Upwards he curls, and his large floe-black eyes
Melt in foft blandifhments, and humble joy ;
His gloffy fkin, or yellow-pied, or blue,
In lights or fhades by nature's pencil drawn,
Reflects the various tints ; his ears and legs
Fleckt here and there in gay enamel'd pride,
Rival the fpeckled part ; his rufh-grown tail
O'er his broad back bends in an ample arch ;
On fhoulders clean, upright and firm he ftands ;
His round cat foot, ftraight hams, and wide-fpread thighs,
And his low dropping cheft, confefs his fpeed,
His ftrength, his wind, or on the fteepy hill,

                           Or

Or far extended plain ; in every part
So well proportion'd, that the nicer ſkill
Of Phidias himſelf can't blame thy choice.
Of ſuch compoſe thy pack.——

The colour, I think of little moment ; and am of opinion, with our friend Foote, reſpecting his negro friend, that a good dog, like a good candidate, cannot be of a bad colour.

Men are too apt to be prejudiced by the ſort of hound they themſelves have been moſt accuſtomed to. Thoſe who have been uſed to the ſharp-noſed fox-hound, will hardly allow a large-headed hound to *be* a fox-hound ; yet they both equally are.—Speed and beauty are the chief excellencies of the one ; whilſt ſtoutneſs and tenderneſs of noſe in hunting,* are characteriſtic of the other. I could tell you, that I have ſeen very good ſport with very unhandſome packs, conſiſting of hounds of various ſizes, differing from one another as much in ſhape and look, as in their colour ; nor could there be traced the leaſt ſign of conſanguinity amongſt them : conſidered ſeparately, the hounds were good ; as a pack of hounds they were not to be commended ; nor would you be ſatisfied with any thing that looks ſo very incom-

---

* Il paroit que la fineſſe de l'odorat, dans les chiens, dépend de la groſſeur plus que de la longueur du muſeau.

BUFFON.

3

pletc.

plete.—You will find nothing fo effential to your fport, as, that your hounds fhould run well together; nor can this end be better attained, than by confining yourfelf, as near as you can to thofe of the fame fort, fize, and fhape.

A great excellence in a pack of hounds is the head they carry; and that pack may be faid to go the fafteft, that can run ten miles the fooneft; notwithftanding the hounds, feparately, may not run fo faft as many others. A pack of hounds, confidered in a collective body, go faft in proportion to the excellence of their nofes, and the head they carry; as that traveller generally gets fooneft to his journey's end, who ftops leaft upon the road.——Some hounds that I have hunted with, would creep all through the fame hole, though they might have leapt the hedge, and would follow one another in a ftring, as true as a team of cart-horfes.—I had rather fee them, like the horfes of the fun, *all a-breaft*.

A friend of mine killed thirty-feven brace of foxes in one feafon: twenty nine of the foxes were killed without any intermiffion. I muft tell you at the fame time, that they were killed with hounds bred from a pack of harriers; nor had they, I believe, a fingle fkirter belonging to them. There is a pack now in my neighbourhood of all forts and fizes, which feldom mifs a fox; when
                                                    they

they run, there is a long ſtring of them, and every fault is hit off by an old ſouthern hound. However, out of the laſt eighteen foxes they hunted, they killed ſeventeen; and I have no doubt, that as they become more complete, more foxes will eſcape from them. Packs which are compoſed of hounds of various kinds, ſeldom run well together, nor do their tongues harmonize; yet they generally, I think, kill moſt foxes; but unleſs I like their ſtyle of killing them, whatever may be their ſucceſs, I cannot be completely ſatisfied. I once aſked the famous Will Crane, how his hounds behaved—" *very well, Sir,*" he reply'd; " *they never come to a fault, but they ſpread like a* " *ſky rocket.*"—Thus it ſhould always be.

A famous ſportſman aſked a gentleman what he thought of his hounds.---" Your pack is com-" poſed, Sir," ſaid he, " of dogs which any other " man would *hang*;---they are all *ſkirters.*"--- This was taken as a compliment.---However, think not that I recommend it to you as ſuch; for though I am a great advocate for ſtyle in the killing of a fox, I never forgive a profeſſed ſkirter; where game is plenty, they are always changing, and are the loſs of more foxes than they kill.

You aſk me, how many hounds you ought to keep? It is a queſtion not eaſy to anſwer—from

D

twenty

twenty to thirty couple, are as many, I think, as
you fhould ever take into the field. The propriety of any number muft depend upon the
ftrength of your pack, and the country in which
you are to hunt: the quantity of hounds neceffary to furnifh that number for a whole feafon,
muft alfo depend on the country *where* you hunt;
as fome countries lame hounds more than others.
The taking out too many hounds, Mr. Somervile
very properly calls *an ufelefs incumbrance.* It is
not fo material what the number is, as it is that
all your hounds fhould be fteady, and as nearly
as poffible of equal fpeed.

When packs are very large, the hounds are feldom fufficiently hunted to be good. Few people
choofe to hunt every day; and if they did, it is
not likely the weather in winter would give them
leave. You would always be obliged therefore,
either to take out a very large pack, or a great number of hounds muft be left behind: in the firft
cafe, too many hounds in the field would probably fpoil your fport; in the fecond, hounds that
remain long without work, always get out of wind,
and oftentimes become riotous. About forty
couple, I think, will beft anfwer your purpofe.
Forty couple of hunting hounds will enable you
to hunt three, or even four times in a week; and
I will venture to fay, will kill more foxes than a

greater

greater number. Hounds, to be good, muft be kept conftantly hunted; and if I fhould hereafter fay, a fox-hound fhould be above his work, it will not be a young fox-hound I fhall mean; for he fhould feldom be left at home, as long as he is able to hunt: the old and lame, and fuch as are low in flefh, you fhould leave; and fuch as you are fure idlenefs cannot fpoil.

It is a great fault to keep too many old hounds. If you choofe that your hounds fhould run well together, you fhould not continue *any*, longer than five or fix feafons; though there is no faying with certainty, what number of feafons a hound will laft. Like us, fome of them have better conftitutions than others, and confequently will bear more work; and the duration of all bodies depends as much on the ufage that they may meet with as on the materials of which they are made.

You afk, whether you had not better buy a complete pack at once, than be at the trouble of breeding one? Certainly you had, if fuch an opportunity fhould offer. It fometimes happens, that hounds are to be bought for lefs money than you could breed them. The gentleman to whom my houfe formerly belonged, had a moft famous pack of fox-hounds. His goods, &c. were appraifed and fold; which, when the appraifer had

D 2

done

done, he was put in mind of the hounds.—" Well,
gentlemen," faid he, " what fhall I appraife *them*
" *at? a fhilling a-piece?*—" Oh! it is too little!"
" is it fo?" faid the appraifer; " why it is more
" than *I would give for them, I affure you.*"——

Hounds are not bought fo cheap *at Tatterfall's.*

LET-

LETTER IV.

I AM glad that you do not difapprove the advantage I have made of my friend Somervile. I was doubtful whether you would not have cenfured me for it, and have compared me to fome of thofe would-be fine gentlemen, who, to cut a figure, tack an embroidered edging on their coarfe cloth.—I fhall be cautious, however, of abufing your indulgence, and fhall not quote my poet oftener than is neceffary ; but where we think the fame thing, you had better take it in his words than mine.—I fhall now proceed to the feeding of hounds, and management of them in the kennel.

A good feeder is an effential part of your eftablifhment.—Let him be young and active ; and have the reputation at leaft, of not difliking work : he fhould be good-tempered, for the fake of the animals entrufted to his care ; and who, however they may be treated by him, cannot complain. He fhould be one who will ftrictly obey any orders that you may give ; as well with regard to the management, as to the breeding of the hounds ; and fhould not be folely under the direction of your huntfman. It is true I have feen it otherwife : I have known a pack of hounds belong, as it were, entirely to the huntfman—a

D 3

ftable

ftable of horfes belong to the groom—whilft the mafter had little more power in the direction of either, than a perfect ftranger.—This you will not fuffer. I know you choofe to keep the fupreme command in your own hands; and though you permit your fervants to remonftrate, you do not fuffer them to difobey.—He who allows a huntfman to manage his hounds without controul, literally keeps them for the huntfman's amufement.——You defire to know what is required of a feeder;—I will tell you as well as I can.

As our fport depends entirely on that exquifite fenfe of fmelling, fo peculiar to the hound, care muft be taken to preferve it; and cleanlinefs is the fureft means. The keeping your kennel *fweet* and *clean* cannot therefore be too much recommended to the feeder; nor fhould you on any account admit the leaft deviation from it. If he fees *you* exact, he will be fo himfelf.—This is a very effential part of his bufinefs.——The boiling for the hounds; mixing of the meat; and getting it ready for them at proper hours, your huntfman will of courfe take care of; nor is it ever likely to be forgotten. I muft caution you not to let your dogs eat their meat too hot; for I have known it attended with bad confequences; you fhould alfo order it to be mixed up as thick as poffible.—When the feeder has cleaned his kennel in the morning, and prepared his meat, it is

ufual

ufual for him on hunting-days, (in an eftablifhment like your's) to exercife the horfes of the
huntfman and whipper-in ; and in many ftables
it is alfo the feeder who looks after the huntfman's
horfe when he comes in from hunting, whilft the
huntfman feeds the hounds. When the hounds
are not out, the huntfman, and whipper-in, of
courfe, will exercife their own horfes ; and that day
the feeder has little elfe to mind but the cleaning of his kennel. Every poffible contrivance
has been attended to in the defcription I fent you,
to make that part of his work eafy ; all the courts,
except the grafs-court, being bricked, and floped
on purpofe. There is alfo plenty of water, without any trouble in fetching it ; and a thorough air
throughout the kennels, to affift in drying them
again.---Should you choofe to increafe your number of fervants in the ftable, in that cafe, the bufinefs of the feeder may be confined entirely to the
kennel.---There fhould be always two to feed
hounds properly ; the feeder and huntfman.

Somervile ftrongly recommends cleanlinefs in
the following lines,

" O'er all let cleanlinefs prefide, no fcraps
Beftrew the pavement, and no half-pick'd bones,
To kindle fierce debate, or to difguft
That nicer fenfe, on which the fportfman's hope,
And all his future triumphs muft depend.
Soon as the growling pack with eager joy

Have

> Have lapp'd their fmoaking viands, morn or eve,
> From the full ciftern lead the ductile ftreams,
> To wafh thy court well-pav'd, nor fpare thy pains,
> For much to health will cleanlinefs avail.
> Seek'ft thou for hounds to climb the rocky fteep,
> And brufh th' entangled covert, whofe nice fcent
> O'er greafy fallows, and frequented roads,
> Can pick the dubious way ? Banifh far off
> Each noifome ftench, let no offenfive fmell
> Invade thy wide inclofure, but admit
> The nitrous air, and purifying breeze."

So perfectly right is the poet in this, that if you can make your kennel a vifit every day, your hounds will be the better for it. When I have been long abfent from mine, I have always perceived a difference in their looks. I fhall now take notice of that part of the management of hounds in the kennel, which concerns the huntfman as well as the feeder.---Your huntfman muft always attend the feeding of the hounds, which fhould be drafted, according to the condition they are in. In all packs, fome hounds will feed better than others; fome there are that will do with lefs meat ; and it requires a nice eye, and great attention, to keep them all in equal flefh :---it is what diftinguifhes a good kennel-huntfman, and has its merit.---It is feldom that huntfmen give this particular all attention it deferves: they feed their hounds in too great a hurry ; and not often, I believe, take the trouble of cafting their eye over them before they begin ;

and

and yet, to diftinguifh with any nicety, the order
a pack of hounds are in, and the different degrees
of it, is furely no eafy tafk; and to be done well,
requires no fmall degree of circumfpection: you
had better not expect your huntfman to be very
exact; where precifion is required, he will moft
probably fail.

When I am prefent myfelf, I make feveral
drafts. When my huntfman feeds them, he calls
them all over by their names, letting in each
hound as he is called; it has its ufe—it ufes them
to their names, and teaches them to be obedient.
Were it not for this, I fhould difapprove of it entirely; fince it certainly requires more coolnefs
and deliberation to diftinguifh with precifion
which are beft entitled to precedence, than this
method of feeding will admit of; and unlefs flefh
be in great plenty, thofe that are called in laft,
may not have a tafte of it. To prevent this inconvenience, fuch as are low in flefh, had better
be all drafted off into a feparate kennel;* by this
means, the hounds that require *flefh*, will all have
a fhare of it. If any be much poorer than the

* By thus feparating from the reft, fuch as are poor, you will
proceed to the feeding of your hounds with more accuracy, and
lefs trouble; and though they be at firft drafted off, in the manner above defcribed, it is ftill meant that they fhould be let in to
feed, one by one, as they anfwer to their names; or elfe, as it
will frequently happen, they may be better fed than taught.

reft,

reft, they fhould be fed again—fuch hounds cannot be fed too often. If any in the pack be too
fat, *they* fhould be drafted off, and not fuffered
to fill themfelves. The others fhould eat what
they will of the meat. The days my hounds have
greens or fulphur, they generally are let in all
together; and fuch as require *flefh*, have it given
to them afterwards. Having a good kennel-
huntfman, it is not often that I take this trouble;
yet I feldom go into my kennel, but I indulge
myfelf in the pleafure of feeing food given to fuch
hounds, as appear to me to be in want of it. I
have been told that in one kennel in particular,
the hounds are under fuch excellent management,
that they conftantly are fed with the door of the
feeding-yard open; and the rough nature of the
fox-hound is changed into fo much politenefs,
that he waits at the door, till he is invited in; and
what perhaps is not lefs extraordinary, he comes
out again, whether he has fatisfied his hunger or
not, the moment he is defired—The effect of dif-
cipline. However, as this is not abfolutely neceffary, and hounds may be good without it; and
as I well know your other amufements will not
permit you to attend to fo much manœuvring, I
would by no means wifh you to give fuch power
to your huntfman. The bufinefs would be injudicioufly done, and moft probably would not anfwer
your expectations—The hound would be tor-
mented *mal-à-propos*;—an animal fo little deferving

ing of it from our hands, that I fhould be forry to
difturb his hours of repofe by unneceffary feverity.
You will perceive it is a nice affair; and I affure
you I know no huntfman who is equal to it. The
gentleman who has carried this matter to its
moft perfection, has attended to it regularly himfelf; has conftantly acted on fixed principles,
from which he has never deviated; and I believe
has fucceeded to the very utmoft of his wifhes.—
All hounds, (and more efpecially young ones)
fhould be called over often in the kennel;* and
moft huntfmen practife this leffon, as they feed
their hounds.—They flog them while they feed
them—and if they have not always a belly-full
one way, they feldom fail to have it the other.†

* There is no better method of teaching a hound obedience;
when you call him, he fhould approach you; when you touch
him with your ftick, he fhould follow you any where.

† "Thus we find, eat or not eat, work or play, whipping is
always in feafon." (vide Monthly Review) The critic treats this
paffage with great feverity. He would have fpared it, without
doubt, had he underftood that it was introduced on purpofe to
correct the abufe of kennel difcipline. Unacquainted, as the
Reviewer feems to be with the fubject, it is no wonder that he
fhould miftake a meaning, perhaps rather unfairly ftated by the
author, in favor of that humanity he is fuppofed fo much to
want.—Hounds are called in to feed, one by one, and fuch only
are corrected, as come uncalled for: nor is correction unjuft, fo
long as it fhall fall on the difobedient only. Obedience is an ufeful leffon, and though it cannot be *practifed* too often, it fhould
be *taught* them at a more idle time.

It

It is not, however, my intention to oppofe fo general a practice, in which there may be fome
utility; I fhall only obferve, that it fhould be
ufed with difcretion, left the whip fhould fall
heavily in the kennel on fuch as never deferve it
in the field.

My hounds are generally fed about eleven
o'clock;* and when I am prefent myfelf, I take
the fame opportunity to make my draft for the
next day's hunting. I feldom, when I can help
it, leave this to my huntfman, though it is neceffary he fhould be prefent when the draft is
made, that he may know what hounds he has
out.

* Having found it neceffary to alter my method of feeding
hounds, it may not be improper to take notice of it here.
They are now fed at eight o'clock, inftead of eleven. Their
firft feed is of barley and oatmeal mixed, an equal quantity of
each. Flefh is afterwards mixed up with the remainder for
fuch hounds as are poor, who are then drafted off into another
kennel, and let in to feed all together. When the flefh is all
eaten, the pack are again let in, and are by this means cheated
into a fecond appetite. At three o'clock thofe that are to hunt
the next day are drafted into the hunting kennel; they are
then let into the feeding-yard, where a fmall quantity of oatmeal (about three buckets) is prepared for them; not mixed
up thin, as mentioned in page 45, but mixed up thick. Such
as are tender, or bad feeders, have a handful of boiled flefh
given to them afterwards. When they are not to hunt the next
day, they are fed once only—at eleven o'clock.

It

It is a bad cuſtom to uſe hounds to the boiling-houſe; it is apt to make them nice, and may prevent them from ever eating the kennel-meat. What they have, ſhould always be given them in the feeding-yard, and for the ſame reaſon, though it be fleſh, it ſhould have ſome meal mixed with it.

If your hounds be low in fleſh, and have far to go to cover, they may all have a little thin lap again in the evening; but this ſhould never be done if you hunt early.* Hounds, I think, ſhould be ſharp-ſet before hunting; they run the better for it.†

If many of your hounds, after long reſt, ſhould be too fat,‡ by feeding them for a day or two on thinner meat than you give the others, it will be found, I believe, to anſwer better than the uſual method of giving them the ſame meat, and ſtinting them in the quantity of it.

* Hounds that are tender feeders cannot be fed too late, or with meat too good.

† Vid. Note, page 44.

‡ Hounds that reſt, ſhould not be ſuffered to become fat.— It would be accounting very badly for the fatneſs of a hound, to ſay he is fat, becauſe he has not worked lately, ſince he ought to have been kept lower on that account.

If

If your hounds be not walked out, they fhould be turned into the grafs-court to empty them-felves after they have been fed, it will contribute not a little to the cleanlinefs of the kennel.

I have heard that it is a cuftom in fome ken-nels to fhut up the hounds for a couple of hours after they come in from hunting, before they are fed; and that other hounds are fhut up with them, to lick them clean.* *My* ufual way is to fend on a whipper-in before them, that the meat may be gotten ready againft they come, and they are fed *immediately:* having filled their bellies, they are naturally inclined to reft. If they have had a fevere day, they are fed again fome hours after.† As to the method above-mentioned, it may be more convenient perhaps to have the hounds all together: but I cannot think it neceí-fary, for the reafon that is given; and I fhould apprehend a parcel of idle hounds, fhut up amongft fuch as are tired and inclined to reft,

* If hounds be fhut up, as foon as they come in from hunting, they will not readily leave the benches afterwards; for if they be much fatigued, they will prefer reft to food.

† My hounds are generally fed twice on the days they hunt. Some will feed better the fecond time than the firft; befides, the turning them out of the lodging-houfe refrefhes them; they ftretch their limbs; empty their bodies; and, as during this time their kennel is cleaned out, and litter fhaken up, they fet-tle themfelves better on the benches afterwards.

would

would difturb them more than all their licking would make amends for. When you feed them twice, keep them feparate till after the fecond feeding; it would be ftill better were they not put together till the next morning.

Every day, when hounds come in from hunt-ing, they ought carefully to be looked over, and invalids fhould immediately be taken care of.*
Such as have fore feet, fhould have them well wafhed out with brine, or pot liquor. If you permit thofe hounds that are unable to work to run about your houfe, it will be of great fervice to them. Such as are ill, or lame, ought to be turned out into another kennel; it will be more eafy to give them *there* the attention they may re-quire, both as to medicine and food.

Every Thurfday during the hunting feafon, my hounds have one pound of fulphur given them in their meat; and every Sunday through-out the year they have plenty of greens boiled up with it: I find it better to fix the days, as it is then lefs liable to be forgotten. I ufed to give them the wafh from the kitchen, but I found it

* Hounds that come home lame fhould not be taken out the next hunting day, fince they may appear found without be-ing fo. At the beginning of the feafon the eyes of hounds are frequently injured; fuch hounds fhould not be hunted, and if their eyes continue weak they fhould lofe a little blood.

made them thirfty, and it is now omitted in the hunting feafon. A horfe frefh-killed is an excellent meal for hounds after a very hard day; but they fhould not hunt till the third day after it. The bones broken are good food for poor hounds, as there is great proof in them. Sheep trotters are very fweet food, and will be of fervice when horfe-flefh is not to be had. Bullocks' bellies may be alfo of fome ufe, if you can get nothing elfe. Oatmeal, I believe, makes the beft meat for hounds; barley is certainly the cheapeft; and in many kennels they give barley on that account; but it is heating, does not mix up fo well, nor is there fo much proof in it as in oatmeal. If mixed, an equal quantity of each, it will then do very well, but barley alone will not. Much alfo depends on the goodnefs of the meal itfelf, which is not often attended to. If you do not ufe your own, you fhould buy a large quantity of it any time before harveft, and keep it by you: there is no other certainty, I believe, of having it *old*; which is more material than, perhaps, you are aware of. I have heard that a famous Chefhire huntfman feeds his hounds with wheat; which he has found to be the beft food. He gives it them with the bran; it would caufe no little difturbance in many neighbourhoods, if other fportfmen were to do the fame.

I am

I am not fond of *bleeding* hounds, unlefs they want it; though it has long been a cuftom in my kennel to *phyfic* them twice a year; after they leave off hunting, and before they begin. It is given in hot weather, and at an idle time. It cools their bodies, and without doubt is of fervice to them. If a hound be in want of phyfic, I prefer giving it in balls.* It is more eafy to give in this manner the quantity he may want, and you are more certain that he takes it. In many kennels, they alfo bleed them twice a year, and fome people think that it prevents madnefs. The anointing of hounds, or *dreffing* them, as huntfmen call it, makes them fine in their coats: it may be done twice a year, or oftner, if you find it neceffary. As I fhall hereafter have occafion to write on the difcafes of hounds, and their cures, I will fend you at the fame time a receipt for this purpofe. During the fummer months, when my hounds do not hunt, they have feldom any flefh allowed them, and are kept low, contrary, I believe, to the ufual practice of moft kennels, where mangy hounds in fummer are but too often feen. Huntfmen fometimes content themfelves with checking this diforder, when, with lefs trouble, perhaps, they

* One pound of antimony, four ounces of fulphur, and fyrup of buckthorn q. f. to give it the confiftency of a ball. Each ball weighs about feven drachms.

E

might

might prevent it. A regular courfe of whey and vegetables during the hot months muft, certainly, be wholefome, and is, without doubt, the caufe that a mangy hound is an unufual fight in m kennel. Every Monday and Friday my hounds go for whey till the hunting feafon begins; are kept out feveral hours, and are often made to fwim through rivers during the hot weather. After the laft phyfic, and before they begin to hunt, they are exercifed on the turnpike road, to harden their feet, which are wafhed with ftrong brine, as foon as they come in. Little ftraw is neceffary during the fummer; but when they hunt they cannot have too much, or have it changed too often. In many kennels they do not boil for the hounds in fummer, but give them meal only; in mine it is always boiled; but with this difference, that it is mixed up thin, inftead of thick. Many give fpurge-laurel in fummer, boiled up in their meat; as I never ufe it, I cannot recommend it. The phyfic I give is two pounds of fulphur, one pound of antimony, and a pint and a half of fyrup of buckthorn, for about forty couple of hounds.* In the winter feafon, let your hounds be fhut up warm at night. If any hounds, after hunting, be miffing, the ftraw-houfe door fhould be left open; and if

* Vide page 49, where it is recommended that fuch hounds as require phyfic fhould be phyficked feparately.

they

they have had a hard day, it may be as well to leave fome meat there for them.

I have inquired of my feeder, who is a good one, (and has had more experience in thefe matters than any one you perhaps may get) how he mixes up his meat. He tells me, that in his opinion, oatmeal and barley mixed, an equal quantity of each, make the beft meat for hounds. The oatmeal he boils for half an hour, and then puts out the fire, puts the barley into the copper, and mixes both together. I afked him why he boiled one and not the other—he told me, boiling, which made oatmeal thick, made barley thin; and that when you feed with barley only, it fhould not be put into the copper, but be fcalded with the liquor, and mixed up in a bucket. I find there is in my kennel a large tub on purpofe, which contains about half a hogfhead.

You little think, perhaps, how difficult it is to be a good kennel huntfman, nor can you, as yet, know the nicety that is required to feed hounds properly. You are not aware that fome hounds will hunt beft when fed late; others, when fed early: that fome fhould have but little; that others cannot have too much. However, if your huntfman obferve the rules I have here laid down, his hounds will not do much amifs; but fhould you at any time wifh to *renchérir* upon the

mat-

matter, and feed each particular hound fo as to make the moft of him, you muft learn it of a gentleman in Leiceflerfhire, to whom the noble fcience of fox-hunting is more beholden than to any other. I fhall myfelf fay nothing further on the fubject; for as your huntfman will not have the fenfe of the gentleman I allude to, nor *you* perhaps his patience, an eafier method I know will fuit you beft. I fhall only advife you, while you endeavour to keep your hounds in good order, not to let them become *too fat*; it will be impoffible for them to run, if they be. A fat alderman would cut a mighty ridiculous figure were he inclined to run a race.

LETTER V.

THERE is an active vanity in the minds of men which is favourable to improvement, and in every purfuit, while fomething remains to be attained, fo long will it afford amufement; you, therefore, will find pleafure in the breeding of hounds, in which expectation is never com-pletely fatisfied, and it is on the fagacious management of this bufinefs that all your fuccefs will depend. Is it not extraordinary that no other country fhould equal us in this particular, and that the very hounds procured from hence fhould degenerate in another climate?

> " In thee alone, fair land of liberty!
> Is bred the perfect hound, in fcent and fpeed
> As yet unrivall'd, while in other climes
> Their virtue fails, a weak degen'rate race."
>
> SOMERVILE.

Happy climate for fportfmen! where nature feems as it were to give them an exclufive privilege of enjoying this diverfion. To preferve, however, this advantage, care fhould be taken in the breed; I fhall, therefore, according to your defire, fend you fuch rules as I obferve myfelf. Confider the fize, fhape, colour, conftitution, and natural difpofition of the dog you breed from, as well as

E 3

the

the finenefs of his nofe, his ftoutnefs, and method of hunting.   On no account breed from one
that is not *ftout*, that is not *tender-nofed*, or that
is either a *babbler*,* or a *fkirter*.

> " Obferve with care his fhape, fort, colour, fize:
> Nor will fagacious huntfmen lefs regard
> His inward habits; the vain babbler fhun,
> Ever loquacious, ever in the wrong.
> His foolifh offspring fhall offend thy ears
> With falfe alarms and loud impertinence.
> Nor lefs the fhifting cur avoid, that breaks
> Illufive from the pack; to the next hedge
> Devious he ftrays, there ev'ry mufe he tries,
> ' If haply then he crofs the ftreaming fcent,
> Away he flies vain-glorious; and exults
> As of the pack fupreme and in his fpeed
> And ftrength unrivall'd.   Lo! caft far behind,
> His vex'd affociates pant, and lab'ring ftrain
> To climb the fteep afcent.   Soon as they reach
> Th' infulting boafter, his falfe courage fails,
> Behind he lags, doom'd to the fatal noofe,
> His mafter's hate, and fcorn of all the field.
> What can from fuch be hop'd, but a bafe brood
> Of coward curs, a frantic, vagrant race?"
>   SOMERVILE.

It is the judicious crofs that makes the pack
complete.†   The faults and imperfections in one
breed,

---

* Babbling is one of the worft faults that a hound can be
guilty of, it is conftantly increafing, and is alfo catching.
This fault, like many others, will fometimes run in the blood.

† I have feen fox-hounds that were bred out of a Newfound-
land

breed, may be rectified from another; and if this be properly attended to, I see no reason why the breeding of hounds may not improve, till improvement can go no further. If you find a cross hit, pursue it.* Never put an old dog to an old bitch. Be careful that they be healthy which you breed from, or you are not likely to have a healthy offspring. Should a favourite dog skirt a little, put him to a thorough line-hunting bitch, and such a cross may succeed. My objection to the breeding from such a hound is, that as skirting is what most fox-hounds acquire from practice, it had better not be made natural to them. A very famous sportsman has told me, that he frequently breeds from brothers and sisters. As I should be very unwilling to urge any thing in opposition to such authority, you had better try it; and if it succeed in hounds, it is more I believe than it usually does in other animals. A famous cocker assured a friend of mine, that the third generation (which he called

land bitch and a fox-hound dog: they are monstrously ugly—are said to give their tongues sparingly, and to tire soon. The experiment has not succeeded; the cross most likely to be of service to a fox-hound is the beagle. I am well convinced that a handsome, bony, tender-nosed, stout beagle would, occasionally, be no improper cross for a high-bred pack of fox-hounds.

* After the first season, I breed from all my young dog-hounds who have beauty and goodness to recommend them, to see what whelps they get.

E 4

a nick)

a nick) he had found to fucceed very well, but no nearer: as I have neither tried one nor the other, I cannot fpeak with any certainty about them.

Give particular orders to your feeder to watch over the bitches with a cautious eye, and feparate fuch as are going to be proud, before it be too late. The advances they make frequently portend mifchief as well as love; and, if not prevented in time, will not fail to fet the whole kennel together by the ears, and may occafion the death of your beft dogs: care only can prevent it.*

> " Mark well the wanton females of thy pack,
> That curl their taper tails, and frifking court
> Their pye-bald mates enamour'd; their red eyes
> Flafh fires impure; nor reft, nor food they take,
> Goaded by furious love.   In fep'rate cells
> Confine them now, left bloody civil wars
> Annoy thy peaceful ftate.————"   SOMERVILE.

I have known huntfmen perfectly ignorant of the breed of their hounds, from inattention in this particular; and I have alfo known many good dogs fall a facrifice to it.

---

* When the bitches are off their heat, they fhould be fuffered to run about the houfe a day or two before they are taken out to hunt.

The

The earlier in the year you breed the better: January, February, and March, are the beſt months. Late puppies ſeldom thrive; if you have any ſuch, put them to the beſt walks.* When the bitches begin to get big, let them not hunt any more: it proves frequently fatal to the puppies; ſometimes to the bitch herſelf; nor is it ſafe for them to remain much longer in the kennel. If one bitch have many puppies, more than ſhe can well rear, you may put ſome of them to another bitch; or if you deſtroy any of them, you may keep the beſt coloured. They ſometimes will have an extraordinary number: I have known an inſtance of one having fifteen; and a friend of mine, whoſe veracity I cannot doubt, has aſſured me that a hound in his pack brought forth ſixteen, all alive. When you breed from a very favourite ſort, and can have another bitch warded at the ſame time, it will have this advantage, it will enable you to ſave all the puppies. Give particular orders that the bitches be well fed with fleſh; they ſhould alſo have plenty of milk, nor ſhould the puppies be taken from them till they are able to take care of themſelves: they will ſoon learn to lap milk, which will relieve the mother. The bitches, when their puppies are taken away from them,

* Of the early whelps I keep five or ſix, of the late ones only two or three.

ſhould

should be phyficked; they should have three purging balls given them, one every other morning, and plenty of whey the intermediate day.—If a bitch bring only one or two puppies, and you have another bitch that will take them, by putting the puppies to her, the former will be foon fit to hunt again; she should, however, be phyficked firft; and if her dugs be anointed with brandy and water, it will alfo be of fervice. The diftemper makes dreadful havoc with whelps at their walks; greatly owing, I believe, to the little care that is taken of them there. I am in doubt whether it might not be better to breed them up yourfelf, and have a kennel on purpofe. You have a large orchard, paled in, which would fuit them exactly; and what elfe is wanted might eafily be obtained. There is, however, an objection that perhaps may ftrike you—If the diftemper once get amongft them, they muft all have it: yet, notwithftanding *that*, as they will be conftantly well fed, and will lie warm, I am confident it would be the faving of many lives. If you should adopt this method, you muft remember to ufe them early to go in couples; and when they become of a proper age, they muft be walked out often : for should they remain confined, they would neither have the shape, health, or underftanding, which they ought to have. When I kept harriers, I bred up fome of the puppies at a diftant kennel; but having no fervants

vants

vants there to exercife them properly, I found them much inferior to fuch of their brethren as had the luck to furvive the many difficulties and dangers they had undergone at their walks; thefe were afterwards equal to any thing, and afraid of nothing; whilft thofe that had been nurfed with fo much care were weakly and timid, and had every difadvantage attending private education.

I have often heard as an excufe for hounds not hunting a cold fcent, that they were *too high bred*; I confefs, I know not what that means : but this I know, that hounds are frequently *too ill bred* to be of any fervice. It is judgment in the breeder, and patience afterwards in the huntfman, that make them hunt.

Young hounds are commonly named when firft put out, and fometimes indeed ridiculoufly enough; nor is it eafy, when you breed many, to find fuitable or harmonious names for all ; particularly as it is ufual to name all the whelps of one litter with the fame letter, which (to be fyftematically done) fhould alfo be the initial letter of the dog that got them, or the bitch that bred them. A baronet of my acquaintance, a literal obferver of the above rule, fent three young hounds of one litter to a friend, all their names beginning, as *he faid*, with the letter G— *Gowler*, *Govial*, and *Galloper*.

It

It is indeed of little confequence what huntfmen call their hounds; yet if you diflike an un-
meaning name, would it not be as well to leave
the naming of them till they are brought home?
They foon learn their names, and a fhorter lift
would do.   Damons and Delias would not then
be neceffary; nor need the facred names of Titus and Trajan be thus degraded.   It is true,
there are many odd names which cuftom authorifes; yet I cannot think, becaufe fome drunken
fellow or other has chriftened his dog Tipler, or
Tapfter, that there is the leaft reafon to follow
the example.   Pipers and fiddlers, for the fake
of their mufic, we will not object to; but tiplers
and tapfters your kennel will be much better
without.

However extraordinary you may think it, I
can affure you I have myfelf feen a *white* Gipfey,
a *grey* Ruby, a *dark* Snowball, and a Blueman
of any colour but *blue*.   The huntfman of a
friend of mine being afked the name of a young
hound, faid, it was *Lyman*.   " Lyman!" faid
his mafter; " why, James, what does Lyman
" mean?"—" Lord, Sir!" replied James, " what
" does *any thing mean?*"—A farmer, who bred up
two couple of hounds for me, whofe names were
Merryman and Merrylafs, Ferryman and Furious, upon my inquiring after them, gave this
account: " Merryman and Merrylafs are both
                                        " dead,

" dead, but Ferryman, Sir, is a fine dog, and
" fo is *Ferrylafs*." Madam, an ufual name
among hounds, is often, I believe, very difre-
fpectfully treated : I had an inftance of it the
other day in my own huntfman, who, after having rated Madam a great deal, to no purpofe,
(who, to confefs the truth, was much given to
do otherwife than fhe fhould) flew into a violent
paffion, and hallooed out, as loud as he could—
" *Madam, you d—d bitch!*"

As you defire a lift of names, I will fend you
one. I have endeavoured to clafs them according to their different genders; but you will perceive fome names may be ufed indifcriminately
for either. It is not ufual, I believe, to call a
pointer Ringwood, or a greyhound Harmony;
and fuch names as are expreffive of fpeed,
ftrength, courage, or other natural qualities in a
hound, I think moft applicable to them. Damons and Delias I have left out; the bold Thunder and the brifk Lightning, if you pleafe, may
fupply their places; unlefs you prefer the method
of the gentleman I told you of, who intends
naming his hounds from the p—ge; and, I fuppofe, he at the fame time will not be unmindful
of the p—y c——rs.

If you mark the whelps in the fide, (which is
called branding them) when they are firft put

out,

out, (or perhaps it may be better done after they have been out fome time) it may prevent their being ftolen.

When young hounds are firft taken in, they fhould be kept feparate from the pack; and as it will happen at a time of the year, when there is little or no hunting, you may eafily give them up one of the kennels and grafs-court adjoining. Their play ends frequently in a battle; it therefore is lefs dangerous where all are equally matched. What Somervile fays on this fubject is exceedingly beautiful:

> " But here with watchful and obfervant eye,
> Attend their frolics, which too often end
> In bloody broils and death.   High o'er thy head
> Wave thy refounding whip, and with a voice
> Fierce-menacing o'er-rule the ftern debate,
> And quench their kindling rage; for oft in fport
> Begun, combat enfues, growling they fnarl,
> Then on their haunches rear'd, rampant they feize
> Each other's throats, with teeth, and claws, in gore
> Befmear'd, they wound, they tear, till on the ground,
> Panting, half-dead the conquer'd champion lies:
> Then fudden all the bafe ignoble crowd
> Loud-clam'ring feize the helplefs worried wretch,
> And thirfting for his blood, drag diff'rent ways
> His mangled carcafs on th' enfanguin'd plain.
> O breafts of pity void! t' opprefs the weak,
> To point your vengeance at the friendlefs head,
> And with one mutual cry infult the fall'n!
> Emblem too juft of man's degenerate race."

If

If you find that they take a diflike to any particular hound, the fafeft way will be to remove
him; or it is probable they will kill him at laft.
When a feeder hears the hounds quarrel in the
kennel, he halloos to them to ftop them. He
then goes in amongft them, and flogs every
hound he can come near. How much more reafonable, as well as more efficacious, it would be,
were he to fee which were the combatants before
he fpeaks to them. Punifhment would then fall
as it ought, on the guilty only. In all packs
there are fome hounds more quarrelfome than the
reft; and it is to them we owe all the mifchief
that is done. If you find chaftifement cannot
quiet them, it may be prudent to break their
holders; for fince they are not neceffary to them
for the meat they have to eat, they are not likely
to ferve them in any good purpofe.

Young hounds ought to be fed twice a day, as
they feldom take kindly at firft to the kennel-
meat, and the diftemper is moft apt to feize them
at this time. It is better not to round them till
they are thoroughly fettled; nor fhould it be put
off till the hot weather, for then they would
bleed too much.* If any of the dogs be thin

over

---

* It may be better, perhaps, to round them at their quarters,
when about fix months old; fhould it be done fooner, it would
make their ears tuck up. The tailing of them is ufually done

before

over the back, or any more quarrelfome than the reft, it will be of ufe to cut them: I alfo fpay fuch bitches as I think I fhall not want to breed from; they are more ufeful, are ftouter, and are always in better order: befides, it is abfolutely neceffary if you hunt late in the fpring; or your pack will be very fhort for want of it. It may be right to tell you, that the latter operation does not always fucceed, it will be neceffary, therefore, to employ a fkilful perfon, and one on whom you can depend; for if it be ill done, though they cannot have puppies, they will go to heat notwithftanding, of which I have known many inftances, and that, I apprehend, would not anfwer your purpofe at any rate. They fhould be kept low for feveral days before the operation is performed, and muft be fed on thin meat for fome time after.

You afk me what number of young hounds you fhould breed to keep up your ftock? it is a queftion, I believe, no man can anfwer. It depends altogether on contingencies. The deficiencies of one year muft be fupplied the next. I fhould apprehend from thirty to thirty-five couple

before they are put out; it might be better, perhaps, to leave it till they are taken in. Dogs muft not be rounded at the time they have the diftemper upon them; the lofs of blood would weaken them too much.

of old hounds, and from eight to twelve couple
of young ones would, one year with another,
beft fuit an eftablifhment which you do not intend fhould much exceed forty couple. This
rule you fhould at the fame time obferve—never
to part with an ufeful old hound, or enter an un-
handfome young one.

I would advife you in breeding, to be as little
prejudiced as poffible in favour of your own fort;
but fend your beft bitches to the beft dogs, be
they where they may. Thofe who breed only
a few hounds may by chance have a good pack,
whilft thofe who breed a great many (if at the
fame time they underftand the bufinefs) reduce
it to a certainty. You fay, you wifh to fee your
pack as complete as Mr. Meynell's: believe me,
my good friend, unlefs you were to breed as many
hounds, it is totally impoffible. Thofe who breed
the greateft number of hounds have a right to
expect the beft pack; at leaft it muft be their
own fault if they have it not.

NAMES

NAMES of HOUNDS.

A. *dogs.*

ABLE
Actor
Adamant
Adjutant
Agent
Aider
Aimwell
Amorous
Antic
Anxious
Arbiter
Archer
Ardent
Ardor
Arrogant
Arsenic
Artful
Artist
Atlas
Atom
Auditor
Augur
Awful

———

A. *bitches.*

Accurate
Active
Actress
Affable
Agile
Airy
Amity
Angry
Animate
Artifice
Audible

B. *dogs.*

Bachelor
Banger
Baffler
Barbarous
Bellman
Bender
Blaster
Bluecap
Blueman
Bluster
Boaster
Boisterous
Bonnyface
Bouncer
Bowler
Bravo
Bragger
Brawler
Brazen
Brilliant
Brusher
Brutal
Burster
Bustler
Briton

———

B. *bitches.*

Baneful
Bashful
Bauble
Beauteous
Beauty
Beldam
Belmaid
Blameless
Blithsome
Blowzy
Bluebell
Bluemaid
Bonny
Bonnybell
Bonnylass
Boundless
Bravery
Brevity
Brimstone
Busy
Buxom

C. *dogs.*

C. *dogs.*

Caitiff
Capital
Captain
Captor
Carol
Carver
Cafter
Caftwell
Catcher
Catchpole
Caviller
Cerberus
Challenger
Champion
Charon
Chafer
Chaunter
Chieftan
Chimer
Chirper
Choleric
Claimant
Clamorous
Clangor
Clafher
Climbank
Clinker
Combat
Combatant
Comforter
Comrade
Comus
Conflict
Conqueror

Conqueft
Conftant
Conteft
Coroner
Cottager
Counfellor
Countryman
Courteous
Coxcomb
Craftfman
Crafher
Critic
Critical
Crowner
Cruifer-*oe*
Crufty
Cryer
Curfew
Currier

———

C. *bitches.*

Capable
Captious
Carelefs
Careful
Carnage
Caution
Cautious
Charmer
Chauntrefs
Chearful
Cherriper
Chorus

Circe
Clarinet
Clio
Comely
Comfort
Comical
Concord
Courtefy
Crafty
Crazy
Credible
Credulous
Croney
Cruel
Curious

—•—•—•—•—

D. *dogs.*

Damper
Danger
Dangerous
Dapper
Dafter
Darter
Dafher
Dafhwood
Daunter
Dexterous
Difputant
Downright
Dragon
Dreadnought
Driver
Dufter

D. *bitches.*

D. *bitches.*

Dainty
Daphne
Darling
Dashaway
Dauntless
Delicate
Desperate
Destiny
Dian
Diligent
Docile
Document
Doubtful
Doubtless
Dreadful
Dreadless
Dulcet

E. *dogs.*

Eager
Earnest
Effort
Elegant
Eminent
Envious
Envoy
Errant
Excellent

E. *bitches.*

Easy
Echo
Ecstacy
Endless
Energy
Enmity
Essay

F. *dogs.*

Factious
Factor
Fatal
Fearnought
Ferryman
Fervent
Finder
Firebrand
Flagrant
Flasher
Fleece'em
Flinger
Flippant
Flourisher
Flyer
Foamer
Foiler
Foreman
Foremost
Foresight

Forester
Forward
Fulminant
Furrier
Farmer.

————

F. *bitches.*

Fairmaid
Fairplay
Faithful
Famous
Fancyful
Fashion
Favourite
Fearless
Festive
Fickle
Fidget
Fiery
Fireaway
Firetail
Flighty
Flourish
Flurry
Forcible
Fretful
Friendly
Frisky
Frolic
Frolicsome
Funnylass
Fury

2   **G.** *dogs.*

G. *dogs.*

Gainer
Gallant
Galliard
Galloper
Gamboy
Gameſter
Garrulous
Gazer
General
Genius
Gimcrack
Giant
Glancer
Glider
Glorious
Goblin
Governor
Grapler
Graſper
Griper
Growler
Grumbler
Guardian
Guider
Guiler

———

G. *bitches.*

Gaiety
Gainful
Galley
Gambol

Gameſome
Gameſtreſs
Gaylaſs
Ghaſtly
Giddy
Gladneſs
Gladſome
Governeſs
Graceful
Graceleſs
Gracious
Grateful
Gravity
Guileſome
Guiltleſs
Guilty

⸻

H. *dogs.*

Hannibal
Harbinger
Hardiman
Hardy
Harlequin
Harraſſer
Havock
Hazard
Headſtrong
Hearty
Hector
Heedful
Hercules
Hero
Highflyer

Hopeful
Hotſpur
Humbler
Hurtful

———

H. *bitches.*

Haſty
Handſome
Harlot
Harmony
Hazardous
Heedleſs
Helen
Heroine
Hideous
Honeſty
Hoſtile

⸻

I. J. *dogs.*

Jerker
Jingler
Impetus
Jockey
Jolly
Jolly-boy
Joſtler
Jovial
Jubal
Judgment
Jumper

I. J. *bitches.*

Jealoufy
Induftry
Jollity
Joyful
Joyous

L. *dogs.*

Labourer
Larum
Lafher
Lafter
Launcher
Leader
Leveller
Liberal
Libertine
Lictor
Lifter
Lightfoot
Linguift
Liftener
Lounger
Lucifer
Lunatic
Lunger
Lurker
Lufty

L. *bitches.*

Lacerate

Laudable
Lavifh
Lawlefs
Lenity
Levity
Liberty
Lightning
Lightfome
Likely
Liffome
Litigate
Lively
Lofty
Lovely
Luckylafs
Lunacy

M. *dogs.*

Manager
Manful
Markfman
Marplot
Marfchal
Martial
Marvellous
Match'em
Maxim
Maximus
Meanwell
Medler
Menacer
Mendall
Mender
Mentor

Mercury
Merlin
Merryboy
Merryman
Meffmate
Methodift
Mighty
Militant
Minikin
Mifcreant
Mixture
Monarch
Monitor
Motley
Mounter
Mover
Mungo
Mufical
Mutinous
Mutterer
Myrmidon
mountebank.

M. *bitches.*

Madcap
Madrigal
Magic
Maggoty
Matchlefs
Melody
Merrylafs
Merryment
Mindful
Minion
Miriam
Mifchief

Mifchief
Modifh
Monody
Mufic
millinr.

N. *dogs.*

Nervous
Neftor
Nettler
Newfman
Nimrod
Noble
Nonfuch
Novel
Noxious

———

N. *bitches.*

Narrative
Neatnefs
Needful
Negative
Nicety
Nimble
Noify
Notable
Notice
Notion
Novelty
Novice

P. *dogs.*

Pæan
Pageant
Paragon
Paramount
Partner
Partyman
Pealer
Penetrant
Perfect
Perilous
Pertinent
Petulant
Phœbus
Piercer
Pilgrim
Pillager
Pilot
Pincher
Piper
Playful
Plodder
Plunder
Politic
Potent
Prater
Prattler
Premier
Prefident
Prefto
Prevalent
Primate
Principal
Prodigal
Prowler

F 4

Prompter
Prophet
Profper
Profperous
Pryer
panther

———

P. *bitches.*

Paffion
Paftime
Patience
Phœnix
Phrenetic
Phrenzy
Placid
Playful
Pleafant
Pliant
Pofitive
Precious
Prettylafs
Previous
Prieftefs
Probity
Prudence

R. *dogs.*

Racer
Rager
Rallywood
Rambler
Ramper

Ramper	Rumor	Sampler
Rampant	Runner	Sampſon
Rancour	Rural	Sanction
Random	Ruſher	Sapient
Ranger	Ruſtic	Saucebox
Ranſack		Saunter
Rantaway	———	Scalper
Ranter		Scamper
Rapper	R. *bitches.*	Schemer
Ratler		Scourer
Ravager	Racket	Scrambler
Ravenous	Rally	Screamer
Raviſher	Rampiſh	Screecher
Reacher	Rantipole	Scuffler
Reaſoner	Rapid	Searcher
Rector	Rapine	Settler
Regent	Rapture	Sharper
Render	Rarity	Shifter
Reſonant	Raſhneſs	Signal
Reſtive	Rattle	Singer
Reveller	Raviſh	Singwell
Rifler	Reptile	Skirmiſh
Rigid	Reſolute	Smoker
Rigour	Reſtleſs	Social
Ringwood	Rhapſody	Solomon
Rioter	Riddance	Solon
Riſker	Riot	Songſter
Rockwood	Rival	Sonorous
Romper	Roguiſh	Soundwell
Rouſer	Ruin	Spanker
Router	Rummage	Special
Rover	Ruthleſs	Specimen
Rudeſby		Speedwell
Ruffian		Spinner
Ruffler	S. *dogs.*	Splendor
		Splenetic
	Salient	Spoiler
		Spokeſman

Spokefman
Sportfman
Squabbler
Squeaker
Statefman
Steady
Stickler
Stinger
Stormer
Stranger
Stripling
Striver
Strivewell
Stroker
Stroller
Struggler
Sturdy
Subtile
Succour
Suppler
Surly
Swaggerer
Sylvan

———

S. *bitches.*

Sanguine
Sappho
Science
Scrupulous
Shrewdnefs
Skilful
Songftrefs
Specious
Speedy

Spiteful
Spitfire
Sportful
Sportive
Sportly
Sprightly
Stately
Stoutnefs
Strenuous
Strumpet
Surety
Sybil
Symphony
Sweetlips

⊷⊶⊷⊷

T. *dogs.*

Tackler
Talifman
Tamer
Tangent
Tarter
Tatler
Taunter
Teafer
Terror
Thrafher
Threatner
Thumper
Thunderer
Thwacker
Thwarter
Tickler
Tomboy
Topmoft
Topper

Torment
Torrent
Torturer
Toffer
Touchftone
Tracer
Tragic
Trampler
Tranfit
Tranfport
Traveller
Trimbufh
Trimmer
Triumph
Trojan
Trouncer
Truant
Trudger
Trueboy
Trueman
Trufty
Tryal
Tryer
Trywell
Tuner
Turbulent
Twanger
Twig'em
Tyrant

———

T. *bitches.*

Tattle
Telltale
Tempeft
Tentative

Tentative
Termagant
Terminate
/ Terrible
Tetty
Thankful
Thoughtful
/ Tidings
Toilsome
Tractable
/ Tragedy
Trespass
Trifle
Trivial
/ Trollop
Troublesome
' Truelass
Truemaid
/ Tunable
Tuneful

V. dogs.

Vagabond
' Vagrant
/ Valiant
Valid
Valorous
Valour
/ Vaulter
/ Vaunter
Venture
' Venturer
Venturous

Vermin
Vexer
/ Victor
/ Vigilant
Vigorous
Vigour
/ Villager
Viper
/ Volant
Voucher

V. bitches.

Vanquish
Vehemence
Vehement
/ Vengeance
/ Vengeful
/ Venomous
Venturesome
Venus
Verify
Verity
Vicious
/ Victory
Victrix
Vigilance
Violent
Viperous
Virulent
Vitiate
Vivid
/ Vixen
/ Vocal

/ Volatile
Voluble

W. dogs.

Wanderer
Warbler
/ Warning
/ Warrior
Warwhoop
Wayward
/ Wellbred
/ Whipster
/ Whynot
Wildair
/ Wildman
Wilful
Wisdom
/ Woodman
Worker
Workman
Worthy
/ Wrangler
Wrestler

W. bitches.

Waggery
Waggish
Wagtail
/ Wanton
Warfare
Warlike

Warlike	Welldone	Wifhful
Wafpifh	Whimfey	Wonderful
Wafteful	Whirligig	Worry
Watchful	Wildfire	Wrathful
Welcome	Willing	Wreakful

L E T-

LETTER VI.

AFTER the young hounds have been round-ed, and are well reconciled to the kennel, know the huntſman, and begin to know their names, they ſhould be put into couples, and walked out amongſt ſheep.

If any be particularly ſnappiſh and trouble-ſome, you ſhould leave the couples looſe about their necks in the kennel, till you find they are more reconciled to them. If any be more ſtubborn than the reſt, you ſhould couple them to old hounds rather than to young ones; and you ſhould not couple *two dogs* together when you can avoid it. Young hounds are awkward at firſt; I ſhould, therefore, adviſe you to ſend out a few only at a time with your people on foot; they will ſoon afterwards become handy enough to follow a horſe; and care ſhould be taken that the couples be not too looſe, leſt they ſhould ſlip their necks out of the collar, and give trouble in catching them again.

When they have been walked often in this manner amongſt the ſheep, you may then uncouple

a few

a few at a time, and begin to chaſtiſe ſuch as offer to run after them; but you will ſoon find that the cry of *ware ſheep* will ſtop them ſufficiently without the whip; and the leſs this is uſed the better. With proper care and attention you will ſoon make them aſhamed of it, but if once ſuffered to taſte the blood, you may find it difficult to reclaim them. Various are the methods uſed to break ſuch dogs from ſheep; ſome will couple them to a ram, but that is breaking them with a vengeance; you had better hang them.—A late lord of my acquaintance, who had heard of this method, and whoſe whole pack had been often guilty of killing ſheep, determined to puniſh them, and to that intent put the largeſt ram he could find into his kennel. The men with their whips and voices, and the ram with his horns, ſoon put the whole kennel into confuſion and diſmay, and the hounds and the ram were then left together. Meeting a friend ſoon after, " come," ſays he, " come with me to the kennel, and ſee " what rare ſport the ram makes among the " hounds; the old fellow lays about him ſtoutly, " I aſſure you—egad he trims them—there is " not a dog dares look him in the face."—His friend, who is a compaſſionate man, pitied the hounds exceedingly, and aſked, if he was not afraid that ſome of them might be ſpoiled :— " No, d—n them," ſaid he, " they deſerve it, " and let them ſuffer."—On they went—all was

quiet

quiet—they opened the kennel door, but faw neither ram nor hound. The ram by this time was
entirely eaten up, and the hounds having filled
their bellies, were retired to reft.

It without doubt is beft when you air your
hounds to take them out feparately; the old ones
one day, another day the young;* but as I find
your hounds are to have their whey at a diftant
dairy, on thofe days, both old and young may
be taken out together, obferving only to take
the young hounds in couples when the old ones
are along with them. Young hounds are always
ready for any kind of mifchief, and idlenefs might
make even old ones too apt to join them in it.
Befides, fhould they break off from the huntfman, the whipper-in is generally too ill mounted
at this feafon of the year eafily to head and bring
them back. Run no fuch rifk. My hounds
were near being fpoiled by the mere accident of
a horfe's falling. The whipper-in was thrown
from his horfe; the horfe ran away, and the whole
pack followed: a flock of fheep, which were
at a little diftance, took fright, began to run,
and the hounds purfued them. The moft vicious fet on the reft, and feveral fheep were foon

* It would be ftill better to take out your hounds every day,
the old and young feparately, when it can be done without inconvenience; when it cannot, a large grafs-court will partly
anfwer the fame purpofe.

pulled

pulled down and killed. I mention this to fhew you what caution is neceffary whilft hounds are idle; for though the fall of the horfe was not to be attributed to any fault of the man, yet had the old hounds been taken out by themfelves, or had all the young ones been in couples, it is pro - bable fo common an accident would not have produced fo extraordinary an effect.

It is now time to ftoop them to a fcent.—You had better enter them at their own game—it will fave you much trouble afterwards. Many dogs, I believe, like that fcent beft which they were firft blooded to; but be that as it may, it is cer- tainly moft reafonable to ufe them to that which it is intended they fhould hunt. It may not be amifs, when they firft begin to hunt, to put light collars on them. Young hounds may eafily get out of their knowledge; and fhy ones, after they have been much beaten, may not chufe to return home. Collars, in that cafe, may prevent their being loft.

You fay, you fhould not like to fee your young hounds run a trail-fcent. I have no doubt that you would be glad to fee them run over an open down, where you could fo eafily obferve their action and their fpeed. I cannot think the doing of it once or twice could hurt your hounds; and and yet as a fportfman, I dare not recommend it

to

to you. All that I fhall fay of it is, that it would be lefs bad than entering them *at hare.* A cat is as good a trail as any; but on no account fhould any trail be ufed after your hounds are ftooped to a fcent.

I know an old fportfman who enters his young hounds firft at a cat, which he drags along the ground for a mile or two, at the end of which he turns out a badger, firft taking care to break his teeth; he takes out about two couple of old hounds along with the young ones to hold them on. He never enters his young hounds but at vermin; for he fays, " *train up a child in the way* " *he fhould go, and when he is old he will not de-* " *part from it.*"

Summer hunting, though ufeful to young hounds, is prejudicial to old ones; I think, therefore, you will do well to referve fome of the beft of your draft-hounds to enter your young hounds with, felecting fuch as are moft likely to fet them a good example. I need not tell you they fhould not be fkirters; but, on the contrary, fhould be fair hunting hounds, fuch as love a fcent, and that hunt clofeft on the line of it; it will be ne-ceffary that fome of them fhould be good finders, and all muft be fteady: thus you procure for your young hounds the beft inftructors, and at the fame time prevent two evils, which would necdffarily neceffarily enfue, were they taught by the whole pack; one, that of corrupting, and getting into fcrapes, fuch as are not much wifer than them-felves; and the other, that of occafioning much flogging and rateing, which always fhies and in-terrupts the hunting of an old hound. An old hound is a fagacious animal, and is not fond of trufting himfelf in the way of an enraged whipper-in, who, as experience has taught him, can flog fe-verely, and can flog unjuftly.—By attending to this advice, you will improve one part of your pack without prejudice to the other; whilft fuch as never feparate their young hounds from the old, are not likely to have any of them fteady.

You afk, at what time you fhould begin to en-ter your young hounds?—that queftion is eafily anfwered; for you certainly fhould begin with them *as foon as you can.* The time muft vary in different countries: in corn countries it may not be poffible to hunt till after the corn is cut; in grafs countries you may begin fooner; and in woodlands you may hunt as foon as you pleafe. If you have plenty of foxes, and can afford to make a facrifice of fome of them for the fake of making your young hounds fteady, take them firft where you have leaft riot, putting fome of the fteadieft of your old hounds amongft them. If in fuch a place you are fortunate enough to find a litter of foxes you, may affure yourfelf you will

G

have

have but little trouble with your young hounds afterwards.

Such young hounds as are moſt riotous at firſt, generally ſpeaking, I think, are beſt in the end. A gentleman in my neighbourhood was ſo thoroughly convinced of this, that he complained bitterly of a young pointer to the perſon who gave it him, becauſe he had done *no miſchief*. However, meeting the ſame perſon ſome time after, he told him the dog he believed would prove a good one at laſt.—" How ſo ?" replied his friend, " it " was but the other day that you ſaid he was good " for nothing."—" *True; but he has killed me nine-* " *teen turkies ſince that.*"

If, owing to a ſcarcity of foxes, you ſhould ſtoop your hounds at hare, let them by no means have the blood of her ; nor, for the ſake of conſiſtency, give them much encouragement. Hare-hunting has one advantage—hounds are chiefly in open ground, where you can eaſily command them ; but, notwithſtanding that, if foxes be in tolerable plenty, keep them to their own game, and forget not the advice of the old ſportſman.

Frequent *hallooing* is of uſe with young hounds ; it keeps them forward, prevents their being loſt, and hinders them from hunting after the reſt. The oftener therefore a fox is ſeen and hallooed, the better ;

better; it ferves to let them in, makes them eager, makes them exert themfelves, and teaches them to be handy. I muft tell you, at the fame time I fay this, that I by no means approve of much hallooing to old hounds; and though I frequently am guilty of it myfelf, it is owing to my fpirits, which lead me into an error which my judgment condemns. It is true, there is a time when hallooing is of ufe; a time when it does hurt; and a time when it is perfectly indifferent : but it is long practice, and great attention to hunting, that muft teach you the application.

Hounds, at their firft entering, cannot be encouraged too much. When they become handy, love a fcent, and begin to know what is *right*, it will be foon enough to chaftife them for doing *wrong*; in which cafe, one fevere beating will fave a deal of trouble. You fhould recommend to your whipper-in, when he flogs a hound, to make ufe of his voice as well as his whip; and let him remember, that the fmack of the whip is often of as much ufe as the lafh, to one that has felt it. If any be very unfteady, it will not be amifs to fend them out by themfelves, when the men go out to exercife their horfes. If you have hares in plenty, let fome be found fitting, and turned out before them; and you will foon find the moft riotous will not run after them. If you intend them to be made fteady from deer, they

G 2

fhould

ſhould often ſee deer, and they will not regard them; and if, after a probation of this kind, you turn out a cub before them, with ſome old hounds o lead them on, you may aſſure yourſelf they will not be unſteady long; for as Somervile rightly obſerves,

> " Eaſy the leſſon of the youthful train,
> When inſtinct prompts, and when example guides."

Flogging hounds in the kennel, the frequent practice of moſt huntſmen, I hold in abhorrence: it is unreaſonable, unjuſt, and cruel; and carried to the exceſs we ſometimes ſee it, is a diſgrace to humanity. Hounds that are old offenders, that are very riotous, and at the ſame time very cunning, it may be difficult to catch: ſuch hounds may be excepted——they deſerve puniſhment wherever taken, and you ſhould not fail to give it them *when you can.*—This you will allow is a particular caſe, and neceſſity may excuſe it—but let not the peace and quiet of your kennel be often thus diſturbed. When your hounds offend, puniſh them:—when caught in the fact, then let them ſuffer—and if you be ſevere, at leaſt be juſt.

When your young hounds ſtoop to a ſcent, are become handy, know a rate and ſtop eaſily, you may then begin to put them into the pack, a few only at a time; nor do I think it adviſeable to begin
this,

this, till the pack have been out a few times by themfelves, and are gotten well in blood. I fhould alfo advife you to take them the firft day where they are moft fure to find; as long reft makes all hounds riotous, and they may do that *en gaieté de cœur*, which they would not think of at another time. Let your hounds be low in flefh, when you begin to hunt; the ground is generally hard at that feafon, and they are liable to be fhaken.

If your covers be large, you will find the ftrait horn of ufe, and I am forry to hear that you do not approve of it.—You afk me why I like it?— not as a *mufician*, I can affure you.—It fignifies little in our way what the noife is, as long as it is underftood.

LETTER VII.

UNLESS I had kept a regular journal of all that has been done in the kennel from the time when my young hounds were firſt taken in, to the end of the laſt feafon, it would be impoffible, I think, to anfwer all the queſtions which in your laſt letter you aſk concerning them. I wiſh that a memory, which is far from a good one, would enable me to give the information you defire. If I am to be more circumſtantial than in my former letter, I muſt recollect, as well as I can, the regular fyſtem of my own kennel; and if I am to write from memory, you will, without doubt, excufe the want of the *lucidus ordo :*—it ſhall be my endeavour, that the information thefe letters contain, ſhall not miflead you.

You wiſh me to explain what I mean by hounds being *handy*—it reſpects their readinefs to do whatever is required of them ; and particularly, when caſt, to turn eafily which way the huntſman pleafes.*

* My hounds are frequently walked about the courts of the kennel, the whipper-in following them, and rating them after the huntſman ; this, and the fending them out, (after they have been fed,) with the people on foot, contribute greatly to make them handy.

I was

I was told the other day by a sportsman, that he considers the management of hounds as a regular system of education, from the time when they are first taken into the kennel: I perfectly agree with this gentleman; and am well convinced, that if you expect sagacity in your hound when he is old, you must be mindful what instruction he receives from you in his youth; for as he is of all animals the most docile, he is also most liable to bad habits. A diversity of character, constitution, and disposition, are to be observed amongst them; which, to be made the most of, must be carefully attended to, and differently treated. I do not pretend to have succeeded in it myself; yet you will perceive, perhaps, that I have paid some attention to it.

I begin to hunt with my young hounds in August. The employment of my huntsman the preceding months is to keep his old hounds healthy and quiet, by giving them proper exercise; and to get his young hounds forward.* They are called over often in the kennel; it uses them to their names, to the huntsman, and to the whipper-in.

* Nothing will answer this purpose so well as taking them out often. Let your huntsman lounge about with them---nothing will make them so handy. Let him get off his horse frequently, and encourage them to come to him,---nothing will familiarize them so much.---Too great restraint will oftentimes incline hounds to be riotous.

G 4

They

They are walked out often among sheep, hares, and deer: it uses them to a rate. Sometimes he turns down a cat before them, which they hunt up to, and kill: and, when the time of hunting approaches, he turns out badgers or young foxes, taking out some of the steadiest of his old hounds to lead them on—this teaches them to hunt. He draws small covers and furze brakes with them, to use them to a halloo, and to teach them obedience. If they find improper game, and hunt it, they are stopped and brought back; and as long as they will stop at a rate, they are not chastised. Obedience is all that is required of them, till they have been sufficiently taught the game they are to pursue. An obstinate deviation from it afterwards is *never pardoned*. It is an observation of the Marchese Beccaria, that " La certezza di un " castigo, benche moderato, fara sempre una " maggiore impressione, che non il timore di un " altro piu terribile, unito colla speranza, della " 'impunita."

When my young hounds are taken out to air, my huntsman takes them into that country in which they are to hunt. It is attended with this advantage; they acquire a knowledge of the country, and when left behind at any time, cannot fail to find their way home more easily.

When

When they begin to hunt, they are firſt taken into a large cover of my own, which has many ridings cut in it; and where young foxes are turned out every year on purpoſe for them. *Here* they are taught the ſcent they are to follow, are encouraged to purſue it, and are ſtopped from every other. *Here* they are blooded to fox. I muſt alſo tell you that as foxes are plentiful in this cover, the principal earth is not ſtopped, and the foxes are checked back, or ſome of them let in, as may beſt ſuit the purpoſe of blooding. After they have been hunted a few days in this manner, they are then ſent to more diſtant covers, and more old hounds are added to them; there they continue to hunt till they are taken into the pack, which is ſeldom later than the beginning of September; for by that time they will have learned what is required of them, and they ſeldom give much trouble afterwards.* In September I begin to hunt in earneſt, and after the old hounds have killed a few foxes, the young hounds are put into the pack, two or three couple at a time, till all have hunted. They are then divided; and as I ſeldom have occaſion to take in more than nine or ten couple, one half are taken out one day, the other half the next, till all are ſteady.

* Sport in fox-hunting cannot be ſaid to begin before Octo-
ber, but in the two preceding months, a pack is either made or
marred.

Two

Two other methods of entering young hounds I have practised occasionally, as the number of hounds have required; for instance, if that number be confiderable, (fifteen or fixteen couple,) I make a large draft of my fteadieft hounds, which are kept with the young hounds in a feparate kennel, and are hunted with them all the firft part of the feafon. This, when the old hounds begin to hunt, makes two diftinct packs, and is always attended with great trouble and inconvenience. Nothing hurts a pack fo much as to enter many young hounds, fince it muft be confiderably weakened by being robbed of thofe which are the moft fteady; and yet young hounds can do nothing without their affiftance. Such, therefore, as conftantly enter their young hounds in this manner, will, fometimes at leaft, have two indifferent packs, inftead of one good one.

In the other method the young hounds are well awed from fheep, but never ftooped to a fcent, till they are taken out with the pack; they are then taken out a few only at a time; and if your pack be perfectly fteady, and well manned, may not give you much trouble. The method I firft mentioned, is that I moft commonly practife, being moft fuitable to the number of young hounds I ufually enter—nine or ten couple: if you have fewer, the laft will be moft convenient. The one which requires two diftinct packs, is on too ex-

4

tenfive

tenfive a plan to fuit your eftablifhment, requiring more horfes and hounds than you intend to keep.*

Though I have mentioned, in a former letter, from eight to twelve couple of young hounds, as a fufficient number to keep up your pack to its prefent eftablifhment; yet it is always beft to have a referve of a few couple more than you want, in cafe of accidents: fince from the time you make your draft, to the time of hunting, is a long period; and their exiftence at that age and feafon very precarious: befides, when they are fafe from the diforder, they are not always fafe from each other; and a fummer feldom paffes without fome

---

* To render fox-hunting perfeft, no young hounds fhould be taken into the pack the firft feafon—a requifite too expenfive for moft fportfmen. The pack fhould confift of about forty couple of hounds, that have hunted, one, two, three, four, or five feafons. The young pack fhould confift of about twenty couple of young hounds, and about an equal number of old ones. They fhould have a feparate eftablifhment, nor fhould the two kennels be near enough to interfere with each other. The feafon over, the beft of the young hounds fhould be taken into the pack, and the draft of old ones exchanged for them. To enable you every feafon to take in twenty couple of young hounds, many muft be bred; and of courfe the greater your choice, the handfomer your pack will become. It will always be eafy to keep up the number of old hounds, for when your own draft is not fufficient, drafts from other packs may eafily be obtained, and at a fmall expence. When young hounds are hunted together the firft feafon, and have not a fufficient number of old hounds along with them, it does them more harm than good.

loffes

loffes of that kind. At the fame time I muft tell you, that I fhould decline *entering* more than are neceffary to keep up the pack, fince a greater number would only create ufelefs trouble and vexation.

You wifh to know what number of old hounds you fhould hunt with the young ones:—that muft depend on the firength of your pack, and the number which you choofe to fpare; if good and fteady, ten or twelve couple will be fufficient.

My young hounds, and fuch old ones as are intended to hunt along with them,* are kept in a kennel by themfelves, till the young hounds are hunted with the pack. I need not, I am fure, enumerate the many reafons that make *this regulation* neceffary.

I never truft my young hounds in the foreft till they have been well blooded to fox, and feldom put more than a couple into the pack at a time.†

* Some alfo take out their unfteady hounds, when they enter the young ones; I doubt the propriety of it.

† I fometimes fend all my young hounds together into the foreft, with four or five couple of old hounds only; fuch as I know they cannot fpoil. As often as any of them break off to deer, they are taken up, and flogged. When they lofe one fox, they try for another; and are kept out, till they are all made tolerably fteady.

The

The others are walked out amongſt the deer, when the men exerciſe their horſes, and are ſeverely chaſtiſed if they take any notice of them. They alſo draw covers with them; chooſing out ſuch, where they can beſt ſee their hounds, and moſt eaſily command them; and where there is the leaſt chance to find a fox. On theſe occaſions I had rather they ſhould have to rate their hounds than encourage them. It requires leſs judgment; · and, if improperly done, is leſs dangerous in its conſequences. One halloo of encouragement to a wrong ſcent, more than undoes all that you have been doing.

When young hounds begin to love a ſcent, it may be of uſe to turn out a badger before them; you will then be able to diſcover what improvement they have made; I mention a badger, on a ſuppoſition that young foxes cannot ſo well be ſpared; beſides, the badger, being a ſlower animal, he may eaſily be followed, and driven the way you chooſe he ſhould run.

The day you intend to turn out a fox, or badger, you will do well to ſend them amongſt hares, or deer. A little rating and flogging, before they are encouraged to vermin, is of the greateſt uſe, as it teaches them as well what they ſhould not, as what they ſhould do. I have known a badger run ſeveral miles, if judiciouſly

5 managed;

managed; for which purpofe he fhould be turned out in a very open country, and followed by a perfon who has more fenfe than to ride on the line of him. If he do not meet with a cover or hedge in his way, he will keep on for feveral miles; if he do, you will not be able to get him any farther. You fhould give him a great deal of law, and you will do well to break his teeth.*

If you run any cubs to ground in an indifferent country, and do not want blood, bring them home, and they will be of ufe to your young hounds. Turn out bag foxes to your young hounds, but never to your old ones. I object to them on many accounts; but of bag foxes I fhall have occafion to fpeak hereafter.

The day after your hounds have had blood, is alfo a proper time to fend them where there is riot, and to chaftife them if they deferve; it is always beft to correct them when they cannot help knowing what they are corrected for. When you fend out your hounds for this purpofe, the later they go out the better, as the worfe the fcent is the lefs inclinable will they be to run it, and of

* The critic fays, " there is neither juftice nor equity in breaking his teeth." (Vide Monthly Review.) I confefs there is not, and I never know that it is done, but I feel all the force of the obfervation. Let *neceffity*, if it be able, plead in its excufe.

courfe

courfe will give lefs trouble in ftopping them. It is a common practice with huntfmen to flog their hounds moft unmercifully in the kennel: I have already mentioned my difapprobation of it: but if many of your hounds be obftinately riotous,* you may with lefs impropriety put a live hare into the kennel to them, flogging them as often as they appproach her; they will then have fome notion, at leaft, for what they are beaten: but let me entreat you, before this *charivari*† begins, to draft off your hounds; an animal to whom we owe fo much good diverfion fhould not be ill ufed unneceffarily. When a hare is put into the kennel, the huntfman and both the whippers-in fhould be prefent; and the whippers-in fhould flog every hound, calling him by his name, and rateing him as often as he is near the hare; and, upon this occafion, they cannot cut them too hard, or rate them too much. When·

---

* This paffage has alfo been thought deferving of cenfure, though its motive is humane. By thefe means, the difobedient are taught obedience, and a more general punifhment prevented; which the effect of bad example might otherwife make neceffary.

† A confufion arifing from a variety of noifes. It is a cuftom in France, and in Switzerland, if a woman marry fooner than is ufual after the death of her hufband; or a woman get the better of her hufband when attempting to chaftife her, and return the beating with intereft—the neighbours give them a *charivari*—a kind of concert compofed of tongs, fire-fhovels, kettles, brafs pans, &c. &c.

they

they think they have chaſtiſed them enough, the hare ſhould then be taken away, the huntſman ſhould halloo off his hounds, and the whippers-in ſhould rate them to him. If any one love hare more than the reſt, you may tie a dead one round his neck, flogging him and rating him at the ſame time. This poſſibly may make him aſhamed of it. I never bought a lot of hounds, ſome of which were not obliged to undergo this diſcipline. Either hares are leſs plentiful in other countries, or other ſportſmen are leſs nice in making their hounds ſteady from them.

I would adviſe you to hunt your large covers with your young hounds : it will tire them out ;* a neceſſary ſtep towards making them ſteady ; will open the cover againſt the time you begin in earneſt, and by diſturbing the large covers early in the year, foxes will be ſhy of them in the ſeaſon, and ſhew you better chaces ; beſides, as they are not likely to break from thence, you can

* Provided that you have old hounds enough out, to carry on the ſcent; if you have not a body of old hounds to keep up a cry on the right ſcent, the young ones, as ſoon as the ground becomes foiled, will be ſcattered about the cover, hunting old ſcents, and will not get on faſt enough to tire themſelves. Young hounds ſhould never be taken into large covers, where there is much riot, unleſs whippers-in can eaſily get at them.

do

do no hurt to the corn, and may begin before it is cut.

If your hounds be very riotous, and you are obliged to ſtop them often from hare, it will be adviſeable to try on (however late it may be) till you find a fox; as the giving them encouragement ſhould, at ſuch a time, prevail over every other conſideration.

Though all young hounds are given to riot, yet the better they are bred, the leſs trouble they will be likely to give. Pointers well-bred ſtand naturally, and high-bred fox-hounds love their own game beſt. Such, however, 'as are very riotous, ſhould have little reſt; you ſhould hunt them one day in large covers where foxes are in plenty; the next day they ſhould be walked out amongſt hares and deer, and ſtopped from riot; the day following be hunted again as before. Old hounds, which I have had from other packs, (particularly ſuch as have been entered at hare) I have ſometimes found incorrigible; but I never yet knew a young hound ſo riotous, but, by this management, he ſoon became ſteady.

When hounds are rated, and do not anſwer the rate, they ſhould be coupled up immediately, and be made to know the whipper-in; in all probability this method will ſave any farther

H

trouble.

trouble. Thefe fellows fometimes flog hounds unmercifully, and fome of them feem to take pleafure in their cruelty; I am fure, however, I need not defire you to prevent any excefs in cor-rection.

I have heard that no fox-hounds will break off to deer after once a fox is found.—I cannot fay the experience I have had of this diverfion will in any wife juftify the remark; let me advife you, therefore, to feek a furer dependence. Before you hunt your good hounds where hares are in plenty, let them be awed and ftopped from hare: before you hunt amongft deer, let them not only fee deer, but let them draw covers where deer are; for you muft not be furprifed, if, after they are fo far fteady as not to run them in view, they fhould challenge on the fcent of them. Unlefs you take this method with your young hounds before you put them into the pack, you will run a rifk of corrupting the old ones, and may fuffer continual vexation by hunting with unfteady hounds. I have already told you, that after my young hounds *are* taken into the pack, I ftill take out but very few at a time when I hunt among deer. I alfo change them when I take out others, for the fteadinefs they may have ac-quired could be but little depended on, were they to meet with any encouragement to be riotous.

I con-

I confefs I think firft impreffions of more confequence than they are in general thought to be;
I not only enter my young hounds to vermin on
that account, but I even ufe them, as early as I
can, to the ftrongeft covers and thickeft brakes;
and I feldom find that they are fhy of them afterwards. A friend of mine has affured me, that
he once entered a fpaniel to fnipes, and the dog
ever after was partial to them, preferring them to
every other bird.

If you have martin cats within your reach, as
all hounds are fond of their fcent, you will do
well to enter your young hounds in the covers
they frequent. The martin cat being a fmall
animal, by running the thickeft brakes it can
find, teaches hounds to run cover, and is therefore of the greateft ufe. I do not much approve
of hunting them with the old hounds; they fhew
but little fport; are continually climbing trees;
and as the cover they run feldom fails to fcratch
and tear hounds confiderably, I think you might
be forry to fee your whole pack disfigured by it.
The agility of this little animal is really wonderful; and though it falls frequently from a tree,
in the midft of a whole pack of hounds, all intent on catching it, there are but few inftances,
I believe, of a martin's being caught by them in
that fituation.

In fummer hounds might hunt in an evening:
—I know a pack, that after having killed one
fox in the morning with the young hounds, killed
another in the evening with the old ones. Scent
generally lies well at the clofe of the day, yet
there is a great objection to hunting at that time;
—animals are then more eafily difturbed, and
you have a greater variety of fcents than at an
earlier hour.

Having given you all the information that I
can poffibly recollect, with regard to my own
management of young hounds, I fhall now take
notice of that part of your laft letter, where, I
am forry to find, our opinions differ.—Obedience,
you fay, is every thing neceffary in a hound, and
that it is of little confequence by what means it
is obtained. I cannot concur altogether in that
opinion; for I think it very neceffary, that the
hound fhould at the fame time underftand you.
Obedience, under proper management, will be a
neceffary confequence of it. Obedience, furely,
is not all that is required of them; they fhould
be taught to diftinguifh of themfelves right from
wrong, or I know not how they are to be managed; when, as it frequently happens, we cannot fee what they are at, and muft take their
words for it. A hound that hears a voice which
has often rated him, and that hears the whip he
has often felt, I know, will ftop. I alfo know,

he

he will commit the fame fault again, if he has been accuftomed to be guilty of it.

Obedience, you very rightly obferve, is a neceffary quality in a hound, for he is ufelefs without it. It is, therefore, an excellent principle for a huntfman to fet out upon; yet, good as it is, I think it may be carried too far. I would not have him infift on too much, or torment his hounds *mal-à-propos*, by forcibly exacting from them what is not abfolutely neceffary to your diverfion. You fay, he intends to enter your hounds at hare :—is it to teach them obedience? Does he mean to encourage vice in them for the fake of correcting it afterwards?—I have heard, indeed, that the way to make hounds fteady from hare, is to enter them at hare :* that is, to encourage them to hunt her. The belief of fo ftrange a paradox requires more faith than I can pretend to.

It concerns me to be under the neceffity of differing from you in opinion; but fince it cannot now be helped, we will purfue the fubject, and examine it throughout. Permit me then to afk

* In proper hands either method may do. The method here propofed feems beft fuited to fox-hounds in general, as well as to thofe who have the direction of them. The talents of fome men are fuperior to all rules; nor is their fuccefs any pofitive proof of the goodnefs of their method.

H 3

you

you, what it is you propofe from entering your hounds at hare? Two advantages, I fhall pre-fume, you expect from it—the teaching of your hounds to hunt, and teaching them to be obe-dient. However neceffary you may think thefe requifites in a hound, I cannot but flatter myfelf that they are to be acquired by lefs exceptionable means. The method I have already mentioned to make hounds obedient, as it is practifed in my own kennel—that of calling them over often in the kennel, to ufe them to their names,* and walking them out often amongft fheep, hares, and deer, from which they are ftopped to ufe them to a rate, in my opinion, would anfwer your purpofe better. The teaching your hounds to hunt, is by no means fo neceffary as you feem to imagine. *Nature* will teach it them, nor need you give yourfelf fo much concern about it. *Art* only will be neceffary to prevent them from hunt-ing what they ought *not to hunt*; and do you think your method a proper one to accom-plifh it?

The firft and moft effential thing towards making hounds obedient, I fuppofe, is to make them underftand you; nor do I apprehend that you will find any difficulty on their parts, but fuch

* Vide note page 43.

as may be occafioned on your's.* The language
we ufe to them to convey our meaning fhould
never vary; ftill lefs fhould we alter the very
meaning of the terms we ufe. Would it not be
abfurd to encourage when we mean to rate ? and
if we did, could we expect to be obeyed ? You
will not deny this, and yet you are guilty of no
lefs an inconfiftency, when you encourage your
hounds to run a fcent to-day, which you know,
at the fame time, you muft be obliged to break
them from to-morrow—is it not running counter
to juftice and to reafon ?

I confefs there is fome ufe in hunting young
hounds, where you can eafily command them;
but even this you may pay too dearly for. Enter
your hounds in fmall covers, or in fuch large
ones as have ridings cut in them; whippers-in
can then get at them, can always fee what they
are at, and I have no doubt that you may have a
pack of fox-hounds ready to fox by this means,
without adopting fo prepofterous a method as
that of firft making hare-hunters of them. You
will find, that hounds thus taught what game
they are to hunt, and what they are not, will

* Were huntfmen to fcream continually to their hounds,
ufing the fame halloo whether they were drawing, cafting, or
running, the hounds could not underftand them, and probably
would fhew, on every occafion, as little attention to them as
they would deferve.

H 4

ftop

ftop at a word, becaufe they will underftand you: and, after they have been treated in this manner, a fmack only of the whip will fpare you the inhumanity of cutting your hounds in pieces (not very juftly) for faults which you yourfelf have encouraged them to commit.

In your laft letter you feem very anxious to get your young hounds well blooded to fox, at the fame time that you talk of entering them at hare. How am I to reconcile fuch contradictions? If the blood of fox be of fo much ufe, furely you cannot think the blood of hare a matter of indifference; unlefs you fhould be of opinion, that a fox is better eating. You may think, perhaps, it was not intended they fhould hunt fheep; yet we very well know, when once they have killed fheep, that they have no diflike to mutton afterwards.

You have conceived an idea, perhaps, that a fox-hound is defigned by nature to hunt a fox. Yet, furely, if that were your opinion, you would not think of entering him at any other game. I cannot, however, fuppofe nature defigned the dog, which we call a fox-hound, to hunt fox only, fince, we very well know, he will alfo hunt other animals. That a well bred fox-hound may give a preference to vermin, *cæteris paribus*, I will not difpute: it is very poffible he may; but,

of

of this I am certain—that every fox-hound will leave a bad fcent of fox for a good one of either hare or deer, unlefs he has been made fteady from them; and in this I fhall not fear to be contradicted. But as I do not wifh to enter into abftrufe reafoning with you, or think it in anywife material to our prefent purpofe, whether the dogs we call fox-hounds were originally defigned by nature to hunt fox or not; we will drop the fubject. I muft at the fame time beg leave to obferve, that dogs are not the only animals in which an extraordinary diverfity of fpecies has happened fince the days of Adam: yet a great naturalift tells us, that man is nearer, by eight degrees, to Adam, than is the dog to the firft dog of his race; fince the age of man is fourfcore years, and that of a dog but ten. It therefore follows, that if both fhould equally degenerate, the alteration would be eight times more remarkable in the dog than in man.

The two moft neceffary queftions which refult from the foregoing premifes, are—whether hounds entered at hare are perfectly fteady, afterwards, to fox—and, whether fteadinefs be not attainable by more reafonable means? Having never hunted with gentlemen who follow this practice, I muft leave the firft queftion for others to determine; but having always had my hounds fteady, I can myfelf anfwer the fecond.

The

The objections I have now made to the treat-
ment of young hounds by fome huntfmen, though
addreffed, my friend, to you, are general objections, and fhould not perfonally offend you. I
know no man more juft, or more humane, than
yourfelf. The difapprobation you fo ftrongly
marked in your laft letter of the feverity ufed in
fome kennels, the noble animal we both of us
admire is much beholden to you for. Your intention of being prefent yourfelf the firft time a
hound is flogged, to fee how your new whipper-in
behaves himfelf, is a proof of benevolence, which
the Italian author of the moft humane book,*
could not fail to commend you for. Huntfmen
and whippers-in are feldom fo unlucky as to have
your feelings; yet cuftom, which authorifes them
to flog hounds unmercifully, does not do away
the barbarity of it.—A gentleman feeing a girl
fkinning eels alive, afked her, " if it was not
" very cruel!"—" O not at all, Sir," replied the
girl, " *they be ufed to it.*"

* Dei delitti e delle pene.

LETTER VIII.

YOU defire to know if there be any remedy for the diftemper among dogs. I fhall, therefore, mention all the diforders which my hounds have experienced, and point out the remedies which have been of fervice to them. The diftemper you inquire about is, I believe, the moft fatal (the plague only excepted) that any animal is fubject to. Though not long known in this country, it is almoft inconceivable what numbers have been deftroyed by it in fo fhort a period; feveral hundreds I can myfelf place to this mortifying account. It feems happily to be now on the decline; at leaft, is lefs frequent and more mild; and probably in time may be entirely removed. The effects of it are too generally known to need any defcription of them here; I wifh the remedies were known as well!

A brother fportfman communicated to me a remedy, which, he faid, his hounds had found great benefit from, viz. *an ounce of Peruvian bark, in a glafs of Port wine, taken twice a day.*— It is not infallible; but in fome ftages of this

dif-

diforder is certainly of ufe. The hound moft infected, that ever I knew to recover, was a large
ftag-hound; he lay five days without being able
to get off the bench; receiving little nourifhment
during the whole time of the diforder, except
the medicine, with which he drank three bot-
tles of Port wine. You may think, perhaps,
the feeder drank his fhare—it is probable he
might, had it not been fent ready mixed up with
the bark. I once tried the *poudre unique*, thinking it a proper medicine for a diforder which is
faid to be putrid; but I cannot fay any thing in
its favour, with regard to dogs, at leaft. Norris's drops I have alfo given, and with fuccefs. I
gave a large table-fpoonful of them in an equal
quantity of Port wine, three times a day; as the
dog grew better, I leflened the quantity. When
dogs run much at the nofe, nothing will contribute more to the cure of them than keeping that
part clean; when that cannot conveniently be
done, emetics will be neceflary: the beft I know
is a large fpoonful of common falt, diffolved in
three fpoonfuls of warm water.* The firft fymp-
tom of this diforder generally is a cough. As
foon as it is perceived amongft my young hounds,
great attention is paid to them: they have plenty

* The quantity of falt muft be proportioned to the fize of
the dog, and to the difficulty there may be to make him vo-
mit.

of clean ſtraw, and are fed oftener and better than at other times; as long as they continue to eat the kennel meat, they are kept together; as ſoon as any of them refuſe to feed, they are removed into another kennel, the door of the lodging-room is left open in the day, and they are only ſhut up at night: being out in the air is of great ſervice to them. To ſuch as are very bad, I give Norris's drops; to others, emetics; whilſt ſome only require to be better fed than ordinary, and need no other remedy.* They ſhould be fed from the kitchen, when they refuſe the kennel meat. Sometimes they will loſe the uſe of their hinder parts; bleeding them, by cutting of the laſt joint of the tail, may, perhaps, be of ſervice to them. I cannot ſpeak of it with any certainty, yet I have reaſon to think that I once ſaved a favourite dog by this operation. In ſhort, by one method or another, I think they may always be recovered.

The likelieſt preſervative for thoſe that are well is keeping them warm at night, and feeding them high. This diſorder being probably infectious, it is better to provide an hoſpital for ſuch as are ſeized with it, which ſhould be in the

---

* Hounds that have the diſtemper upon them have but little appetite. By feeding two or three together, they eat more greedily.

back

back part of the kennel. There is no doubt, that fome kennels are healthier than others, and confequently lefs liable to it. I apprehend mine to be one of thofe; for in a dozen years I do not believe that I have loft half that number of old hounds, although I lofe fo great a number of whelps at their walks. Neighbouring kennels have not been equally fortunate: I have obferved, in fome of them, a diforder unknown in mine; I mean a fwelling in the fide, which fometimes breaks, but foon after forms again, and generally proves fatal at laft. I once heard a friend of mine fay, whofe kennel is fubject to this complaint, that he never knew but one inftance of a dog who recovered from it. I have, however, fince known another, in a dog I had from him, which I cured by frequently rubbing with a digeftive ointment: the tumour broke, and formed again feveral times, till at laft it entirely difappeared. The diforder we have now been treating of has this, I think, in common with the putrid fore throat, that it ufually attacks the weakeft. Women are more apt to catch the fore throat than men; children, than women; and young hounds more readily catch this diforder than old. When it feizes whelps at their walks, or young hounds, when firft taken from them, it is then moft dangerous. I alfo think that madnefs, *their* inflammatory fever, is lefs frequent than it was before this diforder was known.

I   There

There are few diforders which dogs are fo fubject to as the mange. Air and exercife, whol-
fome food, and cleanlinefs, are the beft prefer-
vatives againft it. Your feeder fhould be particularly attentive to it, and when he perceives any
fpot upon them, let him rub it with the following mixture:

> A pint of train oil,
> Half a pint of oil of turpentine,
> A quarter of a pound of ginger, in powder,
> Half an ounce of gunpowder, finely powdered,
> Mixed up cold.

If the diforder fhould be bad enough to refift
that, three mild purging balls, one every other
day, fhould be given, and the dog laid up for a
little while afterwards. For the red mange, you
may ufe the following:

> Four ounces of quickfilver,
> Two ounces of Venice turpentine,
> One pound of hog's lard.

The quickfilver and turpentine are to be rubbed
together, till the globules all difappear. When
you apply it, you muft rub an ounce, once a
day, upon the part affected, for three days fucceffively. This is to be ufed when the hair
comes off, or any rednefs appears.

How wonderful is the fatigue which a fox-
hound undergoes! Could you count the miles

he

he runs, the number would appear almoſt incredible. This he undergoes cheerfully; and, perhaps, three times a week, through a long ſeaſon: his health, therefore, well deſerves your care; nor ſhould you ſuffer the leaſt taint to injure it. Huntſmen are frequently too negligent in this point. I know one in particular, a famous one too, whoſe kennel was never free from the mange, and the ſmell of brimſtone was oftentimes ſtronger, I believe, in the noſes of his hounds than the ſcent of the fox.—If you chuſe to try a curious preſcription for the cure of the mange, in the Phil. Tranſ. No. 25, p. 451, you will find the following:

“ Mr. Cox procured an old mungrel cur, all
“ over mangy, of a middle ſize, and having,
“ ſome hours before, fed him plentifully with
“ cheeſe-parings and milk, he prepared his ju-
“ gular vein; then he made a ſtrong ligature on
“ his neck, that the venal blood might be emit-
“ ted with the greater impetus; after this, he
“ took a young land ſpaniel, about the ſame
“ bigneſs, and prepared his jugular vein like-
“ wiſe, that the deſcendent part might receive
“ the mangy dog's blood, and the aſcendent diſ-
“ charge his own into a diſh; he transfuſed
“ about fourteen or ſixteen ounces of the blood
“ of the *infected* into the veins of the *ſound* dog;
“ by this experiment there appeared no alteration
“ in

" in the found one, but the mangy dog was, in
" about ten days, or a fortnight's time, perfectly
" cured; and poffibly this is the quickeft and
" fureft remedy for that difeafe, either in man
" or beaft."

Hounds fometimes are bitten by vipers: fweet
oil has been long deemed a certain antidote;
fome fhould be applied to the part, and fome
taken inwardly. Though a friend of mine informs me, that the common cheefe rennet, ex-
ternally applied, is a more efficacious remedy
than oil, for the bite of a viper. They are liable
to wounds and cuts: Friar's balfam is very good,
if applied immediately; yet, as it is apt to fhut
up a bad wound too foon, the following tincture
in fuch cafes may, perhaps, be preferable; at
leaft, after the firft dreffing or two—

> Of Barbadoes aloes, two ounces,
> Of myrrh, pounded, three ounces,
> Mixed up with a quart of brandy.

The bottle fhould be well corked, and put into
a bark bed, or dunghill, for about ten days or a
fortnight. The tongue of the dog, in moft
cafes, is his beft furgeon; where he can apply
that, he will feldom need any other remedy. A
green, or feton, in the neck, is of great relief in
moft diforders of the eyes; and I have frequently
known dogs almoft blind, recovered by it. It is

I   alfo

alſo of ſervice when dogs are ſhaken in the ſhoulders, and has made many ſound.* .In the latter caſe, there ſhould be two, one applied on each ſide, and as near to the ſhoulder as it is poſſible. The following ointment may be uſed to diſperſe ſwellings:

> Of freſh mutton ſuet, *tried*, two pounds,
> Of gum elemi, one pound,
> Of common turpentine, ten ounces.

The gum is to be melted with the ſuet, and, when taken from the fire, the turpentine is to be mixed with it, ſtraining the mixture whilſt it is hot. Dogs frequently are ſtubbed in the foot: the tincture before-mentioned, and this, or any digeſtive ointment, will ſoon recover them.† For ſtrains, I uſe two-thirds of ſpirits of wine, and one of turpentine, mixed up together; the Britiſh oil is alſo good: hounds, from blows, or other accidents, are often lame in the ſtifle: either of theſe, frequently applied, and long reſt, are the likelieſt means that I know of to recover

---

* Turning a hound out of the kennel will ſometimes cure a lameneſs in the ſhoulders. An attentive huntſman will perceive, from the manner of a hound's galloping, when this lameneſs takes place; and the hound ſhould be turned out immediately. Care ſhould be taken that a hound, turned out, do not become fat.

† An obſtinate lameneſs ſometimes is increaſed by humours. Phyſic, in that caſe, may be neceſſary to remove it.

them.

them. The following excellent remedy for a ftrain, with which I have cured myfelf, and many others, I have alfo found of benefit to dogs, when ftrained in the leg or foot.

Diffolve two ounces of camphire in half a pint of fpirits of wine, and put to it a bullock's gall. The part affected muft be rubbed before the fire three or four times a day.

Sore feet are foon cured with brine, pot-liquor, or falt and vinegar, a handful of falt to a pint of vinegar; if neither of thefe will do, mercurial ointment may then be neceffary. A plafter of black pitch is the beft cure for a thorn in either man, horfe, or dog; and I have known it fucceed after every thing elfe had failed. If the part be much inflamed, a common poultice bound over the plafter will affift in the cure. Hounds frequently are lame in the knee, fometimes from bruifes, fometimes from the ftab of a thorn; digeftive ointment, rubbed in upon the part, will generally be of fervice.*

If hounds be much troubled with worms, the following is the beft cure that I am acquainted with:

---

* If the knee continue foul, blifters and long reft afterwards are the moft likely means to recover it.

> Of pewter, pulverized, 1 drachm 10 grs.
> Of Æthiops mineral, 16 grs.

This is to be taken three times; every other day,
once: the dog fhould be kept warm, and from
cold water. Whey, or pot-liquor, may be given
him two or three hours after, and fhould be
continued, infiead of meat, during the time he
is taking the medicine. The beft way of giving
it is to mix it up with butter, and then to make
it into balls with a little flour.

When a dog is rough in his coat, and fcratches
much, two or three purging balls, and a little
reft afterwards, feldom fail to get him into order
again. To make dogs fine in their coats, you
fhould ufe the following drefling:

> One pound of native fulphur,
> One quart of train oil,
> One pint of oil of turpentine,
> Two pounds of foap.

My hounds are dreffed with it two or three times
only, in a year: in fome kennels, I am told
they drefs them once in two months. The more
frequently it is done, the cleaner, I fuppofe,
your hounds will look. Should you choofe to
drefs your puppies before they are put out to
their walks, the following receipt, which I received from a friend of mine in Staffordfhire,

(the

(the perfon already mentioned in this letter, an excellent fportfman, to whom I have many obligations) will anfwer the purpofe beft, and on their change of diet, from milk to meat, may be fometimes neceffary:

> Three quarters of an ounce of quickfilver,
> Half a pint of fpirits of turpentine,
> Four ounces of hog's lard,
> One pound of foft foap,
> Three ounces of common turpentine, in which the quickfilver muft be killed.

Inftinct directs dogs, when the ftomach is out of order, to be their own phyfician; and it is from their example that we owe our knowledge how to relieve it. It may appear foreign to our prefent purpofe; yet as it is much (if true) to the honour of animals in general, I muft beg leave to add, what a French author tells us:— that alfo by the hippopotamus, we are inftructed how to bleed, and by the crane, how to give a clyfter. I have already declared my difapprobation of bleeding hounds, unlefs they abfolutely want it: when they refufe their food, from having been over worked; or when they have taken a chill, to which they are very fubject, then the lofs of a little blood may be of ufe to recover them. Sick hounds will recover fooner, if fuffered to run about the houfe, than if they be confined in the kennel.

I 3

Mad-

Madnefs, thou dreadful malady; what fhall I fay to thee! or what prefervative fhall I find againft thy envenomed fang! Somervile, who declines writing of leffer ills, is not filent on the fubject of this:

> " Of leffer ills the mufe declines to fing,
> Nor ftoops fo low; of thefe each groom can tell
> The proper remedy."

I wifh this worthy gentleman, to whom we have already been fo much obliged, had been lefs fparing of his inftructions; fince it is poffible grooms may have all the knowledge he fuppofes them to have, and their mafters may ftand in need of it. No man, I believe, will complain of being too well informed: nor is any knowledge unneceffary which is likely to be put in practice. The executive part is fully fufficient to truft in the groom's hands. Somervile's advice on the fubject of madnefs, is worthy your notice:

> " When Sirius reigns, and the fun's parching beams
> Bake the dry gaping furface, vifit thou
> Each ev'n and morn, with quick obfervant eye,
> The panting pack. If in dark fullen mood,
> The glouting hound refufe his wonted meal,
> Retiring to fome clofe obfcure retreat,
> Gloomy, difconfolate; with fpeed remove
> The poor infectious wretch, and in ftrong chains
> Bind him fufpected. Thus that dire difeafe
> Which art can't cure, wife caution may prevent."

Plenty

Plenty of water, whey, greens, phyfic, air, and exercife, fuch as I have before mentioned, have hitherto preferved my kennel from its baneful influence; and, without doubt, you will alfo find their good effects.   If, notwithftanding, you fhould at any time have reafon to fufpect the approach of this evil, let your hounds be well obferved at the time when they feed; there will be no danger whilft they can eat.   Should a whole pack be in the fame predicament, they muft be chained up feparately; and I fhould be very cautious what experiment I tried to cure them; for I have been told by thofe who have had madnefs in their kennels, and who have drenched their hounds to cure it, that it was the occafion of its breaking out a long time afterwards, and that it continued to do fo, as long as they give them any thing to put it off.—If a few dogs only have been bitten, you had better hang them.—If you fufpect any, you had better feparate them from the reft; and a fhort time, if you ufe no remedy, will determine whether they really were bitten or not.— Should you, however, be defirous of trying a remedy, the following prefcription, I am told, is a very good one :

  Of Turbith's mineral eight grains,
  Ditto fixteen grains,
  Ditto thirty-two grains.

I 4   This

This is to be given for three mornings fuccef-fively; beginning the firft day with eight grains, and increafing it according to the above direc-tion. The dog fhould be empty when he takes it, and fhould have been bled the day before. The dofe fhould be given early in the morning, and the dog may have fome thin broth, or pot-liquor, about two or three o'clock, but nothing elfe during the time h; takes the medicine; he fhould alfo be kept from water. The beft way to give it is in butter, and made up into balls with a little flour. Care muft be taken that he does not throw it up again. After the laft day of the medicine, he may be fed as ufual. Various are the drenches and medicines which are given for this diforder, and all faid to be infallible: this laft, however, I prefer. The whole pack belong-ing to a gentleman in my neighbourhood were bitten; and he affures me, he never knew an in-fiance of a dog who went mad, that had taken this medicine.—The caution, which I have re-commended to you, I flatter myfelf will pre-ferve you from this dreadful malady; a malady, for which I know not how to recommend a re-medy. Several years ago I had a game-keeper much bitten in the flefhy part of his thigh; a horfe, that was bitten at the fame time, died raving mad; the man was cured by Sir George Cob's medicine.—I have heard that the Ormfkirk medicine is alfo very good. I have given it to

feveral

feveral people in my neighbourhood, and, I believe, with fuccefs; at leaft, I have not, as yet,
heard any thing to the contrary—Though I mention thefe as the two moft favourite remedies, I
recommend neither. Somervile's advice, which I
have already given, is what I recommend to you—
if properly attended to, it will prevent the want
of any remedy.

P. S. A Treatife on canine madnefs, written
by Dr. James, is worth your reading. You will
find, that he prefcribes the fame remedy for the
cure of madnefs in dogs, as I have mentioned
here, but in different quantities. I have, however taken the liberty of recommending the quantities above-mentioned, as they have been known
to fucceed in my neighbourhood, and as the ef-
ficacy of them has been very frequently proved.

LET-

LETTER IX.

THE variety of queſtions which you are pleaſed to aſk concerning the huntſman, will, perhaps, be better anſwered, when we are on the ſubjeçt of hunting. In the mean time, I will endeavour to deſcribe what a good huntſman ſhould be. He ſhould be young, ſtrong, açtive, bold and enterpriſing; fond of the diverſion, and indefatigable in the purſuit of it; he ſhould be ſenſible and good-tempered; he ought alſo to be ſober; he ſhould be exaçt, civil, and cleanly; he ſhould be a good horſeman, and a good groom; his voice ſhould be ſtrong and clear, and he ſhould have an eye ſo quick, as to perceive which of his hounds carries the ſcent, when all are running; and ſhould have ſo excellent an ear, as always to diſtinguiſh the foremoſt hounds, when he does not ſee them. He ſhould be quiet, patient, and without conceit. Such are the excellencies which conſtitute a good huntſman: he ſhould not, however, be too fond of diſplaying them, till neceſſity calls them forth.—He ſhould let his hounds alone, whilſt they *can hunt*, and he ſhould have genius to aſſiſt them, *when they cannot.*

With

With regard to the whipper-in, as you keep two
of them, (and no pack of fox-hounds is complete
without) the firſt may be conſidered as a ſecond
huntſman, and ſhould have nearly the ſame good
qualities. It is neceſſary beſides, that he ſhould
be attentive and obedient to the huntſman; and
as his horſe will probably have moſt to do, the
lighter he is, the better; though if he be a good
horſeman, the objection of his weight will be ſufficiently overbalanced.—He muſt not be conceited.——I had one formerly, who, inſtead of
ſtopping hounds as he ought, would try to kill a
fox by himſelf.—This fault is unpardonable;—
he ſhould always maintain to the huntſman's
halloo, and ſtop ſuch hounds as divide from it.
When ſtopped, he ſhould get forward with them
after the huntſman.

He muſt always be contented to act an under
part, except when circumſtances may require that
he ſhould act otherwiſe;* and the moment they
ceaſe, he muſt not fail to reſume his former ſta-
tion.—You have heard me ſay, that where there
is much riot, I prefer an excellent whipper-in to
an excellent huntſman.—The opinion, I believe,
is new; I muſt therefore endeavour to explain it.

* When the huntſman cannot be up with the hounds, the
whipper-in ſhould; in which caſe it is the buſineſs of the huntſman to bring on the tail hounds along with him.

My

My meaning is this: that I think I ſhould have better ſport, and kill more foxes with a moderate huntſman, and an excellent whipper-in, than with the beſt of huntſmen without ſuch an aſſiſt-ant. You will ſay, perhaps, that a good huntſ-man will make a good whipper-in;—not ſuch, however, as I mean;—his talent muſt be born with him. My reaſons are, that good hounds, (and bad I would not keep) oftener need the one than the other; and genius, which in a whipper-in, if attended by obedience, his firſt requiſite, can do no hurt; in a huntſman, is a dangerous, though a deſirable quality; and if not accom-panied with a large ſhare of prudence, and I may ſay humility, will oftentimes ſpoil your ſport, and hurt your hounds. A gentleman told me that he heard the famous Will Dean, when his hounds were running hard in a line with Daventry, from whence they were at that time many miles diſtant, ſwear exceedingly at the whipper-in, ſaying, " *What buſineſs have you here?*" the man was amazed at the queſtion, " *why don't you know*" ſaid he, " *and be d---d to you, that the great earth* " *at Daventry is open?*"—The man got forward, and reached the earth juſt time enough to ſee the fox go in.—If therefore whippers-in be left at liberty to act as they ſhall think right, they are much leſs confined than the huntſman himſelf, who muſt follow his hounds; and, conſequently

they

they have greater scope to exert their genius, if they have any.

I had a dispute with an old sportsman, who contended, that the whipper-in should always attend the huntsman, to obey his orders; (a stable-boy, then, would make as good a whipper-in as the best) but this is so far from being the case, that he should be always on the opposite side of the cover from him, or I am much mistaken in my opinion: if within hearing of his halloo, he is near enough; for that is the hunting signal he is to obey.—The station of the second whipper-in may be near the huntsman, for which reason any boy that can halloo, and make a whip smack, may answer the purpose.

Your first whipper-in being able to hunt the hounds occasionally, will answer another good purpose;—it will keep your huntsman in order. They are very apt to be impertinent when they think you cannot do without them.

When you go from the kennel, the place of the first whipper-in is before the hounds; that of the second whipper-in should be some distance behind them; if not, I doubt if they will be suffered even to empty themselves, let their necessities be ever so great; for as soon as a boy is made a whipper-in, he fancies he is to whip the

hounds

hounds whenever he can get at them, whether they deferve it or not.

I have always thought a huntfman a happy man; his office is pleafing, and at the fame time flattering; we pay him for that which diverts him, and he is enriched by his greateft pleafure;* nor is a General after a victory, more proud, than is a huntfman who returns with his fox's head.

I have heard that a certain Duke who allowed no vails to his fervants, afked his huntfman what he generally made of his field-money, and gave him what he afked, inftead of it: this went on very well for fome time, till at laft the huntfman defired an audience.—" Your Grace," faid he, " is very generous, and gives me more than ever " I got from field-money in my life, yet I come " to beg a favour of your Grace—that you " would let me take field-money again; for I " have not half the pleafure now in killing a fox, " that I had before."

As you afk me my opinion of fcent, I think I had better give it you before we begin on the fub-ject of hunting. I muft, at the fame time, take the liberty of telling you, that you have puzzled me exceedingly; for fcent is, I believe, what we

* The *field-money* which is collected at the death of a fox.

fportfmen

fportfmen know leaft about; and, to ufe the words of a great claffic writer;

Hoc fum contentus, quòd etiam fi quo quidque fiat ignorem, quid fiat intelligo.---Cic. de div.

Somervile, who, as I have before obferved, is the only one I know of, who has thrown any light on the fubject of hunting, fays, I think, but little about fcent; I fend you his words; I fhall afterwards add a few of my own.

" Should fome more curious fportfmen here inquire,
Whence this fagacity, this wond'rous power
Of tracing ftep by ftep, or man, or brute?
What guide invincible points out their way,
O'er the dark marfh, bleak hill, and fandy plain ?
The courteous mufe fhall the dark caufe reveal.
The blood that from the heart inceffant rolls
In many a crimfon tide, then here, and there
In fmaller rills difparted, as it flows
Propell'd, the ferous particles evade,
Thro' th' open pores, and with the ambient air
Entangling mix, as fuming vapours rife,
And hang upon the gently purling brook,
There by the incumbent atmofphere comprefs'd
The panting chace grows warmer as he flies,
And thro' the net-work of the fkin perfpires ;
Leaves a long—fteaming—trail behind ; which by
The cooler air condens'd remains, unlefs
By fome rude ftorm difpers'd, or rarefy'd
By the meridian fun's intenfer heat,
To every fhrub the warm effluvia cling,
Hang on the grafs, impregnate earth and fkies.

With

> With noſtrils opening wide, o'er hill, o'er dale,
> The vig'rous hounds purſue, with ev'ry breath
> Inhale the grateful ſteam, quick pleaſures ſting
> Their tingling nerves, while their thanks repay,
> And in triumphant melody confeſs
> The titillating joy.   Thus on the air
> Depends the hunters hopes."

I cannot agree with Mr. Somervile, in thinking that ſcent depends on the air only; it depends alſo on the ſoil. Without doubt, the beſt ſcent is that, which is occaſioned by the effluvia, as he calls it, or particles of ſcent, which are conſtantly perſpiring from the game as it runs, and are ſtrongeſt and moſt favourable to the hound, when kept by the gravity of the air, to the height of his breaſt; for then, it neither is above his reach, nor is it neceſſary that he ſhould ſtoop for it. At ſuch times, ſcent is ſaid to lie *breaſt high*. Experience tells us, that difference of ſoil occaſions difference of ſcent; and on the richneſs and moderate moiſture of the ſoil does it alſo depend, I think, as well on the air. At the time leaves begin to fall, and before they are rotted, we know that the ſcent lies ill in cover. This alone would be a ſufficient proof, that ſcent does not depend on the air only. A difference of ſcent is alſo occaſioned by difference of motion; the faſter the game goes, the leſs ſcent it leaves. When game has been ridden after, and hurried on by imprudent ſportſmen, the ſcent is leſs favourable to

I

hounds;

hounds; one reafon of which may be, that the particles of fcent are then more diffipated. But if the game fhould have been run by a dog not belonging to the pack, feldom will any fcent remain.

I believe it is very difficult to afcertain what fcent exactly is; I have known it alter very often in the fame day. I believe, however, that it depends chiefly on two things, " *the condition the " ground is in, and the temperature of the air*; both of which, I apprehend, fhould be moift, without being wet: when both are in this condition, the fcent is then perfect; and vice verfâ, when the ground is hard, and the air dry, there feldom will be any fcent.—It fcarce ever lies with a north, or an eaft wind; a foutherly wind without rain, and a wefterly wind that is not rough, are the moft favourable.—Storms in the air are great enemies to fcent, and feldom fail to take it entirely away.—A fine fun fhiny day is not often a good hunting day; but what the French call, *jour des dames*, warm without fun, is generally a perfect one: there are not many fuch in a whole feafon.—In fome fogs, I have known the fcent lie high; in others, not at all; depending, I believe, on the quarter the wind is then in.—I have known it lie very high in a mift, when not too wet; but if the wet fhould hang on the boughs and bufhes, it will fall upon the fcent, and deaden it.

K   **When**

When the dogs roll, the scent, I have frequently observed, seldom lies; for what reason, I know not; but, with permission, if they smell strong, when they first come out of the kennel, the proverb is in their favour; and that smell is a prognostic of good luck.—When cobwebs hang on the bushes, there is seldom much scent.—During a white frost the scent lies high; as it also does when the frost is quite gone: at the time of its going off, scent never lies: it is a critical minute for hounds, in which their game is frequently lost. In a great dew the scent is the same. In heathy countries, where the game brushes as it goes along, scent seldom fails. Where the ground carries, the scent is bad for a very evident reason, which hare-hunters, who pursue their game over greasy fallows, and through dirty roads, have great cause to complain of.——A wet night frequently produces good chaces, as then, the game neither like to run the cover, nor the roads.—It has been often remarked, that scent lies best in the richest soils; and countries which are favourable to horses, are seldom so to hounds. I have also observed that, in some particular places, let the temperature of the air be as it may, scent never lies.

Take not out your hounds on a very windy, or bad day.

" These

R. Fairbrother, Huntsman to   . Newman, Esq.r of Knavestock, Essex

Published by J. Wheble March 1 1794

" These auspicious days, on other cares
Employ thy precious hours; th' improving friend
With open arms embrace, and from his lips
Glean science, season'd with good-natur'd wit;
But if th' inclement skies, and angry Jove,
Forbid the pleasing intercourse, thy books
Invite thy ready hand, each sacred page
Rich with the wise remarks of heroes old."

The sentiments of Mr. Somervile always do him honour, but on no occasion, more than on this.

In reading over my letter, I find I have used the word *smell*, in a sense that perhaps you will criticize.——A gentleman, who, I suppose, was not the sweetest in the world, sitting in the front boxes at the play-house, on a crowded night, his neighbour very familiarly told him, that he *smelt strong* :—" No, Sir," replied he, with infinite good humour,—" it is you that *smell, I stink*."

[The qualifications necessary to make a good huntsman, Mr. Beckford has dwelt upon with much ingenuity in the former part of this letter, it is therefore hoped, that our presenting the readers of his admired production, in this place, with a portrait of one who is reputed to be the best in the kingdom, will be deemed appropriate; his name is RICH-ARD FAIRBROTHER, and hunts the pack belong-

ing to Mr. Newman, of Navefrock, in Effex:—
the horfe on which he is feated, called JOLLY
ROGER, is an old favourite, having carried
him through fome of the fevereft chaces ever
known.]

LETTER X.

I THOUGHT that I had been writing all this time to a fox-hunter; and hitherto my letters have had no other object. I now receive a letter from you, full of queftions about hare-hunting; to all of which you expect an anfwer. I muft tell you, at the fame time, that though I kept harriers many years, it was not my intention, if you had not afked it, to have written on the fubject. By inclination, I was never a hare-hunter; I followed this diverfion more for air and exercife, than amufement; and if I could have perfuaded myfelf to ride on the turnpike road to the three-mile ftone, and back again, I fhould have thought that I had had no need of a pack of harriers.—Excufe me, brother hare-hunters! I mean not to offend; I fpeak but relatively to my own particular fituation in the country, where hare-hunting is fo bad, that it is more extraordinary I fhould have perfevered in it fo long, than that I fhould forfake it now. I refpect hunting in whatever fhape it appears; it is a manly, and a wholefome exercife, and feems, by nature, defigned to be the amufement of a Briton.

You afk, how many hounds a pack of harriers fhould confift of? and what kind of hound is beſt ſuited to that diverſion?——You ſhould never exceed twenty couple in the field; it might be difficult to get a greater number to run well together, and a pack of harriers cannot be complete if they do not:* beſides, the fewer hounds you have, the leſs you foil the ground, which you otherwiſe would find a great hindrance to your hunting.——Your other queſtion is not eaſily anſwered; the hounds, I think, moſt likely to ſhew you ſport, are between the large ſlow hunting harrier, and the little fox beagle: the former are too dull, too heavy, and too ſlow; the latter, too lively, too light, and too fleet. The firſt ſpecies, it is true, have moſt excellent notes, and I make no doubt, will kill their game at laſt, if the day be long enough; but, you know, the days are ſhort in winter, and it is bad hunting in the dark. The other, on the contrary, fling and daſh, and are all alive; but every cold blaſt affects them, and if your country be deep and wet, it is not impoſſible that ſome of them may be drowned. My hounds were a croſs of both theſe kinds, in which it was my endeavour to get as much bone and ſtrength, in as ſmall a compaſs as poſſible.——It was a difficult undertaking.——

* A hound that runs too faſt for the reſt, ought not to be kept. Some huntſmen load them with heavy collars; ſome tie a long ſtrap round their necks; a better way would be to part with them. Whether they go too ſlow, or too faſt, they ought equally to be drafted.

I bred

I bred many years, and an infinity of hounds, before I could get what I wanted : I, at laſt, had the pleaſure to ſee them very handſome; ſmall, yet very bony; they ran remarkably well together; ran faſt enough; had all the alacrity that you could defire, and would hunt the coldeſt ſcent.—When they were thus perfect, I did, as many others do—I parted with them.

It may be neceſſary to unſay, now that I am turned hare-hunter again, many things I have been ſaying, as a fox-hunter; as I hardly know any two things of the ſame genus, (if I may be allowed the expreſſion) that differ ſo entirely. What I ſaid in a former letter, about the huntſman and whipper-in, is in the number : as to the huntſman, he ſhould not be young : I ſhould moſt certainly prefer one, as the French call it, *d'un certain age,* as he is to be quiet and patient ; for patience, he ſhould be a very Grizzle; and the more quiet he is, the better. He ſhould have infinite perſeverance; for a hare ſhould never be given up, whilſt it is poſſible to hunt her : ſhe is ſure to ſtop, and therefore may always be recovered. Were it uſual to attend to the breed of our huntſmen, as well as to that of our hounds, I know no family that would furniſh a better croſs than that of the *ſilent gentleman,* mentioned by the Spectator : a female of his line, croſſed

K 4   with

with a knowing huntſman, would probably produce a perfeƈt hare-hunter.

The whipper-in alſo has little to do with him, whom I before deſcribed: yet he may be like the ſecond whipper-in to a pack of fox-hounds; the ſtable-boy who is to follow the huntſman: but I would have him ſtill more confined, for he ſhould not dare even to ſtop a hound, or ſmack a whip, without the huntſman's order. Much noiſe and rattle is direƈtly contrary to the firſt principles of hare-hunting, which is, to be perfeƈtly quiet, and to let your hounds alone. I have ſeen few hounds ſo good as town packs, that have no profeſſed huntſman to follow them. If they have no one to aſſiſt them, they have at the ſame time, no one to interrupt them; which, I believe, for this kind of hunting, is ſtill more material. I ſhould, however, mention a fault I have obſerved, and which ſuch hounds muſt of neceſſity ſometimes be guilty of; that is, *running back the heel.* Hounds are naturally fond of ſcent; if they cannot carry it forward, they will turn, and hunt it back again: hounds, that are left to themſelves, make a fault of this; and it is, I think, the only one they commonly have.—Though it be certainly beſt to let your hounds alone, and thereby to give as much ſcope to their natural inſtinƈt, as you can; yet, in this particular inſtance, you ſhould check it mildly; for, as it is almoſt an

invariable

invariable rule in all hunting, to make the head good, you fhould encourage them to try forward firft; which may be done without taking them off their nofes, or without the leaft prejudice to their hunting. If trying forward fhould not fucceed, they may then be fuffered to try back again, which you will find them all ready enough to do; for they are fenfible how far they brought the fcent, and where they left it. The love of fcent is natural to them, and they have infinitely more fagacity in it than we ought to pretend to— I have no doubt, that they often think us very obftinate, and very foolifh.

Harriers, to be good, like all other hounds, muft be kept to their own game: if you run fox with them, you fpoil them: hounds cannot be perfect unlefs ufed to one fcent and one ftile of hunting. Harriers run fox in fo different a ftile from hare, that it is of great difiervice to them when they return to hare again: it makes them wild, and teaches them to fkirt. The high fcent which a fox leaves, the ftraightnefs of his running, the eagernefs of the purfuit, and the noife that generally accompanies it, all contribute to fpoil a harrier.

I hope you agree with me, that it is a fault in a pack of harriers to go too faft; for a hare is a little timorous animal, which we cannot help

feeling

feeling fome compaffion for, at the very time when we are purfuing her deftruction: we fhould give fcope to all her little tricks, nor kill her foully and over-matched.* Inftinct inftructs her to make a good defence when not unfairly treated; and I will venture to fay, that, as far as her own fafety is concerned, fhe has more cunning than the fox, and makes many fhifts to fave her life, far beyond all his artifice. Without doubt, you have often heard of hares, who, from the miraculous efcapes they have made, have been thought *witches*; but, I believe, you never heard of a fox that had cunning enough to be thought a *wizard*.

They who like to rife early have amufement in feeing the hare trailed to her form; it is of great fervice to hounds; it alfo fhews their good-nefs to the huntfman more than any other hunting, as it difcovers to him thofe who have the moft ten-der nofes. But, I confefs, I feldom judged it worth while to leave my bed a moment fooner on that

* The critic terms this " a mode of deftruction fomewhat beyond brutal." (Vide Monthly Review.) I fhall not pretend to juftify that conventional cruelty, which feems fo univerfally to prevail—neither will I afk the gentleman, who is fo fevere on me, why he feeds the lamb, and afterwards cuts his throat; I mean only to confider cruelty under the narrow limits which concern hunting—if it may be defined to be, a pleafure which refults from giving pain, then certainly a fportfman is much lefs cruel than he is thought.

account

GOING OUT IN THE MORNING.

account. I always thought hare-hunting fhould
be taken as a ride after breakfaft, to get us an
appetite to our dinner. If you make a ferious
bufinefs of it, you fpoil it. Hare-finders, in this
cafe, are neceffary: it is agreeable to know where
to go immediately for your diverfion, and not
beat about, for hours perhaps, before you find.
It is more material with regard to the fecond hare
than the firft; for if you are warmed with your
gallop, the waiting long in the cold afterwards
is, I believe, as unwholefome as it is difagreeable.
Whoever does not mind this, had better let his
hounds find their own game; they will certainly
hunt it with more fpirit afterwards, and he will
have a pleafure himfelf in expectation which no
certainty can ever give. Hare-finders make hounds
idle; they alfo make them wild. Mine knew
the men as well as I did myfelf, could fee them
as far, and would run, full cry, to meet them.
Hare-finders are of one great ufe; they hinder
your hounds from chopping hares, which they,
otherwife, could not fail to do. I had in my
pack one hound in particular that was famous for
it; he would challenge on a trail very late at
noon, and had a good knack at chopping a hare
afterwards; he was one that liked to go the
fhorteft way to work, nor did he choofe to take
more trouble than was neceffary.—Is it not wonderful, that the trail of a hare fhould lie after fo

many

many hours, when the scent of her dies away so
soon?

Hares are said (I know not with what truth) to
foresee a change of weather, and to seat themselves accordingly. This is however certain, that
they are seldom found in places much expofed to
the wind. In inclosures they more frequently
are found near to a hedge than in the middle of a
field. They who make a profession of hare-finding (and a very advantageous one it is in some
countries) are directed by the wind where to look
for their game. With good eyes and nice observation they are enabled to find them in any weather. You may make forms, and hares will sit
in them. I have heard it is a common practice
with shepherds on the Wiltshire downs; and, by
making them on the side of hills, they can tell
at a diftance off, whether there are hares in them
or not. Without doubt people frequently do not
find hares, from not knowing them in their forms.
A gentleman, courfing with his friends, was
shewn a hare that was found fitting—" *Is that*
" *a hare?*" he cried, " *then, by Jove, I found two*
" *this morning as we rode along.*"

Though the talent of hare-finding is certainly
of ufe, and the money collected for it, when
given to shepherds, is money well beftowed by
fportfman, as it tends to the prefervation of his
game

game, yet I think, when it is indiſcriminately given, that hare-finders are often too well paid. I have known them frequently get more than a guinea for a ſingle hare. I myſelf have paid five ſhillings in a morning for hares found ſitting. To make our companions pay dearly for their diverſion, and oftentimes ſo much more than it is worth; to take from the pockets of men who oftentimes can ill afford it, as much as would pay for a good dinner afterwards, is, in my opinion, an ungenerous cuſtom; and this conſideration induced me to collect but once, with my hounds, for the hare-finders. The money was afterwards divided amongſt them, and if they had leſs than half a crown each, I myſelf ſupplied the deficiency.—An old miſer, who had paid his ſhilling, complained bitterly of it afterwards, and ſaid, *" he had been made to pay a ſhilling for two penny-" worth of ſport."*

When the game is found you cannot be too quiet: the hare is an animal ſo very timorous, that ſhe is frequently headed back, and your dogs are liable to over-run the ſcent at every inſtant; it is beſt, therefore, to keep a conſiderable way behind them, that they may have room to turn as ſoon as they perceive they have loſt the ſcent; and, if treated in this manner, they will ſeldom over-run it much. Your hounds, through the whole chace, ſhould be left almoſt entirely to

them-

themſelves, nor ſhould they be hallooed much: when the hare doubles, they ſhould hunt through thoſe doubles; nor is a hare hunted fairly when hunted otherwiſe. They ſhould follow her every ſtep ſhe takes, as well over greaſy fallows as through flocks of ſheep; nor ſhould they ever be caſt, but when nothing can be done without it. I know a gentleman, a pleaſant ſportſman, but a very irregular hare-hunter, who does not ex-actly follow the method here laid down. As his method is very extraordinary I will relate it to you:—His hounds are large and fleet; they have at times hunted every thing; red deer, fallow deer, fox, and hare; and muſt in their nature have been moſt excellent, ſince, notwithſtanding the variety of their game, they are ſtill good. When a hare is found ſitting, he ſeldom fails to give his hounds a view; and as the men all halloo, and make what noiſe they can, ſhe is half fright-ened to death immediately. This done, he then ſends his whipper-in to ride after her, with par-ticular directions not to let her get out of his ſight; and he has found out, that this is the only proper uſe of a whipper-in. If they come to a piece of fallow, or a flock of ſheep, the hounds are not ſuffered to hunt any longer, but are cap-ped and hallooed as near to the hare as poſſible; by this time the poor devil is near her end, which the next view generally finiſhes; the ſtrongeſt hare, in this manner, ſeldom ſtanding twenty

minutes;

minutes; but, my friend fays, a hare is good eating, and he therefore thinks, that he cannot kill too many of them. By what Martial fays, I fuppofe *he* was of the fame opinion,

" Inter quadrupedes gloria prima lepus."

A propos to eating them.—I muft tell you, that in the Encyclopedic, a book of univerfal knowledge, where, of courfe, I expected to find fomething on hunting, which might be of fervice to you, as a fportfman, to know, I found the following advice about the dreffing of a hare, which may be of ufe to your cook; and the regard I have for your health will not fuffer me to conceal it from you.—" *On mange le levraut roti dans* " *quelques provinces du royaume, en Gafcogne et en* " *Languedoc, par exemple, avec une fauce compofée* " *de vinaigre et de fucre, qui eft mauvaife, malfaine* " *en foi effentiellement, mais qui eft furtout abomina-* " *ble pour tous ceux qui n'y font pas accoutumés.*" You, without doubt, therefore, will think yourfelf obliged to the authors of the Encyclopedic for their kind and friendly information.

Having heard of a fmall pack of beagles to be difpofed of in Derbyfhire, I fent my coachman, the perfon whom I could at that time beft fpare, to fetch them. It was a long journey, and not having been ufed to hounds, he had fome trouble in getting them along; alfo, as ill-luck would

have

have it, they had not been out of the kennel for many weeks before, and were fo riotous, that they ran after every thing they faw; fheep, cur-dogs, and birds of all forts, as well as hares and deer, I found, had been his amufement, all the way along: however, he loft but one hound; and when I afked him what he thought of them, he faid—" they could not fail of being good " hounds, for they would hunt *any thing*."

In your anfwer to my laft letter, you afk, of what fervice it can be to a huntfman to be a good groom? and, whether I think he will hunt hounds the better for it?—I wonder you did not afk, why he fhould be *cleanly?*—I fhould be more at a lofs how to anfwer you. My huntfman has always the care of his own horfes; I never yet knew one who did not think himfelf capable of it; it is for that reafon I wifh him to be a *good groom.*

You fay, that you cannot fee how a huntfman of genius can fpoil your fport, or hurt your hounds? —I will tell you how:—by too much foul play he frequently will catch a fox before he is half tired; and by lifting his hounds too much, he will teach them to fhuffle.—An improper ufe of the one may fpoil your fport; too frequent ufe of the other muft hurt your hounds.

L E T-

TRYING FOR A HARE,

LETTER XI.

I HAVE already obferved, that a trail in the morning is of great fervice to hounds; and, that to be perfect, they fhould always find their own game: for the method of hare-finding, though more convenient, will occafion fome vices in them which it will be impoffible to correct.

Mr. Somervile's authority ftrengthens my obfervation; that, when a hare is found, all fhould be quiet: nor fhould you ride near your hounds, till they are well fettled to the fcent.

> "——————————let all be hufh'd,
> No clamour loud, no frantic joy be heard;
> Left the wild hound run gadding o'er the plain
> Untractable, nor hear thy chiding voice."

The natural eagernefs of the hounds will, at fuch a time, frequently carry even the beft of them wide of the fcent; which too much encouragement, or preffing too clofe upon them, may continue beyond all poffibility of recovery: this fhould be always guarded againft. After a little while, you have lefs to fear. You may then approach them nearer, and encourage them more: leaving, however, at all times, fufficient room for them to turn, fhould they over-run the fcent. On high roads and dry paths be always doubtful of the fcent, nor give them much encouragement; but when a hit is made on either fide, you may halloo as much as you pleafe; nor can you then encourage your hounds too much. A hare generally defcribes a circle as fhe runs; larger or lefs, according to her ftrength, and the opennefs of the country. In inclofures, and where there is much cover, the circle is for the moft part fo fmall that it is a conftant puzzle to the hounds. They have a Gordian knot, in that cafe, ever to unloofe; and though it may afford matter of fpeculation to the philofopher, it is always contrary to the wifhes of the fportf-man. Such was the country I hunted in for many years.

> " Huntfman! her gait obferve: if in wide rings
> She wheels her mazy way, in the fame round
> Perfifting ftill, fhe'll foil the beaten track.
> But if fhe fly, and with the fav'ring wind
> Urge her bold courfe, lefs intricate thy tafk:
> Pufh on thy pack."
>
> SOMERVILE.

Befides running the foil, they frequently make doubles, which is going forward, to tread the fame fteps back again, on purpofe to confufe their purfuers: and the fame manner in which they make the firft double, they generally continue,

nue, whether long or fhort. This information, therefore, if properly attended to by the huntf-man, may be of ufe to him in his cafts.

When they make their double on a high road, or dry path, and then leave it with a fpring, it is often the occafion of a long fault: the fpring which a hare makes on thefe occafions is hardly to be credited, any more than is her ingenuity in making it; both are wonderful!

> " ———————————— let cavillers deny
> That brutes have reafon; fure 'tis fomething more:
> 'Tis Heaven directs and ftratagems infpire,
> Beyond the fhort extent of human thought."
>
> SOMERVILE.

She frequently, after running a path a confider-able way, will make a double, and then ftop till the hounds have paft her; fhe will then fteal away as fecretly as fhe can, and return the fame way fhe came. This is the greateft of all trials for hounds. It is fo hot a foil, that in the beft packs there are not many hounds that can hunt it; you muft follow thofe hounds that can, and try to hit her off where fhe breaks her foil, which in all probability fhe will foon do, as fhe now flatters herfelf fhe is fecure. When the fcent lies bad in cover, fhe will fometimes feem to hunt the hounds.

L 2

" — The

> "——————————— The covert's utmoſt bound
> Slily ſhe ſkirts; behind them cautious creeps,
> And in that very track, ſo lately ſtain'd
> By all the ſteaming crowd, ſeems to purſue
> The foe ſhe flies."——   SOMERVILE.

When the hounds are at a check, make your huntſman ſtand ſtill, nor ſuffer him to move his horſe one way or the other: hounds lean naturally toward the ſcent, and if you ſay not a word to them, will ſoon recover it. If you ſpeak to a hound at ſuch a time, calling him by his name, which is too much the practice, he ſeldom fails to look up in your face, as much as to ſay, *what the deuce do you want?*—when he ſtoops to the ſcent again, is it not probable that he means to ſay, *You fool, you, let me alone.*

When your hounds are at fault, let not a word be ſaid: let ſuch as follow them ignorantly and unworthily ſtand all aloof—*Procul, O procul eſte profani!* for whilſt ſuch are chattering, not a hound will hunt. *A propos*, Sir, a politician will ſay—What news from America? *A propos*—Do you think both the admirals will be tried? Or, *propos*—Did you hear what has happened to my grandmother? Such queſtions are, at ſuch a time, extremely troubleſome, and very *mal-à-propos.* Amongſt the ancients, it was reckoned *an ill omen* to ſpeak in hunting—I wiſh it were thought ſo now. *Hoc age* ſhould be one

of

of the firſt maxims in hunting, as in life; and I can aſſure you, when I am in the field, I never wiſh to hear any other tongue than that of a hound. A neighbour of mine was ſo truly a hare-hunter in this particular, that he would not ſuffer any body to ſpeak a word when his hounds were at fault: a gentleman happened to cough; he rode up to him immediately, and ſaid, *" I wiſh, Sir, with all my heart, that your cough " was better."*

In a good day, good hounds ſeldom give up the ſcent at head; if they do, there is generally an obvious reaſon for it: this obſervation a huntſman ſhould always make; it will direct his caſt. If he be a good one, he will attend, as he goes, not only to his hounds, nicely obſerving which have the lead, and the degree of ſcent they carry; but alſo to the various circumſtances that are continually happening from change of weather, and difference of ground. He will likewiſe be mindful of the diſtance which the hare keeps before the hounds, and of her former doubles; he will alſo remark what point ſhe makes to. All theſe obſervations will be of uſe, if a long fault make his aſſiſtance neceſſary; and if the hare ſhould have headed back, he will carefully obſerve whether ſhe met with any thing in her courſe to turn her, or turned of her own accord. When he caſts his hounds, let him begin by making a ſmall

L 3

circle;

circle; if that will not do, then let him try a larger; he afterwards may be at liberty to perfevere in any caft he fhall judge moft likely. As a hare generally revifits her old haunts, and returns to the place where fhe was firft found, if the fcent be quite gone, and the hounds can no longer hunt; *that* is as likely a caft as any to recover her. Let him remember, in all his cafts, that the hounds are not to follow his horfe's heels, nor are they to carry their heads high, and nofes in the air. At thefe times they muft try for the fcent, or they will never find it; and he is either to make his caft quick or flow, as he perceives his hounds try, and as the fcent is either good or bad.

Give particular directions to your huntfman to prevent his hounds, as much as he can, from chopping hares. Huntfmen like to get blood at any rate; and when hounds are ufed to it, it would furprize you to fee how attentive they are to find opportunities. A hare muft be very wild, or very nimble, to efcape them. I remember, in a furzy country, that my hounds chopped three hares in one morning; for it is the nature of thofe animals either to leap up before the hounds come near them, and *fteal away*, as it is called, or elfe to lie clofe, till they put their very nofes upon them. Hedges, alfo, are very dangerous; if the huntfman beat the hedge himfelf, which

is

Hare Hunting _ Plate 6.th

THE DEATH.

is the ufual practice, the hounds are always upon the watch, and a hare muft have good luck to efcape them all. The beft way to prevent it, is to have the hedge well beaten at fome diftance before the hounds.

Hares feldom run fo well as when they do not know where they are. They run well in a fog, and generally take a good country. If they fet off down the wind, they feldom return: you then cannot pufh on your hounds too much. When the game is finking, you will perceive your old hounds get forward; they then will run at head.

> " Happy the man, who with unrivall'd fpeed
> Can pafs his fellows, and with pleafure view
> The ftruggling pack; how in the rapid courfe
> Alternate they prefide, and joftling pufh
> To guide the dubious fcent; how giddy youth
> Oft babbling errs, by wifer age reprov'd;
> How, niggard of his ftrength, the wife old hound
> Hangs in the rear, till fome important point
> Roufe all his diligence, or till the chace
> Sinking he finds; then to the head he fprings,
> With thirft of glory fir'd, and wins the prize."
>
> SOMERVILE.

Keep no babblers; for though the pack foon find them out, and mind them not, yet it is unpleafant to hear their noife; nor are fuch fit companions for the reft.

L 4

Though

Though the Spectator makes us laugh at the oddity of his friend, Sir Roger, for returning a hound, which he faid was an excellent *bafs*, becaufe he wanted a *counter-tenor*; yet I am of opinion, that if we attended more to the variety of notes frequently to be met with in the tongues of hounds, it might greatly add to the harmony of the pack. I do not know that a complete concert could be attained, but it would be eafy to prevent difcordant founds.

Keep no hound that runs falfe: the lofs of one hare is more than fuch a dog is worth.

It is but reafonable to give your hounds a hare fometimes: I always gave mine the laft they killed, if I thought they deferved her.

It is too much the cuftom, firft to ride over a dog, and then cry, *ware horfe*. Take care not to ride over your hounds; I have known many a good dog fpoiled by it: in open ground caution them firft; you may afterwards ride over them, if you pleafe; but in roads and paths they frequently cannot get out of your way; it furely, then, is your bufinefs either to ftop your horfe or break a way for them, and the not doing it, give me leave to fay, is not lefs abfurd than cruel; nor can that man be called a good fportfman who thus wantonly deftroys his own fport. Indeed,

good

good sportsmen seldom ride on the line of the tail hounds.

An acquaintance of mine, when he hears any of his servants say, *ware horse!* halloos out—ware horse!—*ware dog!* and be hanged to you.

You ask how my warren hares are caught ?—it shall be the subject of my next letter.

LETTER XII.

YOU wifh to know how my warren hares are caught? they are caught in traps, not unlike to the common rat-traps. I leave mine always at the meufes, but they are *fet* only when hares are wanted: the hares, by thus conftantly going through them, have no miftruft, and are eafily caught. Thefe traps fhould be made of old wood, and even then it will be fome time before they will venture through them. Other meufes muft be alfo left open, left a difiafte fhould make them forfake the place. To my warren I have about twenty of thefe traps; though, as the flock of hares is great, I feldom have occafion to fet more than five or fix, and fcarcely ever fail of catching as many hares. The warren is paled in, but I found it neceffary to make the meufes of brick; that is, where the traps are placed. Should you at any time wifh to make a hare-warren, it will be neceffary for you to fee one firft, and examine the traps, boxes, and ftoppers, to all which there are particularities not eafy to be defcribed. Should you perceive the hares, towards the end of the feafon, to become fhy of the traps, from having

been

been often caught, it will be neceſſary to drive them in with ſpaniels. Should this be the caſe, you will find them very thick round the warren; for the warren-hares will be unwilling to leave it, and when diſturbed by dogs will immediately go in.

If you turn them out before greyhounds, you cannot give them too much law; if before hounds, you cannot give them too little; for reaſons which I will preſently add. Though hares, as I told you before, never run ſo well before hounds as when they do not know where they are, yet, before greyhounds, it is the reverſe; and your trap-hares, to run well, ſhould always be turned out within their knowledge: they are naturally timid, and are eaſily diſheartened, when they have no point to make to for ſafety.

If you turn out any before your hounds, (which, if it be not your wiſh, I ſhall by no means recommend) give them not much time, but lay on your hounds as ſoon as they are out of view; if you do not, they will be likely to ſtop, which is oftentimes fatal. Views are at all times to be avoided, but particularly with trap-hares; for, as theſe know not where they are, the hounds have too great an advantage over them. It is beſt to turn them down the wind; they hear the hounds better, and ſeldom turn

I   again.

again. Hounds, for this bufinefs, fhould not be too fleet. Thefe hares run ftraight, and make no doubles; they leave a ftrong fcent, and have other objections in common with animals turned out before hounds: they may give you a gallop, they will, however, fhew but little hunting.— The hounds are to be hunted like a pack of fox-hounds, as a trap-hare runs very much in the fame manner, and will even top the hedges. What I fhould prefer to catching the hares in traps, would be, a warren in the midft of an open country, which might be ftopped clofe on hunting-days. This would fupply the whole country with hares, which, after one turn round the warren, would moft probably run ftraight at end. The number of hares which a warren will fupply is hardly to be conceived; I feldom turned out lefs in one year than thirty brace of trap-hares, befides many others killed in the environs, of which no account was taken. My warren is a wood of near thirty acres; one of half the fize would anfwer the purpofe perhaps as well. Mine is cut out into many walks; a fmaller warren fhould have only *one*, and *that* round the outfide of it. No dog fhould ever be fuffered to go into it, and traps fhould be conftantly fet for ftoats and polecats. It is faid parfley makes hares ftrong; they certainly are very fond of eating it: it therefore cannot be amifs to

fow

fow fome about the warren, as it may be the means of keeping your hares more at home.

I had once fome converfation with a gentleman about the running of my trap-hares, who faid he had been told that catching a hare, and tying *a piece of ribbon to her ear*, was a fure way to make her run *ftrait*.---I make no doubt of it---and fo would *a canifter tyed to her tail*.

I am forry you fhould think I began my firft letter on the fubject of hare-hunting in a manner that might offend any of my brother fportfmen. It was not hare-hunting I meant to depreciate, but the country I had hunted hare in.—It is good diverfion in a good country:—you are always certain of fport; and if you really love to fee your hounds hunt; the hare, when properly hunted, will fhew you more of it, than any other animal.

You afk me, what is the right time to leave off hare-hunting?—You fhould be guided in that by the feafon: you fhould never hunt after March; and, if the feafon be forward, you fhould leave off fooner.

Having now fo confiderably exceeded the plan I firft propofed, you may wonder, if I omit to fay any thing of *ftag-hunting*. Believe me, if I do, it will not be for want of refpect; but becaufe I

have

have feen very little of it. It is true, I hunted two winters at Turin; but their hunting, you know, is no more like our's, than is the hot meal we *there* flood up to eat, to the Englifh breakfaft we fit down to *here*.—Were I to defcribe their manner of hunting, their infinity of dogs, their number of huntfmen, their relays of horfes, their great faddles, great bitts, and jack boots, it would be no more to our prefent purpofe, than the defcription of a wild boar chafe in Germany, or the hunting of jackalls in Bengal. *C'eft une chaffe magnifique, et voila tout.*—However, to give you an idea of their huntfmen, I muft tell you that one day the flag, which is very unufual, broke cover and left the foreft; a circumftance, which gave as much pleafure to me, as difpleafure to all the reft—it put every thing into confufion. I followed one of the huntfmen, thinking he knew the country beft, but it was not long before we were feparated; the firft ditch we came to ftopped him: I, eager to go on, hallooed out to him, *allons, Piqueur, fautez donc.*—" *Non pardi*," replied he, very coolly, " *c'eft un double foffé—je ne* " *faute pas des doubles foffés.*——There was alfo an odd accident the fame day, which, has it happened to a great man, even to the King himfelf, you may think interefting; befides, it was the occafion of a *bon mot* worth your hearing.—The King, eager in the purfuit, rode into a bog, and was difmounted—he was not hurt—he was foon

on

on his legs, and we were all ftanding round him. One of his old generals, who was at fome diftance, behind, no fooner faw the king off his horfe, but he rode up full gallop to know the caufe, " *Qu'eft* " *ce que c'eft? qu'eft ce que c'eft?*" cries the good old general, and in he tumbles into the fame bog. Count Kevenhuller, with great humour replied, pointing to the place, " *voila ce que c'eft! voila ce* " *que c'eft.*"

With regard to the ftag-hunting in this country, as I have already told you, that I know but little of it; but you will, without doubt, think it a fufficient reafon for my being filent concerning it.

LETTER XIII.

IN some of the preceding letters we have, I think, settled the business of the kennel in all its parts; and determined what should be the number, and what the qualifications of the attendants on the hounds: we also agree in opinion, that a pack should consist of about twenty-five couple; I shall now proceed to give some account of the use of them. You desire that I would be as particular, as if you were to hunt the hounds yourself: to obey you, therefore, I think I had better send you a description of an imaginary chace, in which I shall be at liberty to describe such events as probably may happen, and to which your present inquiries seem most to lead; a further and more circumstantial explanation of them will necessarily become the subject of my future letters. I am, at the same time, well aware of the difficulties attending such an undertaking. A fox-chace is not easy to be described—yet as even a faint description of it may serve, to a certain degree, as an answer to the various questions which you are pleased to make concerning that diversion, I shall prosecute my attempt in such a manner, as I think may suit your purpose best.—As I fear it may read ill, it

shall

fhall not be long. A gentleman, to whofe underftanding nature had moft evidently been fparing of her gifts, as often as he took up a book, and
met with a paffage which he could not compre-
hend, was ufed to write in the margin oppofite *matiere embrouillée,* and gave himfelf no
further concern about it. As different caufes
have been known to produce the fame effects,
fhould *you* treat *me* in like manner, I fhall think
it the fevereft cenfure that can be paffed upon me.
Our friend Somervile, I apprehend, was no great
fox-hunter; yet all he fays on the fubject of hunting is fo fenfible and juft, that I fhall turn to his
account of fox-hunting, and quote it where I can.
The hour moft favourable to the diverfion, is
certainly an early one; nor do I think I can fix
it better than to fay, the hounds fhould be at the
cover at fun-rifing. Let us fuppofe that we are
arrived at the cover fide.————

> " ———————————— Delightful fcene!
> Where all around is gay, men, horfes, dogs;
> And in each fmiling countenance appears
> Frefh blooming health, and univerfal joy."
>
> SOMERVILE.

Now let your huntfman throw in his hounds
as quietly as he can, and let the two whippers-in
keep wide of him on either fide, fo that a fingle
hound may not efcape them; let them be attentive to his halloo, and be ready to encourage, or

M   rate,

rate, as that directs; he will, of courſe, draw up the wind, for reaſons which I ſhall give in another place.—Now, if you can keep your brother ſportſmen in order, and put any diſcretion into them, you are in luck; they more frequently do harm than good: if it be poſſible, perſuade thoſe who wiſh to halloo the fox off, to ſtand quiet under the cover ſide, and on no account to halloo him too ſoon; if they do, he moſt certainly will turn back again: could you entice them all into the cover, your ſport, in all probability, would not be the worſe for it.

How well the hounds ſpread the cover! the huntſman, you ſee, is quite deſerted, and his horſe, who ſo lately had a crowd at his heels, has not now one attendant left. How ſteadily they draw! you hear not a ſingle hound; yet none are idle. Is not this better than to be ſubject to continual diſappointment, from the eternal babbling of unſteady hounds?

> "———————————— See! how they range
> Diſpers'd, how buſily this way and that,
> They croſs, examining with curious noſe
> Each likely haunt. Hark! on the drag I hear
> Their doubtful notes, preluding to a cry
> More nobly full, and ſwell'd with every mouth."
>
> SOMERVILE.

How

DRAWING COVER.

Published Dec.r 1.st 1794 by J. Wheble, Warwick Square, Warwick Lane, LONDON.

BREAKING COVER.

Publish'd by J. Wheble, Warwick Square, January 1.st 1793.

How mufical their tongues!—And as they get nearer to him, how the chorus fills!—Hark! he is found.—Now, where are all your forrows, and your cares, ye gloomy fouls! Or where your pains, and aches, ye complaining ones! one halloo has difpelled them all.—What a crafh they make! and echo feemingly takes pleafure to repeat the found. The aftonifhed traveller forfakes his road, lured by its melody; the liftening plowman now ftops his plow; and every diftant fhepherd neglects his flock, and runs to fee him break.—— What joy! what eagernefs in every face!

> " How happy art thou, man, when thou'rt no more
> Thyfelf! when all the pangs that grind thy foul,
> In rapture and in fweet oblivion loft,
> Yield a fhort interval, and eafe from pain!"
>
> SOMERVILE.

Mark how he runs the cover's utmoft limits, yet dares not venture forth; the hounds are ftill too near!—That check is lucky!—now, if our friends head him not, he will foon be off—hark! they halloo: by G—d he's gone!

> " ———————————— Hark! what loud fhouts
> Re-echo thro' the groves! he breaks away:
> Shrill horns proclaim his flight. Each ftraggling hound
> Strains o'er the lawn to reach the diftant pack.
> 'Tis triumph all, and joy."
>
> SOMERVILE.

M 2

Now

Now huntſman get on with the head hounds; the whipper-in will bring on the others after you: keep an attentive eye on the leading hounds, that ſhould the ſcent fail them, you may know at leaſt how far they brought it.

Maid *Galloper*, how he leads them!—It is difficult to diſtinguiſh which is firſt; they run in ſuch a ſtile; yet *he* is the foremoſt hound.—The goodneſs of his noſe is not leſs excellent than his ſpeed:—how he carries the ſcent! and when he loſes it, ſee how eagerly he flings to recover it again!—There—now he's at head again!—ſee how they top the hedge!——Now, how they mount the hill!——Obſerve what a head they carry, and ſhew me, if thou canſt, one ſhuffler or ſkirter amongſt them all: are they not like a parcel of brave fellows, who, when they engage in an undertaking, determine to ſhare its fatigue and its dangers, equally amongſt them?

    "——— Far o'er the rocky hills we range,
And dangerous our courſe; but in the brave
True courage never fails.   In vain the ſtream
In foaming eddies whirls, in vain the ditch
Wide gaping threatens death.   The craggy ſteep,
Where the poor dizzy ſhepherd crawls with care,
And clings to every twig, gives us no pain;
But down we ſweep, as ſtoops the falcon bold
To pounce his prey.   Then up the opponent hill,
By the ſwift motion flung, we mount aloft:
So ſhips in winter ſeas now ſliding ſink

                        Adown

In VIEW.

Published Feb.y 1.st 1795. by J.Wheble, Warwick Square, London.

> Adown the fteepy wave, then tofs'd on high
> Ride on the billows, and defy the ftorm."   Som.

It was then the fox I faw, as we came down the hill;—thofe crows directed me which way to look, and the fheep ran from him as he paft along. The hounds are now on the very fpot, yet the fheep ftop them not, for they dafh beyond them. Now fee with what eagernefs they crofs the plain!—*Galloper* no longer keeps his place, *Brufher* takes it—fee how he flings for the fcent, and how impetuoufly he runs!—How eagerly he took the lead, and how he ftrives to keep it—yet *Victor* comes up apace.—He reaches him!—See what an excellent race it is between them!——It is doubtful which will reach the cover firft.—How equally they run!—how eagerly they ftrain! now Victor—Victor!——Ah! Brufher, you are beaten; Victor firft tops the hedge.—See there! fee how they all take it in their ftrokes! the hedge cracks with their weight, fo many jump at once.——

Now haftes the whipper-in to the other fide of the cover; he is right unlefs he head the fox.

> " Heav'ns! what melodious ftrains! how beat our hearts
> Big with tumultuous joy! the loaded gales
> Breathe harmony; and as the tempeft drives
> From wood to wood, thro' ev'ry dark recefs
> The foreft thunders, and the mountains fhake."   Som.

                    Liften!

Liften!—the hounds have turned. They are now in two parts: the fox has been headed back, and we have changed at laft.

Now, my lad, mind the huntfman's halloo, and ftop to thofe hounds which he encourages. He is right!—that, doubtlefs, is the hunted fox;—Now they are off again.

" What lengths we pafs! where will the wand'ring chace
Lead us bewilder'd! fmooth as fwallows fkim
The new-fhorn mead, and far more fwift we fly.
See my brave pack; how to the head they prefs,
Juftling in clofe array, then more diffufe
Obliquely wheel, while from their op'ning mouths
The vollied thunder breaks.
————————————Look back and view
The ftrange confufion of the vale below,
Where fore vexation reigns;————————
——————————Old age laments
His vigour fpent; the tall, plump, brawny youth
Curfes his cumbrous bulk? and envies now
The fhort pygmean race, he whilom kenn'd
With proud infulting leer. A chofen few
Alone the fport enjoy, nor droop beneath
Their pleafing toils."   Som.

Ha! a check.—Now for a moment's pa-
tience!—We prefs too clofe upon the hounds!—
Huntfman, ftand ftill! as they want you not.—
How admirably they fpread! how wide they caft!
Is there a fingle hound that does not try? if there
be, ne'er fhall he hunt again. There, *Trueman*

is

Cook Sculp.

AT FAULT.

is on the fcent—he feathers, yet ftill is doubtful
—'tis right! how readily they join him! See thofe
wide-cafting hounds, how they fly forward to recover the ground they have loft!—Mind *Lightning*, how fhe dafhes; and *Mungo*, how he works!
Old *Frantic*, too, now pufhes forward; fhe knows,
as well as we, the fox is finking.

> "————————Ha! yet he flies, nor yields
> To black defpair.   But one loofe more, and all
> His wiles are vain.   Hark! thro' yon village now
> The rattling clamour rings.   The barns, the cots,
> And leaflefs elms return the joyous founds.
> Thro' ev'ry homeftall, and thro' ev'ry yard,
> His midnight walks, panting, forlorn, he flies.
>
> Som.

Huntfman! at fault at laft? How far did you
bring the fcent?—Have the hounds made their
own caft?—Now make your's.   You fee that
fheep-dog has courfed the fox;—get forward with
your hounds, and make a wide caft.

Hark! that halloo is indeed a lucky one.—If
we can hold him on, we may yet recover him;
for a fox, fo much diftreffed, muft ftop at laft.
We fhall now fee if they will hunt as well as
run; for there is but little fcent, and the impend-
ing cloud ftill makes that little, lefs.   How they
enjoy the fcent!—fee how bufy they all are, and
how each in his turn prevails!

M 4

Huntf-

Huntfman! be quiet! Whilft the fcent was good, you prefs'd on your hounds; it was well done: when they came to a check, you ftood ftill, and interrupted them not: they were afterwards at fault; you made your caft with judgment, and loft no time. You now muft let them hunt;— with fuch a cold fcent as this you can do no good; they muft do it all themfelves;—lift them now, and not a hound will ftoop again.—Ha! a high road, at fuch a time as this, when the tendereft-nofed hound can hardly own the fcent!—Another fault! That man at work, then, has headed back the fox. Huntfman! caft not your hounds now, you fee they have over-run the fcent; have a little patience, and let them, for once, try back.

We now muft give them time:—fee where they bend towards yonder furze brake—I wifh he may have ftopped there!—Mind that old hound, how he dafhes o'er the furze; I think he winds him.—Now for a frefh *entapis!* Hark! they halloo!—Aye, there he goes.

It is nearly over with him; had the hounds caught view, he muft have died.—He will hardly reach the cover; fee how they gain upon him at every ftroke!—It is an admirable race! yet the cover faves him.

Now

THE DEATH.

Now be quiet, and he cannot efcape us; we have the wind of the hounds, and cannot be better placed:—how fhort he runs!—he is now in the very ftrongeft part of the cover.—What a crafh! every hound is in, and every hound is running for him. That was a quick turn!—Again another!—he's put to his laft fhifts.—Now *Mifchief* is at his heels, and death is not far off.—Ha! they all ftop at once;—all filent, and yet no earth is open. Liften!—now they are at him again!—Did you hear that hound catch him? they over-ran the fcent, and the fox had laid down behind them. Now, Reynard, look to yourfelf!—How quick they all give their tongues!—Little *Dreadnought*, how he works him! the terriers too, they are now fqueaking at him.—How clofe *Vengeance* purfues! how terribly fhe preffes!—it is juft up with him!—Gods! what a crafh they make; the whole wood refounds!—That turn was very fhort!—There!—now!—aye, now they have him! Who-hoop!

LETTER XIV.

FOX-HUNTING, however lively and animating it may be in the field, is but a dull,
dry fubject to write upon; and I can now affure
you, from experience, that it is much lefs difficult to follow a fox-chace than to defcribe one.
You will eafily imagine, that to give enough of
variety to a fingle action, to make it interefting,
and to defcribe in a few minutes, the events of,
perhaps, as many hours; though it pretend to no
merit, has at leaft fome difficulty and trouble; and
you will as eafily conclude that I am glad they
are over.

You defire me to explain that part of my laft
letter, which fays, *if we can hold him on, we may
now recover him.*—It means, if we have fcent to
follow on the line of him, it is probable he will
ftop, and we may hunt up to him again. You
alfo object to my faying *catch* a fox; you call it
a bad expreffion, and fay, that it is not *fportly*; I
believe I have not often ufed it; and when I have,
it has been to diftinguifh betwixt the hunting a
fox down, as you do a hare, and the killing of
him with hard running.—You tell me, I fhould
always

always *kill* a fox. I might anfwer—I muft *catch* him firft.

You fay, that I have not enlivened my chace with many halloos: it is true, I have not; and what is worfe, I fear I am never likely to meet your approbation in that particular; for fhould we hunt together, then, I make no doubt, you will think that I halloo too much; a fault which every one is guilty of who real'y loves this animating fport, and is eager in the purfuit of it. Believe me, I never could halloo in my life, unlefs after hounds; and the writing a halloo appears to me almoft as difficult as to *pen a whifper.*

Your friend A——, you fay, is very fevere on us fox-hunters;—no one is more welcome. However, even he might have known, that the profeffion of fox-hunting is much altered fince the time of Sir John Vanburgh; and the intemperance, clownifhnefs, and ignorance of the old fox-hunter, are quite worn out: a much truer definition of one might now be made than that which he has left. Fox-hunting is now become the amufement of *gentlemen*; nor need any gentleman be afhamed of it.

I fhall now begin to anfwer your various queftions as they prefent themfelves. Though I was glad of this expedient, to methodife, in fome de-

gree,

gree, the variety we have to treat of, yet I was well aware of the impoffibility of fufficiently explaining myfelf in the midft of a fox-chace, whofe rapidity, you know very well, brooks no delay; now is the time, therefore, to make good that deficiency: what afterwards remains on the fubject of hunting will ferve as a fupplement to the reft; in which I fhall ftill have it in my power to introduce whatever may be now forgotten, or, give a further explanation of fuch parts as may feem to you to require it: for fince my principal view in writing thefe letters is to make the inftruction they contain of fome ufe to you, if you fhould want it; if not, to others; the being as clear and explicit as I can, will be far beyond all other confiderations. Repetitions, we know, are fhocking things; yet, in writing fo many letters on the fame fubject, I fear it will be difficult to avoid them.

Firft, then, as to the early hour recommended in my former letter:—I agree with you, it requires explanation; but you will pleafe to confider, that you defired me to fix the hour moft favourable to the fport, and without doubt it is *an early one.** You fay, that I do not go out fo early myfelf:—it is true, I do not; do phyficians

* An early hour is only neceffary, where you are not likely to find without a drag.

always

always follow their own prescriptions? Is it not
sufficient that their prescriptions be good? However, if my hounds should be out of blood, I go
out early, for then it becomes necessary to give
them every advantage. At an early hour, you
are seldom long before you find. The morning
is the part of the day which generally affords the
best scent; and the animal himself, which, in
such a case, you are more than ever desirous of
killing, is then least able to run away from you.
The want of rest, and perhaps a full belly, give
hounds a great advantage over him. I expect,
my friend, that you will reply to this, " that a
" fox-hunter, then, is not a *fair sportsman.*"—
He certainly is not; and what is more, would be
very sorry to be mistaken for one. He is otherwise
from principle. In his opinion, a fair sportsman,
and a foolish sportsman, are synonimous; he,
therefore, takes every advantage of the fox he
can. You will think, perhaps, that he may
sometimes spoil his own sport by this? It is true,
he sometimes does, but then he *makes* his hounds;
the whole art of fox-hunting being to keep the
hounds well in blood. Sport is but a secondary
consideration with a fox-hunter; the first is, *the
killing of the fox:* hence arises the eagerness of
pursuit, chief pleasure of the chace:—I confess,
I esteem blood so necessary to a pack of fox-
hounds, that with regard to myself, I always return home better pleased with but an indifferent

I   chace.

chace, with death at the end of it, than with the beft chace poffible, if it end with the lofs of the fox. Good chaces, generally fpeaking, are long chaces; and, if not attended with fuccefs, never fail to do more harm to hounds than good. Our pleafures, I believe, for the moft part, are greater during the expectation than the enjoyment: in this cafe, reality itfelf warrants the idea, and your prefent fuccefs is almoft a fure fore-runner of future fport.

I remember to have heard an odd anecdote of the late Duke of R——, who was very popular in his neighbourhood.—A butcher, at Lyndhurft, a lover of the fport, as often as he heard the hounds return from hunting came out to meet them, and never failed to afk the Duke what fport he had? " Very good, I thank you, honeft friend."—" Has your grace killed a fox?"—"*No:* " —We have had a good run, but we have not " killed."—" *Pfhaw!*" cried the butcher, looking archly, and pointing at him with his finger.— This was fo conftantly repeated, that the Duke, when he had not killed a fox, was ufed to fay, *he was afraid to meet the butcher.*

You afk, why the huntfman is to draw fo quietly; and, why up the wind? With regard to his drawing quietly, that may depend on the kind of cover before him; and alfo on the feafon

of

of the year. If your covers be small, or such
from which a fox cannot break unseen, then
noise can do no hurt; if you draw at a late hour,
and when there is no drag, then the more the
cover is difturbed the better; the more likely you
are to find. Late in the feafon foxes are wild,
particularly in covers that are often hunted. If
you do not draw quietly, he will fometimes get
too much the ftart of you: when you have any
fufpicion of this, fend on a whipper-in to the
oppofite fide of the cover before you throw in
your hounds. With regard to the drawing up
the wind, *that* is much more material. You never
fail to give the wind to a pointer and fetter; why
not to a hound?—Befides, the fox, if you draw
up the wind, does not hear you coming; and
your hounds, by this means, are never out of
your hearing; befides, fhould he turn down the
wind, as moft probably he will, it lets them all in.
Suppofe yourfelf acting directly contrary to this,
and then fee what is likely to be the confequence.

You think I am too fevere on my brother
fportfmen: if more fo than they deferve, I am
forry for it. I know many gentlemen who are
excellent fportfmen, yet, I am forry to fay, the
greater number of thofe who ride after hounds
are not; and it is thofe only whom I allude to.
Few gentlemen will take any pains, few of them
will ftop a hound, though he fhould run riot

clofe

clofe befide them, or will ftand quiet a moment, though it be to halloo a fox: it is true, they will not fail to halloo if he fhould come in their way, and they will do the fame to as many foxes as they fee. Some will encourage hounds which they do not know; it is a great fault: were every gentleman who follows hounds to fancy himfelf a huntfman, what noife, what confufion would enfue! I confider many of them as gentlemen riding out, and I am never fo well pleafed as when I fee them ride home again. You may perhaps have thought, that I wifhed them all to be huntfmen—moft certainly not; but the more affifiants a huntfman has, the better, in all probability, his hounds will be. Good fenfe, and a little obfervation, will foon prevent fuch people from doing amifs; and I hold it as an almoft invariable rule in hunting, that thofe who do not know how to do good are always liable to do harm :* there is fcarce an inftant, during a whole chace, when a fportfman ought not to be in one particular place:

* This is a better reafon, perhaps, why gentlemen ought to underftand this diverfion, than for the good they may do in it; fince a pack of hounds that are well manned will feldom need any other affiftance. A gentleman, perceiving his hounds to be much confufed by the frequent halloos of a ftranger, rode up to him, and thanked him with great civility for the trouble he was taking: but at the fame time acquainted him, that the two men he faw in green coats were paid fo much by the year, *on purpofe to halloo*, it would be needlefs for him, therefore, to give himfelf any *further* trouble.

and,

and, I will venture to fay, that if he be not *there*, he might as well be in his bed.

I muft give you an extraordinary inftance of a gentleman's *knowledge* of hunting.—He had hired a houfe in a fine hunting country, with a good kennel belonging to it, in the neighbourhood of two packs of hounds, of which mine was one; and that he might not offend the owner of either, intended, as he faid, to hunt with both. He offered me the ufe of his kennel, which, for fome reafons, I chofe to decline; it was afterwards offered to the other gentleman, who accepted it. The firft day that the hounds hunted this country he did not appear. The fecond day, the hounds were no fooner at the cover fide than my friend faw an odd figure, ftrangely accoutred, riding up, with a *fpaniel* following him. " Sir," faid he, " it gave me great concern not to be able to " attend you when you was here before; I hope " you was not offended at it; for, to fhew you " how well I am inclined to affift your hunt, " you fee, *I have brought my little dog.*"

I will now give you an inftance of another gentleman's *love* of hunting. We were returning from hunting over a very fine country, and upon its being remarked that we had a pleafant ride, he replied, " the beft part of the *fport*, in my opi- " nion, is the riding home to dinner afterwards."

N   He

He is, without doubt, of the same opinion with a fat old gentleman I one day overtook upon the road, who, after having asked me, " how many " foxes we usually killed in one day—why I did " not hunt hare rather than fox, as she was bet- " ter to eat ?"—he concluded, saying, " there is " but one part of hunting I likes—*it makes one* " *very hungry.*"

There are two things, which I particularly recommend to you; the one is, to make your hounds steady, the other, to make them all draw. Many huntsmen are fond of having them at their horses heels ; but, believe me, they never can get so well, or so soon together, as when they spread the cover : besides, I have often known, when there have been only a few finders, that they have found their fox, gone down the wind, and been heard of no more that day.

Never take out an unsteady old hound ; young ones properly awed from riot, and that will stop at a rate, may be put into the pack, a few at a time ; but an old hound that is vicious should not escape hanging ; let him be ever so good in other respects I will not excuse him ; for a pack must be wretched indeed that can stand in need of such assistance.

There

There is infinite pleasure in hearing a fox well found. When you get up to his kennel, with a good drag, the chorus increasing as you go, it inspires a joy more easy to be felt than described. With regard to my own sensations, I would rather hear one fox found in this lively manner, than ride the best hare-chace that ever was run.

Much depends on the first finding of your fox. *Dimidium facti, qui bene cœpit, habet,* which we learned at Westminster, is verified here; for I look upon a fox well found to be half killed. I think people generally are in too great a hurry on this occasion. There is an enthusiasm attending this diversion, which, in this instance in particular, ought always to be restrained.* The hounds are always mad enough when they find their fox; if the men be also mad, they make mad work of it indeed. A gentleman of my acquaintance, who hunts his own hounds, and is not less eager than the rest of us, yet very well knows the bad consequences of being so, to prevent this fault in himself, always begins by taking a pinch of snuff, he then sings part of an old song, " *Some say that* " *care killed the cat,*" &c. By this time his hounds get together, and settle to the scent. He then halloos, and rides as if the d—l drove.

---

* There are but few instances where sportsmen are not too noisy, and too fond of encouraging their hounds, which seldom do their business so well as when little is said to them.

If

If the fox break cover, you will fometimes fee a young fportfman ride after him. He never fails to afk fuch a one, " *Do you think you can* " *catch him, Sir?*"—" *No.*"—" Why then be fo " good as to let my hounds try—*if they can.*"

[The fubject which has been chofen as a frontif-piece to the prefent edition of this work, being in fome degree analogous to moft parts of Letter xiv. it may not be improper in this place to notice the circumftance which occafioned it.

A pack of hounds belonging to his GRACE of BEAUFORT, after a purfuit of many miles, fcented Reynard to a cottage at CASTLE COOMBE, where he had taken refuge in a cradle; little time, how-ever, was given him in this retreat, as they almoft inftantly entered the hovel, feized upon their de-voted victim, and dragged him from his lurking place.]

LETTER XV.

I LEFT off juft as I had found the fox: I
now, therefore, with your leave, will fuppofe, that the hounds are running him. You
defire I would be more particular with regard to
the men; it was always my intention. To begin, then, the huntfman ought certainly to fet off
with his foremoft hounds, and I fhould wifh him
to keep as clofe to them afterwards as he conveniently can; nor can any harm arife from it, unlefs he fhould not have common fenfe. No
hounds then can flip down the wind, and get out
of his hearing; he will alfo fee how far they
carry the fcent; a neceffary requifite; for without it, he never can make a caft with any certainty.

You will find it not lefs neceffary for your
huntfman to be active in preffing his hounds forward,* while the fcent is good, than to be pru-

* Preffing hounds on, is, perhaps, a dangerous expreffion;
as more harm may be done by preffing them beyond the fcent,
when it is good, than when it is bad: however, it means no
more than to get forward the tail-hounds, and to encourage the
others to pufh on as faft as they can, while the fcent ferves
them.

dent

dent in not hurrying them beyond it, when it is bad. Your's, you fay, is a good horfeman; it is of the utmoft confequence to your fport; nor is it poffible for a huntfman to be of much ufe, who is not; for the firft thing, and the very *fine qua non* of a fox-hunter is to ride up to his headmoft hounds. It is his bufinefs to be ready, at all times, to lend them that affiftance they fo frequently need, and which, when they are firft at a fault, is then moft critical. A fox-hound, at that time, will exert himfelf moft; he afterwards cools, and becomes more indifferent about his game. Thofe huntfmen who do not get forward enough to take advantage of this eagernefs and impetuofity, and direct it properly, feldom know enough of hunting to be of much ufe to them afterwards.

You will, perhaps, find it more difficult to keep your whipper-in back, than to get your huntfman forward; at leaft, I always have found it fo.* It is, however, neceffary; nor will a good whipper-in leave a cover whilft a fingle hound remains in it: for this reafon, there fhould

* Though a huntfman cannot be too fond of hunting, a whipper-in eafily may. His bufinefs will feldom allow him to be forward enough with the hounds to fee much of the fport: his only thought, therefore, fhould be to keep the hounds together, and to contribute, as much as he can, to the killing of the fox.

be

be two; one of whom fhould always be forward
with the huntfman. You cannot conceive the
many ills that may happen to hounds that are
left behind. I do not know that I can enumerate one half of them; but of this you may be
certain, that the keeping them together is the
fureft means to keep them fteady. When left to
themfelves, they feldom refufe any blood they can
get; they acquire many bad habits; they become
conceited, a terrible fault in any animal; and
they learn to tye upon the fcent, an unpardonable fault in a fox-hound: befides this, they frequently get a trick of hunting by themfelves, and
they feldom are worth much afterwards. The
lying out in the cold, perhaps the whole night,
can do no good to their confitutions, nor will
the being worried by fheep-dogs or maftifs be of
fervice to their bodies: all this, however, and
much more, they are liable to. I believe I
mentioned, in my fourth letter, that the ftraw-
houfe door fhould be left open when any hounds
are miffing.

Every country is foon known, and nine foxes
out of ten, with the wind in the fame quarter,
will follow the fame track. It is eafy, therefore,
for the whipper-in to cut fhort, and catch the
hounds again; at leaft it is fo in the country
where I hunt. With a high fcent you cannot
pufh on hounds too much. Screams keep the

N 4

fox

fox forward, at the fame time that they keep tho hounds together, or let in the tail-hounds;* they alfo enliven the fport, and if difcreetly ufed, are always of fervice; but, in cover, they fhould be given with the greateft caution.

Moft fox-hunters wifh to fee their hounds run in a, good ftyle; I confefs, I am myfelf one of thofe. I hate to fee a ftring of them, nor can I bear to fee them creep, where they can leap. It is the dafh of the fox-hound which diftinguifhes *him* as truly, as the motto of William of Wickham diftinguifhes *us*. A pack of harriers, if they have time, may kill a fox; but I defy them to kill him in the ftyle in which a fox ought to be killed; they muft hunt him down. If you intend to tire him out, you muft expect to be tired alfo yourfelf: I never wifh a chace to be lefs than one hour, or to.exceed two: it is fufficiently long, if properly followed; it will feldom be longer, unlefs there be a fault fomewhere—either in the day, in the huntfman, or in the hounds. What Lord Chatham once faid

* Halloos feldom do any hurt, when you are running up the wind; for then, none but the tail-hounds can hear you: when you are running down the wind, you fhould halloo no more than may be neceffary to bring the tail-hounds forward, for a hound that knows his bufinefs feldom wants encouragement when he is upon a fcent.

of

of a battle, is particularly applicable to a fox-chace: it should be *short*, *sharp*, and *decisive*.

There is, I believe, but little difference in the speed of hounds of the same size; the great difference is in the head they carry; and in order that they may run well together, you should not keep too many old hounds: after five or six seasons, they generally do more harm than good. If they tie upon the scent, and come hunting after, hang them up immediately, let their age be what it may; there is no getting such conceited devils on; they will never come to a halloo, which every hound that is off the scent, or behind the rest, should not fail to do; and they are always more likely to draw you back than help you forward.*

You think me too severe on skirters. I must confess, that I have but one objection to them,

* From this passage, the critic endeavours to prove the sportsman's ingratitude; and yet common sense, I believe, induces most men to rid themselves of that which if kept would be prejudicial to them. The critic seems to allude to a well-known fable of Æsop, but is not very happy in the application. He has also mis-quoted the passage—the author does not say *tire*, but *tye* upon the scent. Good hounds, when they become aged, are liable to the first; bad ones only are guilty of the last. In either case, death is not meant as a punishment, nor is it considered as a misfortune.—Vide Monthly Review.

and

and it is *this:* I have conſtantly ſeen them do more *harm* than *good.*

Changing from the hunted fox to a freſh one, is as bad an accident as can happen to a pack of fox-hounds, and requires all the obſervation and all the ingenuity that man is capable of to guard againſt it. Could a fox-hound diſtinguiſh a hunted fox, as the deer-hound does the deer that is blown, fox-hunting would then be perfect. There are certain rules that ought to be obſerved by huntſmen. A huntſman ſhould always liſten to his hounds, whilſt they are running in cover; he ſhould be particularly attentive to the head-moſt hounds, and he ſhould be conſtantly on his guard againſt a ſkirter, for if there be two ſcents, he muſt be wrong. Generally ſpeaking, the beſt ſcent is leaſt likely to be that of the hunted fox; and as a fox ſeldom ſuffers hounds to run up to him as long as he is able to prevent it, ſo, nine times out of ten, when foxes are hallooed early in the day, they are all freſh foxes. The hounds moſt likely to be right are the hard-running line-hunting hounds, or ſuch as the huntſman knows had the lead, before there aroſe any doubt of changing. With regard to the fox, if he break over an open country, it is no ſign that he is hard run; for they ſeldom at any time will do that, unleſs they be a great way before the hounds. Alſo, if he run up the wind—they ſel-

dom

dom ever do that when they have been long hunted, and grow weak; and when they run their foil, *that* alfo may direct him. All this, as you will perceive, requires a good ear and nice obfervation; and indeed, in that confifts the chief excellence of a huntfman.

When the hounds divide, and are in two parts, the whipper-in, in ftopping, muft attend to the huntfman, and wait for his halloo, before he attempts to ftop either: for want of proper management in this particular, I have known the hounds ftopped at both places, and both foxes loft by it. If they have many fcents, and it is quite uncertain which is the hunted fox, let him ftop thofe that are fartheft down the wind, as they can hear the others, and will reach them fooneft: in fuch a cafe, there will be little ufe in ftopping thofe that are up the wind.

When hounds are at a check, let every one be filent, and ftand ftill: but as I have already faid fo much on that head in my eleventh letter on hare-hunting, I beg leave to refer you to it. Whippers-in are frequently at this time coming on with the tail-hounds. They fhould never halloo to them, when the hounds are at fault; the leaft thing does hurt at fuch a time, but a halloo more than any other. The huntfman, at a check, had better let his hounds alone, or con-

tent

tent himfelf with holding them forward, without taking them off their nofes. Hounds that are not ufed to be caft, *à tout bout de champ* will of themfelves acquire a better caft than it is in the power of any huntfman to give them; will fpread more, and try better for the fcent; and, if in health and fpirits, will want no encouragement.

Should they be at fault, after having made their own caft, (which the huntfman fhould always firft encourage them to do) it is then his bufinefs to affift them further; but, except in fome particular inftances, I never approve of their being caft as long as they are inclined to hunt. The firft caft I bid my huntfman make is generally a regular one; not choofing to rely entirely on his judgment: if that fhould not fucceed, he is then at liberty to follow his own opinion, and proceed as obfervation and genius may direct. When fuch a caft is made, I like to fee fome mark of good fenfe and meaning in it; whether down the wind, or towards fome likely cover, or ftrong earth: however, as it is at beft uncertain, and as the huntfman and the fox may be of different opinions, I always wifh to fee a regular caft, before I fee a knowing one; which, as a laft refource, fhould not be called forth, till it be wanted: the letting hounds alone is but a negative goodnefs in a huntfman; whereas, it is

true,

true, this laſt ſhows real genius; and to be perfect, it muſt be born with him. There is a
fault, however, which a knowing huntſman is
too apt to commit: he will find a freſh fox, and
then claim the merit of having recovered the
hunted one. It always is dangerous to throw
hounds into a cover to retrieve a loſt ſcent; and,
unleſs they hit him in, is not to be depended on.
Driven to the laſt extremity, ſhould a knowing
caſt not ſucceed, your huntſman is in no wiſe
blameable: mine, I remember, loſt me a good
chace, by perſevering too long in a favourite caſt;
but he gave me ſo many good reaſons why the
fox *ought* to have gone that way, that I returned
perfectly well ſatisfied, telling him, at the ſame
time, that, *if the fox was a fool, he could not
help it.*

Gentlemen, when hounds are at fault, are too
apt themſelves to prolong it. They ſhould always ſtop their horſes ſome diſtance behind the
hounds, and, if it be poſſible to remain ſilent,
this is the time to be ſo: they ſhould be careful
not to ride before the hounds, or over the ſcent;
nor ſhould they ever meet a hound in the face,
unleſs with a deſign to ſtop him. Should you at
any time be before the hounds, turn your horſe's
head the way they are going, get out of their
track, and let them paſs by you.

In

In dry weather, foxes, particularly in heathy countries, will run the roads. If gentlemen, at such times, will ride clofe upon the hounds, they may drive them miles, without any fcent.* High-mettled fox-hounds are feldom inclined to ftop whilft horfes are clofe at their heels.

An acquaintance of mine, a good fportfman, but a very warm one, when he fees the company preffing too clofe upon his hounds, begins with crying out, as loud as he can, *hold hard.* If any one fhould perfift after that, he begins moderately at firft, and fays, *I beg, Sir, you will ftop your horfe :—Pray, Sir, ftop :—God blefs you, Sir, ftop ;—God d—n your blood, Sir, ftop your horfe.*

I am now, as you may perceive, in a very violent paffion; fo I will e'en ftop the continuation of this fubject till I be cool again.

---

* No one fhould ever ride in a direction which, if perfifted in, would carry him amongft the hounds, unlefs he be at a great diftance behind them.

LET-

LETTER XVI.

I ENDED my laſt letter, I think, in a violent paſſion. The hounds, I believe, were at fault alſo. I ſhall now continue the further explanation of my thirteenth letter from that time.

The firſt moment that hounds are at fault is a critical one for the ſport: people then ſhould be very attentive. Thoſe who look forward perhaps may ſee the fox, or the running of ſheep, or the purſuit of crows, may give them ſome tidings of him. Thoſe who liſten may ſometimes take a hint which way he is gone, from the chattering of a magpie; or, perhaps, be at a certainty, from a diſtant halloo: nothing that can give any intelligence, at ſuch a time, is to be neglected. Gentlemen are too apt to ride all together: were they to ſpread more, they might ſometimes be of ſervice; particularly thoſe who, from a knowledge of the ſport, keep down the wind: it would then be difficult for either hounds, or fox, to eſcape their obſervation.

You ſhould, however, be cautious how you go to a halloo. The halloo itſelf muſt, in a great meaſure, direct you; and though it afford no certain rule, yet you may frequently guefs by it whether it may be depended on or not. At the fowing time, when boys are bird-keeping, if you be not very much on your guard, their halloo will fometimes deceive you. It is beft, when you are in doubt, to fend on a whipper-in to know; the worft then that can befall you is the lofs of a little time; whereas, if you gallop away with the hounds to the halloo, and are obliged to return, it is a chance if they try for the fcent afterwards: on the other hand, if, certain of the halloo, you intend going to it; then the fooner you get to it the better. I have been more angry with my huntfman, for being flow at a time like this, than for any other fault whatfoever. Huntfmen who are flow at getting to a halloo, are void of common fenfe.

They frequently commit another fault by being in too great a hurry when they get there. It is hardly credible how much our eagernefs is apt, at fuch a time, to miflead our judgment: for inftance, when we get to the halloo, the firft queftions are natural enough. Did you fee the fox? Which way did he go? The man points with his finger, perhaps, and then away you all ride as faft as you can; and in fuch a hurry, that not one will ftay to hear the anfwer to the queftion which all were fo ready to afk: the general confequence of which is, you miftake the place, and

are

are obliged to return to the man for better information. Depend upon it, the lefs you hurry on
this occafion the more time you fave; and where-
ever the fox was feen for a certainty, whether
near or diftant, that will not only be the fureft,
but alfo the beft place to take the fcent; and,
befides the certainty of going right, you probably will get on fafter than you would by any
other means.

That halloos are not always to be depended on
will be fufficiently evinced by the following inftances :

My hounds being at a long fault, a fellow hallooed to them from the top of a rick, at fome
diftance off. The huntfman, as you may believe, ftuck fpurs to his horfe, hallooed till he
was almoft hoarfe, and got to the man as quickly
as he could: the man ftill kept hallooing, and
as the hounds got near him, " *Here*," faid he—
" *here—here, the fox is gone.*"—" Is he far before
" us?" cried the huntfman. " How long ago
" was it that you faw him?"—" No, mafter, I
" have not *feen him*, but I *fmelt him* here this
" morning, when I came to ferve my fheep."

Another inftance was this: we were trying
with fome deer-hounds for an out-lying ftag,
when we faw a fellow running towards us in his

O

fhirt:

fhirt: we immediately concluded that we fhould hear fome news of the ftag, and fet out joyfully to meet him. Our firft queftion was, if he had feen the ftag? " No, Sir, I have not feen him, " *but my wife dreamt as how fhe faw him t'other* " *night*."

Once a man hallooed us back a mile, only to tell us *that we were right before*, and we loft the fox by it.

A gentleman, feeing his hounds at fault, rode up to a man at plough, and with great eagernefs afked him, if he had feen the fox? " The fox, " Sir!"—" Yes, d—n you, the fox! Did you " never fee a fox?"—" Pray, Sir, if I may be " fo bould, what fort of a looking creature may " he be? has he *fhort ears* and a *long tail*?"— " *Yes*."—" Why then, I can affure you, Sir, I " have feen *no fuch thing*."

We are agreed, that hounds ought not to be caft as long as they are able to hunt; and though the idea, that a hunted fox never ftops, is a very neceffary one to a fox-hunter, that he may be active, and may lofe no time; yet tired foxes will ftop, if you can hold them on; and I have known them ftop, even in wheel-ruts, on the open down, and leap up in the midft of the hounds. A tired fox ought not to be given up,

for

for he is killed fometimes very unexpectedly. If hounds have ever preffed him, he is worth your trouble; perfeverance may recover him, and, if recovered, he moſt probably will be killed ; nor ſhould you defpair, whilſt any fcent remains. The bufinefs of a huntfman is only difficult when the fcent dies quite away; and it is then he may ſhew *his* judgment, when the hounds are no longer able to ſhew *theirs*. The recovering a loſt fcent, and getting nearer to the fox by a long caſt, requires genius, and is, therefore, what few huntfmen are equal to. When hounds are no longer capable of feeling the fcent, it all reſts with the huntfinan; either the game is entirely given up, or is only to be recovered by him, and is the effect of real genius, fpirit, and obferva-tion.

When hounds are at cold hunting, with a bad fcent, it may then be a proper time to fend a whipper-in forward; if he can fee the fox, a lit-tle mobbing, at fuch a time as this, may reafon-ably be allowed.

When hounds are put to a check on a high road, by the fox being headed back, if in that particular inſtance you fuffer them to try back, it gives them the beſt chance of hitting off the fcent again, as they may try on both ſides at once.

O 2

When

When hounds are running in cover, you cannot be too quiet. If the fox be running fhort, and the hounds are catching him, not a word fhould then be faid: it is a difficult time for hounds to hunt him, as he is continually turning, and will fometimes lie down, and let them pafs him.

I have remarked, that the greateft danger of lofing a fox is at the firft finding of him, and when he is finking; at both of which times he frequently will run fhort, and the eagernefs of the hounds is too apt to carry them beyond the fcent. When a fox is firft found, I wifh every one would keep behind the hounds, till they are well fettled to the fcent; and when the hounds are catching him, I wifh them to be as filent as they can.

When he is caught, I like to fee hounds eat him eagerly. In fome countries, I am told, they have a method of *treeing* him;* it is of ufe to make the hounds eager; it lets them all in; they recover their wind, and eat him more readily. I fhould advife you, at the fame time, not to keep him too long, as I do not imagine the hounds

* The intention of it is to make the hounds more eager, and to let in the tail-hounds. The fox is thrown acrofs the branch of a tree, and the hounds are fuffered to bay at him for fome minutes, before he is thrown amongft them.

have

have any appetite to eat him, longer than whilſt they are angry with him.

When two packs of fox-hounds run together, and they kill the fox, the pack that found him is entitled to the head. Should both have found, how is it to be determined then? The huntſman who gets in firſt ſeems, in my opinion, to have the beſt right to it; yet to prevent a diſpute, (which, of courſe, might be thought a wrong-headed one) would he not do well to cut off the head, and preſent it to the other huntſman?

The ſame author, whom I quoted in my tenth letter, and who tells us, how we ſhould *not eat a hare*, is alſo kind enough to tell us when we *ſhould eat a fox*; I wiſh he had alſo aimed me beſt manner of *dreſſing him*: we are obliged to him, however, for the following information:—
" *La chair du Renard eſt moins mauvaiſe que c'elle*
" *du loup; les chiens et même les Hommes en mangent*
" *en automne, ſurtout lorſqu'il s'eſt nourri et en-*
" *graiſſé de raiſins.*"—You would have been better pleaſed, I make no doubt, if the learned gentleman had inſtructed you *how to hunt him,* rather than *when to eat him.*

I ſhall end this letter with an anecdote of a late huntſman of mine, who was a great flip-flop, and always called ſucceſſively, *ſucceſsfully.* One
O 3

day,

day, when he had been out with the young
hounds, I fent for him in, and afkcd him what
fport he had had, and how the hounds behaved?
" Very great fport, Sir, and no hounds could
" behave any better." — " Did you run him
" long?"—" They ran him, and pleafe your
" honour, upwards of three hours *fucccfsfully*."
—" So, then, you *did* kill him ?"—" *Oh, no,*
" *Sir, we loft him at laft.*"

LETTER XVII.

FOX-HUNTING, an acquaintance of mine says, is only to be followed becaufe you can ride hard, and do lefs harm in that than in any other kind of hunting. There may be fome truth in the obfervation; but, to fuch as love the riding part only of hunting, would not a trail fcent be more fuitable? Gentlemen who hunt for the fake of a ride, who are indifferent about the hounds, and know little of the bufinefs, if they do no harm, fulfil as much as we have reafon to expect from them; whilft thofe of a contrary defcription, do good, and have much greater pleafure. Such as are acquainted with the hounds, and can at times affift them, find the fport more interefting; and frequently have the fatisfaction to think, that they themfelves contribute to the fuccefs of the day. This is a pleafure you often enjoy; a pleafure, without any regret attending it. I know not what effect it may have on you; but I know that my fpirits are always good after good fport in hunting; nor is the reft of the day ever difagreeable to me. What are other fports compared to this, which is full of enthufiafm! fifhing is, in my opinion, a dull diverfion;---fhooting, though it admit of a companion, will not allow of many:---both therefore may be

O 4   confidered

confidered as felfifh and folitary amufements, compared with hunting; to which, as many as pleafe are welcome. The one might teach patience to a philofopher; and the other, though it occafion great fatigue to the body, feldom affords much occupation to the mind. Whereas foxhunting is a kind of warfare;---its uncertainties, its fatigues, its difficulties, and its dangers, rendering it interefting above all other diverfions.——— That you may more readily pardon this digreffion, I return to anfwer your letter now before me.

I am glad to hear that your men have good voices; mine, unluckily, have not. There is a friend of mine, who hunts his own hounds; his voice is the ftrangeft, and his halloos the oddeft I ever heard. He has, however, this advantage :--- no dog can poffibly miftake his halloo for another's. Singularity conftitutes an effential part of a huntfman's halloo :---it is for that reafon alone, I prefer the horn, to which, I obferve, hounds fly more readily than to the huntfman's voice. Good voices certainly are pleafing; yet it might be as well, perhaps, if thofe who have them, were lefs fond of exerting them. When a fox is hallooed, thofe who underftand this bufinefs, and get forward, may halloo him again ;*

yet

* Should a fox be hallooed in cover, while the hounds are at fault; if they be long in coming, by getting forward you may
halloo

yet let them be told if the hounds go the contrary way, or do not feem to come on upon the
line of him, to halloo no more. With regard
to its being the hunted fox; the fox which every
man halloos, is the hunted fox in his own opinion,
though he feldom has a better reafon for it, than
becaufe *he* faw him.—Such halloos as ferve to
keep the hounds together, and to get on the tail
hounds, are always of ufe: halloos of encouragement to leading hounds, if injudicioufly given,
may fpoil your fport. I am forry to fay view
halloos frequently do more harm than good.—
They are pleafing to fportfmen, but prejudicial to
hounds. If a ftrong cover be full of foxes, and
they be often hallooed, hounds feldom take much
pains in hunting them; hence arifes that indifference, which fometimes is to be perceived in fox-
hounds while purfuing their game.

You afk me, if I would take off my hounds to
a halloo?—If they be running with a good fcent,
I moft certainly would not; if otherwife, and I

halloo the fox again; perhaps, before the hounds are laid on; by
which means you will get nearer to him. In cafes like this, a
good fportfman may be of great ufe to hounds. There are days
when hounds will do their bufinefs beft if let quite alone; and
there are days, when they can do nothing without affiftance.—
Let them be affifted at no other tim . (f a bad fcenting day,
or when hounds may be over-matche , you can..ot affift them
too much.

could depend upon the halloo, in fome cafes I would : for inftance, when the fox is a great way before them, or perfifts in running his foil ; for fuch foxes are difficult to kill, unlefs you endeavour to get nearer to them by fome means or other.——When you hunt after them, it will frequently happen that the longer you run, the further you will be behind,

If hounds be out of blood, and a fox run his foil, you need not fcruple to ftop the tail hounds, and throw them in at head ; or, if the cover have any ridings cut in it, and the fox be often feen, your huntfman, by keeping fome hounds at his horfe's heels, at the firft halloo that he hears, may throw them in clofe at him.*——This will put him out of his pace, and perhaps, put him off his foil.   It will be neceffary, when you do this, that the whipper-in fhould ftop the pack from hunting after, and get forward with them to the huntfman. I have already given it as my opinion, that hounds may be hallooed too much.   If they

* Nothing is meant more than this—" that the huntfman fhould get the tail hounds off the line of the fcent, (where they do more harm than good,) and encourage them forward; if he fhould hear a halloo, whilft thefe hounds are off the fcent, he fhould lay them on to it; if he fhould not, the tail hounds, by this means, may ftill ftand a chance of getting to the head hounds by the *ear*, which they never could do, if they continued to run by the *nofe*.

fhould

should have been often ufed to a halloo, they will expect it; and may truft, perhaps, to their ears, and eyes, more than to their nofes. If they be often taken from the fcent, it will teach them to fhuffle, and probably will make them flack in cover: it fhould be done, therefore, with great caution; not too often; and always fhould be well-timed. Famous huntfmen, I think, by making too frequent a ufe of this, fometimes hurt their hounds. I have heard of a fportfman, who never fuffers his hounds to be lifted; he lets them pick along the coldeft fcent, through flocks of fheep: this is a particular ftyle of fox-hunting, which, perhaps, may fuit the country in which that gentleman hunts. I confefs to you, I do not think it would fucceed in a bad fcenting country, or indeed, in any country where foxes are wild;— whilft hounds can get on with the fcent, it cannot be right to take them off from it; but when they are ftopped for want of it, it cannot then be wrong to give them every advantage in your power.

It is wrong to fuffer hounds to hunt after others that are gone on with the fcent, particularly in cover; for how are they to get up to them with a worfe fcent; befides, it makes them tye on the fcent, teaches them to run dog, and deftroys that laudable ambition of getting forward, which is the chief excellence of a fox-hound. A good

huntfman

huntfman will feldom fuffer his head hounds to run away from him; if it fhould fo happen, and they be ftill within his hearing, he will fink the wind with the reft of the pack, and get to them as faft as he can.—Though I fuffer not a pack of fox-hounds to hunt after fuch as may be a long way before the reft, for reafons which I have juft given; yet, when a fingle hound is gone on with the fcent, I fend a whip- per-in to ftop him. Were the hounds to be taken off the fcent to get to him, and he fhould no lon- ger have any fcent when they find him, the fox might be loft by it. This is a reafon, why in large covers, and particularly fuch as have many roads in them, fkirting hounds fhould be left at home on windy days.

Skirters, I think, you may find hurtful, both in men and dogs. Such as fkirt to fave their horfes, often head the fox. Good fportfmen never quit hounds, but to be of fervice to them: with men of this defcription, fkirting becomes a neceffary part of fox-hunting, and is of the greateft ufe. Skirters! beware of a furze-brake. If you head back the fox, the hounds moft pro- bably will kill him in the brake. Such as ride after the hounds, at the fame time that they do no good, are leaft likely to do harm; let fuch only as underftand the bufinefs, and mean to be of fervice to the hounds, ride wide of them; I

cannot

cannot however allow, that the riding clofe up to hounds is always a fign of a good fportfman; if it were, a *monkey*, upon a good horfe, would be the beft fportfman in the field.—Here muft I cenfure, (but with refpect) that eager fpirit which frequently interrupts, and fometimes is fatal to fport in fox-hunting; for, though I cannot fubfcribe to the doctrine of my friend ****, " that " a pack of fox-hounds would be better without " a huntfman, than with one; and that if left to " themfelves, they would never lofe a fox;"— yet, allowing them their ufual attendants, had he objected only to the fportfmen who follow them, I muft have joined iffue with him. Whoever has followed hounds, muft have feen them frequently hurried beyond the fcent; and whoever is converfant in hunting, cannot but know, that the fteam of many horfes, carried by the wind, and mixed with a cold fcent, is prejudicial to it.

It fometimes will happen, that a good horfeman is not fo well in with hounds, as an indifferent one; becaufe he feldom will condefcend to get off his horfe. I believe, the beft way to follow hounds acrofs a country, is to keep on the line of them, and to difmount at once, when you come to a leap which you do not choofe to take; for in looking about for eafier places, much time is loft. In following hounds, it may be ufeful to you to know, that when in cover they run up the

the wind, you cannot in reafon be too far behind them, as long as you have a perfect hearing of them, and can command them ; and on the contrary, when they are running down the wind, you cannot keep too clofe to them.

You complain that foxes are in too great plenty ; believe me, it is a good fault. I fhould as foon have expected to have heard your old acquaintance, Jack R——, complain of having too much money ; however, it is not without a remedy ; hunt the fame covers conftantly, and you will foon difperfe them. If your pack be ftrong enough, divide it ; hunt every day, and you will catch many tired foxes. I remember to have killed a brace in one morning, in the ftrongeft feafon ; the firft in ten minutes, the fecond in half an hour.—If your own pack be not ftrong enough to hunt more than every other day, get a pack of harriers to hunt hare in the cover the intermediate day. Foxes thus difturbed, will fhift their quarters ; they know their enemies, and fmell in the night, where they have been in the day, and will not ftay where they are likely to be difturbed by them. Follow them for one week in this manner, and I do not think you will have any reafon, afterwards, to complain that they are in too great plenty.

When

When covers are much difturbed, foxes will fometimes break as foon as they hear a hound. Where the country round is very open, the fox leaft likely to break is that which you are hunting; *he* will be very unwilling to quit the cover, if it be a large one, unlefs he can get a great diftance before the hounds. Should you be defirous to get a run over fuch a country, the likelieft means will be, to poft a quiet and fkilful perfon to halloo one off, and lay on to him. The further he is before you, the lefs likely he will be to return. The beft method, however, to hunt a cover like this, is to ftick conftantly to it, not fuffering the hounds to break, fo long as one fox fhall remain ; do this two or three hunting days following : foxes will then fly, and you will have good chaces.

Nothing is more hurtful to hounds than the frequent changing of their country ; fhould they change from a good fcenting country to a bad one, unlefs they have luck on their fides, they may be fome time without killing a fox; whereas hounds have always a great advantage in a country which they are ufed to. They not only know better where to find their game, but they will alfo purfue it with more alacrity afterwards.

This letter began by a digreffion in favour of hunting; it will end with the opinion of a Frenchman, not fo favourable to it. This Gentleman

tleman was in my neighbourhood on a vifit to the late Lord Caftlehaven, who, being a great fportfman, thought he could not oblige his friend more, than by letting him partake of an amufement, which he himfelf was fo fond of; he therefore mounted him on one of his beft horfes, and fhewed him a fox-chace. The Frenchman, after having been well fhaken, dirted, tired, run away with, and thrown down, was afked, on his return, "*comment il avoit trouvé la chaffe?*"---"*Mor-* "*bleu! Milord,*" faid he, fhrugging up his fhoulders, "*votre chaffe eft une chaffe diabolique.*"

LETTER XVIII.

BEFORE I proceed on my fubject, give me leave to fet you right in one particular, where I perceive you have mifunderſtood me. You ſay, you little expected to fee the abilities of a huntf-man degraded beneath thoſe of a whipper-in. This is a ſerious charge againſt me as a ſportſman; and though I cannot allow that I have put the cart before the horſe, in the manner you are pleaſed to mention: yet you have made it neceſ-ſary for me to explain myſelf further.

I muſt therefore remind you, that I ſpeak of my own country only, a country full of riot; where the covers are large, and where there is a chace full of deer, and full of game. In ſuch a country as this, you that know ſo well how neceſ-ſary it is for a pack of fox-hounds to be ſteady, and to be kept together, ought not to wonder that I ſhould prefer an excellent whipper-in to an excellent huntſman. No one knows better than yourſelf, how eſſential a good adjutant is to a regiment: believe me, a good whipper-in is not leſs neceſſary to a pack of fox-hounds. But I muſt beg you to obſerve, I mean only, *that I*

P   *could*

could do better with mediocrity in the one than in the other. If I have written any thing in a former letter that implies more, I beg leave to retract it in *this.* Yet I muſt confeſs to you, that a famous huntſman I am not very ambitious to have ; unleſs, it neceſſarily followed, that he muſt have *famous hounds:* a concluſion I cannot admit, as long as theſe, ſo famous gentlemen, will be continually attempting themſelves to do what would be much better done if left to their hounds ; beſides, they ſeldom are good ſervants, are always conceited, and ſometimes impertinent. I am very well ſatisfied if my huntſman be acquainted with his country and his hounds; if he ride well up to them, and if he have ſome knowledge of the nature of the animal which he is in purſuit of ; but ſo far am I from wiſhing him to be famous, that I hope he will ſtill continue to think his hounds know beſt how to hunt a fox.

You ſay you agree with me, that a huntſman ſhould ſtick cloſe to his hounds. If then his place be fixed, and that of the firſt whipper-in (where you have two) be not, I cannot but think genius may be at leaſt as uſeful in one as in the other: for inſtance, while the huntſman is riding to his headmoſt hounds, the whipper-in, if he have genius, may ſhew it in various ways; he may clap forward to any great earth that may, by

. . chance,

chance, be open; he may fink the wind to halloo, or mob a fox, when the fcent fails; he may keep him off his foil; he may ftop the tail hounds, and get them forward; and has it frequently in his power to affift the hounds without doing them any hurt, provided he fhould have fenfe to dif-tinguifh where he may be chiefly wanted. Be-fides, the moft effential part of fox-hunting, the making and keeping the pack fteady, depends entirely upon him; as a huntfman fhould feldom rate, and never flog a hound. In fhort, I con-fider the firft whipper-in as a fecond huntfman; and, to be perfect, he fhould be not lefs capable of hunting the hounds than the huntfman himfelf.

You cannot too much recommend to your whipper-in to get to the head of his hounds, be-fore he attempts to ftop them. The rating behind is to little purpofe, and if they fhould be in cover, may prevent him from knowing who the culprits are. When your hounds are running a fox, he then fhould content himfelf with ftopping fuch as are riotous, and fhould get them forward. They may be condemned upon the fpot, but the punifhment fhould be deferred till the next day, when they may be taken out on purpofe to com-mit the fault, and fuffer the punifhment. I agree with you, that young hounds cannot be awed too much; yet fuffer not your punifhment of

P 2

them

them to exceed their offence. I could wish to draw a line betwixt juſtice and barbarity.*

A whipper-in, while breaking in young hounds, fometimes will rate them before they commit the fault: this may, perhaps, prevent them for that time, but they will be juſt as ready to begin the next opportunity. Had he not better let them quite alone till he fee what they would be at? The diſcipline then may be proportioned to the degree of the offence. Whether a riotous young hound run little or much is of fmall confequence if he be not encouraged; it is the blood only that fignifies, which in every kind of riot fhould carefully be prevented.†

* I am forry that it fhould be neceſſary to explain what I mean by *barbarity*. I mean *that* puniſhment, which is either unneceſſarily inflicted; which is inflicted with feverity; or from which no poſſible good can arife. Puniſhment, when properly applied, is not cruelty, is not revenge, it is juſtice; it is even mercy. The intention of puniſhment is to prevent crimes, and, confequently, to prevent the neceſſity of puniſhing.

† It is not meant that hounds fhould be fuffered to continue on a wrong fcent longer than may be neceſſary to know that the fcent *is* a wrong one. This paſſage refers to page 88, where the author's meaning is more fully explained. It is introduced here more ftrongly to mark the danger of encouraging hounds on a wrong fcent, and indulging them afterwards in the blood of it.

My

My general orders to my whipper-in are, if when he rate a hound, the hound does not mind him, to take him up immediately, and give him a fevere flogging. Whippers-in are too apt to continue rating, even when they find that rating will not avail. There is but one way to ftop fuch hounds, which is to get to the heads of them.— I will alfo tell him, never on any account to ftrike a hound, unlefs the hound be at the fame time fenfible what it is for.—What think you of the whipper-in who ftruck a hound as he was going to cover, becaufe he was likely to be noify afterwards, faying, " *you will be noify enough by* " *and by, I warrant you.*" Whippers-in, when left to themfelves, are rare judges of propriety! I wifh they would never ftrike a hound that does not deferve it, and would ftrike thofe hard that do. They feldom diftinguifh fufficiently the degrees of offence which a dog may have committed, to proportion their punifhment accordingly; and fuch is their ftupidity, that when they turn a hound after the huntfman, they will rate him as feverely as if he had been guilty of the greateft fault.

It is feldom neceffary to flog hounds to make them obedient, fince obedience is the firft leffon they are taught. Yet, if any fhould be more riotous than the reft, they may receive a few cuts in the morning before they leave the kennel.

P 3   When

When hounds prove unſteady, every poſſible means ſhould be taken to make them otherwiſe. A hare, or a deer, put into the kennel amongſt them, may then be neceſſary. Huntſmen are too fond of kennel diſcipline. You already know my opinion of it. I never allow it but in caſes of great neceſſity. I then am always preſent myſelf to prevent exceſs. To prevent an improper and barbarous uſe of ſuch diſcipline, I have already told you, is one of the chief objects of theſe letters. If what Montaigne ſays be true, that " there is a certain general claim of kindneſs and " benevolence which every creature has a right " to from us," ſurely we ought not to ſuffer unneceſſary ſeverity towards an animal to whom we are obliged for ſo much diverſion; and what opinion muſt we have of the huntſman who inflicts it on one to whom *he* owes his daily bread.*

* " Perhaps it is not the leaſt extraordinary circumſtance in theſe flogging lectures, that they ſhould be given with Montaigne, or any other moral author whatever, in recollection at the ſame inſtant!" (Vide Monthly Review.) Perhaps it is not the leaſt extraordinary circumſtance in theſe criticiſms, that this paſſage ſhould have been quoted as a proof of the author's inhumanity.—The critic ends his ſtrictures with the following exclamation : " Of a truth, a ſportſman is the moſt uniform, conſiſtent character, from his own repreſentation, that we ever contemplated !" and yet, perhaps, there are ſportſmen to be found, poſſeſſed of as tender feelings of humanity as any critic whatſoever. The motto prefixed to theſe letters, if it had been attended to, might have entitled the author to more candour than the critic has thought fit to beſtow upon him.

If

If any of my hounds be very riotous, they are taken out by themselves on the days when they do not hunt, and properly punished; and this is continued whilst my patience lasts, which, of course, depends on the value of the dog. It is a trial betwixt the whipper in and the dog, which will tire first; and the whipper-in, I think, generally prevails. If this method will not make them steady, no other can; they then are looked upon as incorrigible, and are put away.

Such hounds as are notorious offenders should also feel the lash and hear a rate as they go to the cover; it may be an useful hint to them, and may prevent a severer flogging afterwards. A sensible whipper-in will wait his opportunity to single out his hound; he will then hit him hard, and rate him well, whilst a foolish one will often hit a dog he did not intend to hit; will ride full gallop into the midst of the hounds; will, perhaps, ride over some of the best of them, and put the whole pack into confusion—this is a manoeuvre I cannot bear to see.

Have a care! are words which seldom do any harm; since hounds, when they are on a right scent, will not mind them. Let your whipper-in be careful how he *encourage* the hounds; that, improperly done, may spoil your pack.

P 4

A whip-

A whipper-in will rate a hound, and then en-deavour to flog him. A dog, after having been rated, will naturally avoid the whip. Tell your whipper-in, whenever a hound ſhall deſerve the laſh, to whip him firſt, and rate him afterwards.

When there are two whippers-in, one ought always to be forward. When there is only *one*, he, to be perfect, ſhould be a very *Mungo, here, there,* and *every where.*

You will find it difficult to keep your people in their proper places; I have been obliged to ſlop back myſelf to bring on hounds which my ſervants had left behind. I cannot give you a greater proof how neceſſary it is that a whipper-in ſhould bring home all his hounds, than by telling you, that I had loſt an old hound for ten days, and ſent all the country over to inquire after him; and at laſt, when I thought no more about him, in drawing a large cover in the coun-try where he had been loſt, he joined the pack; he was exceedingly emaciated, and it was a long time before he recovered: how he ſubſiſted all that time I cannot imagine. When any of your hounds may be miſſing, you ſhould ſend the whipper-in back immediately to look for them; it will teach him to keep them more together.

The

The getting forward the tail hounds is a neceffary part of fox-hunting, in which you will find
a good whipper-in of the greateft ufe. He muft
alfo get forward himfelf at times, when the huntfman is not with the hounds; but the fecond
whipper-in (who frequently is a young lad, ignorant of his bufinefs) on no account ought to
encourage or rate a hound, but when he is quite
certain it is right to do it; nor is *he* ever to get
forward, fo long as a fingle hound remains
behind.

Halloo forward is certainly a neceffary and a
good halloo, but is it not ufed too indifcriminately?
it is for ever in the mouth of a whipper-in. If
your hounds be never ufed to that halloo till after
a fox be found, you will fee them fly to it. At
other times other halloos will anfwer the purpofe
of getting them on as well. *Halloo forward* being
ufed as foon as the game is on foot, it feems as if
another halloo were neceffary to denote the breaking cover. *Away! away!* might anfwer that
purpofe. Gentlemen who are kind enough to
flop back to affift hounds, fhould have notice given
them when the hounds leave the cover.

Moft huntfmen, I believe, are jealous of the
whipper-in; they frequently look on him as a
fucceffor, and therefore do not very readily admit
him into the kennel; yet, in my opinion, it is
neceffary

neceffary that he fhould go thither, for he ought to be well acquainted with the hounds, who fhould know and follow him as well as the huntfman.

To recapitulate what I have already faid: if your whipper-in be bold and active; be a good and careful horfeman; have a good ear and a clear voice; if, as I faid, he be a very *Mungo*, having, at the fame time, judgment to diftinguifh where he can be of moft ufe; if, joined to thefe, he be above the foolifh conceit of killing a fox without the huntfman; but, on the contrary, be difpofed to affift him all he can, he then is a perfect whipper-in.

I am forry to hear that your hounds are fo un-fteady; it is fcarcely poffible to have fport with unfteady hounds; they are half tired before the fox is found, and are not to be depended upon afterwards. It is a great pleafure when a hound challenges to be certain he is right: it is a cruel difappointment to hear a rate immediately fucceed it, and the fmacking of whips, inftead of halloos of encouragement. A few riotous and determined hounds do a deal of mifchief in a pack. Never, when you can avoid it, put them amongft the reft; let them be taken out by them-felves and well chaftifed, and if you find them incorrigible hang them. The common faying,

evil

evil communications corrupt good manners, holds good with regard to hounds; they are eafily corrupted. The feparating of the riotous ones from thofe which are fteady anfwers many good purpofes: it not only prevents the latter from getting the blood which they fhould not, but it alfo prevents them from being over-awed by the fmacking of whips, which is too' apt to obftruct drawing and going deep into cover. A couple of hounds, which I received from a neighbour laft year, were hurtful to my pack. They had run with a pack of harriers, and, as I foon found, were never afterwards to be broken from hare. It was the beginning of the feafon, covers were thick, hares in plenty, and we feldom killed lefs than five or fix in a morning. The pack at laft got fo much blood, that they would hunt them as if they were defigned to hunt nothing elfe. I parted with that couple of hounds, and the others, by proper management, are become as fteady as they were before. You will remind me, perhaps, that they were draft-hounds. It is true, they were fo; but they were three or four years hunters, an age when they might be fuppofed to have known better. I advife you, unlefs a known good pack of hounds are to be difpofed of, not to accept old hounds. I mention this to encourage the breeding of hounds, and as the likelieft means of getting a *handfome, good,* and *fleady pack:* though I give you this advice, it is true, I have accepted draft-hounds myfelf, and they have been very good ; but they were the gift of the friend mentioned by me in a former letter, to whom I have already acknowledged many obligations ; and, unlefs you meet with fuch a one, old hounds will not prove worthy your acceptance :* befides, they may bring vices enough along with them to fpoil your whole pack. If old hounds fhould be unfteady, it may not be in your power to make them otherwife ; and I can affure you from experience, that an unfteady old hound will give you more trouble than all your young ones ; the latter will at leaft ftop, but an obftinate old hound will frequently run mute, if he find that he can run no other way ; befides, old hounds that are unacquainted with your people will not readily hunt for them as they ought ; and fuch as were fteady in their own pack may become unfteady in your's. I once faw an extraordinary inftance of this when I kept harriers : hunting one day on the downs, a well-known fox-hound of a neighbouring gentleman came and joined us, and as he both ran fafter than we did, and fkirted more, he broke every fault, and killed many hares. I faw this hound often in his own pack afterwards, where he was perfectly fteady ; and, though he conftantly hunted in covers where hares were in

* The Hon. Mr. Booth Grey, brother to the Earl of Stamford. The hounds here alluded to were from Lord Stamford's kennel.

great

great plenty, I never remember to have feen him run one ftep after them.

A change of country alfo will fometimes occafion a difference in the fteadinefs of hounds. My hounds hunt frequently in Cranborn Chace, and are fteady from deer, yet I once knew them run an outlying deer, which they unexpectedly found in a diftant country.

I am forry to hear fo bad an accident has happened to your pack as that of killing fheep; but, I apprehend, from your account of it, that it proceeded from idlenefs rather than vice. The manner in which the fheep were killed may give you fome infight into it; old practitioners generally feizing by the neck, and feldom, if ever, behind. This, like other vices, fometimes runs in the blood; in an old hound it is, I believe, incorrigible; the beft way, therefore, will be to hang all thofe which, after two or three whippings, cannot be cured of it. In fome countries hounds are more inclined to kill fheep than they are in others. Hounds may be fteady in countries where the covers are fenced, and fheep are only to be feen in flocks, either in large fields, or on open downs; and the fame hounds may be unfteady in forefts and heathy countries where the fheep are not lefs wild than the deer. However hounds, fhould they ftir but a ftep after

them,

them, fhould undergo the fevereft difcipline; if young hounds do it from idlenefs, *that*, and plenty of work, may reclaim them; for old hounds, guilty of this vice, I know, as I faid before, of but one fure remedy—*the halter.*

Though I fo ftrongly recommend to you to make your hounds fteady, from having feen un- fteady packs, yet I muft alfo add, that I have frequently feen the men even more unfteady than the hounds. It is fhocking to hear hounds hal- looed one minute and rated the next: nothing offends a good fportfman fo much, or is in itfelf fo hurtful. I will give you an inftance of the danger of it;—my beagles were remarkably fteady; they hunted hare in Cranborn Chace, where deer are in great plenty, and would draw for hours without taking the leaft notice of them. When tired of hare-hunting, I was inclined to try if I could find any diverfion in hunting of fallow deer. I had been told, that it would be impoffible to do it with thofe hounds that had been made fteady from them; and, to put it to the trial, I took them into a cover of my own, which has many ridings cut in it, and where are many deer. The firft deer we faw we hallooed, and by great encouragement, and conftant hal- looing, there were but few of thefe fteady hounds but would run the fcent. They hunted deer con- ftantly from that day, and never loft one afterwards.

wards. Dogs are senfible animals; they foon find out what is required of them, when we do not confufe them by our own heedlefsnefs: when we encourage them to hunt a fcent which they have been rated from, and, perhaps, feverely chaftifed for hunting, they muft needs think us cruel, capricious, and inconfifient.*

If you know any pack that is very unfteady, depend upon it, either no care has been taken in entering the young hounds to make them fteady; or elfe the men, afterwards, by hallooing them on improperly, and to a wrong fcent, have forced them to become fo.

The firft day of the feafon I advife you to take out your pack where you have leaft riot, and where you are moft fure to find; for, notwith-ftanding their fteadinefs at the end of the laft feafon, long reft may have made them otherwife.

* Though all hounds ought to be made obedient, none re-quire it fo much as fox-hounds, for without it they will be totally uncontroulable; yet, not all the chaftifement that cruelty can inflict will render them obedient, unlefs they be made to underftand what is required of them; when that is effected, many hounds will not need chaftifement, if you do not fuffer them to be corrupted by bad example. Few packs are more obedient than my own, yet none, I believe, are chaftifed lefs; for, as thofe hounds that are guilty of an offence, *are never pardoned*, fo thofe that are innocent, being by this means lefs liable to be corrupted, *are never punifhed*.

If

If you have any hounds more vicious than the reft, they fhould be left at home a day or two, till the others are well in blood: your people, without doubt, will be particularly cautious at the beginning of the featon what hounds they halloo to: fhould they be encouraged on a wrong fcent it will be a great hurt to them.

The firft day that you hunt in the foreft, be equally cautious what hounds you take out. All fhould be fteady from deer; you afterwards may put others to them, a few at a time. I have feen a pack draw fteadily enough; and yet, when running hard, fall on a weak deer, and reft as contented as if they had killed their fox. Thefe hounds were not chaftifed, though caught in the fact, but were fuffered to draw on for a frefh fox; I had rather they had undergone fevere dif-cipline. The finding of another fox with them afterwards might then have been of fervice; otherwife, in my opinion, it could only ferve to encourage them in the vice, and make them worfe and worfe.

I muft mention an inftance of extraordinary fagacity in a fox-beagle, which once belonged to the Duke of Cumberland. I entered him at hare, to which he was immediately fo fteady, that he would run nothing elfe. When a fox was found by the beagles, which fometimes happened, he

would

would inftantly come to the heels of the huntfman's horfe: fome years afterwards I hunted fox
only, and though I parted with moft of the others,
I kept *him:* he went out conftantly with the pack,
and as hares were fcarce in the country I then
hunted, he did no hurt; the moment a fox was
found, he came to the horfe's heels. This continued
fome time, till catching view of a fox that was
finking, he ran in with the reft, and was well
blooded. He, from that time to the day of his
death, was not only as fteady a hound to *fox* as
ever I knew, but became alfo our very beft finder.
I bred fome buck-hounds from him, and they
are remarkable for never changing from a hunted
deer.

Your huntfman's weekly return is a very curious one; he is particularly happy in the fpelling.
The following letter, which is in the fame ftyle,
may make you laugh, and is, perhaps, no un-
fuitable return for your's.

Q

SIR

SIR

HONOURED *   —   —   —   —
—   —   —   —   —   —   —
—   —   —   —   —   —
—   —   —   —   —   —

I have been out with the hounds this day to ayer
the froft is very bad the hounds are all pure well
at prefent and horfes fhephard has had a misfortin
with his mare fhe hung harfelf with the holtar
and throd har felf and broak har neck and frac
tard fkul fo we was forsd to nock har In the head
from your ever dutiful Humbel Sarvant.

                                         **** ******

Wednefday evening.

   * The lines omitted were not upon the fubject of hunting.

LETTER XIX.

FINDING, by your laſt letter, that an early hour does not ſuit you, I will mention ſome particulars which may be of uſe to you when you hunt late: an early hour is only neceſſary where covers are large, and foxes ſcarce; where they are in plenty, you may hunt at any hour you pleaſe. When foxes are weak, by hunting late you have better chaces; when they are ſtrong, give me leave to tell you, you muſt hunt early, or you will not always kill them. I think, however, when you go out late, you ſhould go immediately to the place where you are moſt likely to find; which, generally ſpeaking, is the cover that hounds have been leaſt in. If the cover be large, you ſhould draw only ſuch parts of it as a fox is likely to kennel in; it is uſeleſs to draw any other at a late hour. Beſides, though it be always right to find as ſoon as you can, yet it can never be ſo neceſſary as when the day is far advanced: if you do not find ſoon, a long and tireſome day is generally the conſequence. Where the cover is thick, you ſhould draw it as exactly as if you were trying for a hare: particularly if it be furzy: for, when there is no drag, a fox, at a late hour,

will

will lie till the hounds come clofe upon him.—
Having drawn one cover, let your huntfman ftay
for his hounds, and take them along with him to
another: I have known hounds find a fox after
the huntfman had left the cover. The whippers-
in are not to be fparing of their whips, or voices
on this occafion, and are to come through the
middle of the cover, to be certain that they leave
no hounds behind.

A huntfman will complain of hounds for ftaying behind in cover.—It is a great fault, and
makes the hound addicted to it of but little value;
yet this fault frequently is occafioned by the
huntfman's own mifmanagement. Having drawn
one cover, he hurries away to another, and leaves
the whipper-in to bring on the hounds after him;
but the whipper-in is feldom lefs defirous of getting forward than the huntfman; and, unlefs they
come off eafily, it is not often that he will give
himfelf much concern about them. Hounds alfo
that are left too long at their walks, will acquire
this trick from hunting by themfelves, and are
not eafily broken of it.—Having faid all that I can
at prefent recollect of the duty of a whipper-in,
I fhall now proceed to give you a further account
of *that* of a huntfman. What has already been
faid on the fubject of *drawing* and *cafting*, related
to the fox-chace defcribed in a former letter.---
Much, without doubt, is ftill left to fay; and I

will

will endeavour, as well as I am able, to fupply the deficiency, by confidering, firft, in what manner he fhould draw; and afterwards, how he fhould caft his hounds.

The fixing a day or two beforehand upon the cover in which you intend to hunt, is a great hindrance to fport in fox-hunting. You that have the whole country to yourfelf, and can hunt on either fide of your houfe, as you pleafe, fhould never, (when you can help it) determine on your place of hunting, till you fee what the weather is likely to be.* The moft probable means to have good chaces, is to choofe your country according to the wind.

It will alfo require fome confideration to place hounds to the greateft advantage where foxes either are in great plenty, or very fcarce.

Hounds that lie idle, are always out of wind, and are eafily fatigued. The firft day you go out after a long froft, you cannot expect much fport; take therefore, confiderably more than the ufual number of hounds, and throw them into the largeft cover that you have; if any foxes be

* When the fcent lies badly, fmall covers, or thofe in which a fox cannot move unfeen, are moft favourable to hounds. In fuch covers, good fportfmen will kill foxes in almoft any weather.

in

in the country, it is *there* you will find them.
After once or twice going out in this manner,
you ſhould reduce your number.*

Before a huntſman goes into the kennel to draft
his hounds, let him determine within himſelf the
number of hounds it will be right to take out ; as
likewiſe the number of young hounds that he can
venture in the country where he is going to hunt.
Different countries may require different hounds :
ſome may require more hounds than others : it
is not an eaſy matter to draft hounds properly;
nor can any expedition be made in it, without
ſome method.†

I fel-

* During a froſt, hounds may be exerciſed on downs, or the
turnpike roads; nor will it do any material injury to their feet.
Prevented from hunting, they ſhould be fed ſparingly; and ſuch
as can do without fleſh, ſhould have none given them. A
courſe of vegetables, ſulphur, and thin meat is the likelieſt means
to keep them healthy.

† No hound ought to be left at home, unleſs there be a reaſon for it; it is therefore that I ſay great nicety is required to
draft hounds *properly*. Many huntſmen, I believe, think it of
no great conſequence which they take out, and which they
leave, provided they have the number requiſite. A perfect
knowledge in feeding and drafting hounds, are the two moſt eſſential parts of fox-hunting : good hounds will require but little aſſiſtance afterwards. By *feeding*, I mean the bringing the
hound into the field, in his higheſt vigour. By *drafting*, I particularly mean the taking out no unſteady hound, nor any that
are

I feldom fuffer many unfteady hounds to be taken out together; and when I do, I take care that none fhall go out with them, but fuch as they cannot fpoil.

When the place of meeting, and time are fixed, every huntfman ought to be as exact to them as it is poffible. On no account is he to be *before* the time; yet, on fome occafions, it might be better, perhaps, for the diverfion, were he permitted to be *after it.** The courfe your huntf-man intends to take in drawing, ought alfo to be well underftood before he leaves the kennel.

If your huntfman, without inconveniency, can begin drawing at the fartheft cover down the wind, and fo draw from cover to cover up the

are not likely to be of fervice to the pack :—when you intend to hunt two days following, it is then that the greateft nicety will be requifite to make the moft of a fmall pack. Placing hounds to the greateft advantage, as mentioned in page 228, may alfo be confidered as a neceffary part of fox-hunting

Hounds that are intended to hunt the next day, and are drafted off into the hunting kennel as foon as they are fed, fhould be let out again into the outer court in the evening: my hounds have generally fome thin meat given them at this time, while the feeder cleans out their kennel. (vide note page 44.) I have already faid that cleanlinefs is not lefs effential than food.

* When there is a white froft for inftance, at the going off of which, the fcent never lies.

wind till you find, let him do it: it will have many advantages attending it: he will draw the fame covers in half the time; your people cannot fail of being in their proper places; you will have lefs difficulty in getting your hounds off; and as the fox will moft probably run the covers that have been already drawn, you are leaft likely to change.

If you have a ftring of fmall covers, and plenty of foxes in them, fome caution may be neceffary to prevent your hounds from difturbing them all in one day. Never hunt your fmall covers till you have well rattled the large ones firft; for until the foxes be thinned and difperfed, where they were in plenty, it muft be bad policy to drive others there to increafe the number.—If you would thin your foxes, you muft throw off at the fame cover as long as you can find a fox. If you come off with the fox that breaks, you do not difturb the cover, and may expect to find there again the next day; but where they are fcarce, you fhould never draw the fame cover two days following.

Judicious huntfmen will obferve where foxes like beft to lie. In chaces and forefts, where you have a great tract of cover to draw, fuch obfervation is neceffary, or you will lofe much time in finding. Generally fpeaking, I think they are fondeft

of

of fuch as lie high, and are dry and thick at bottom; fuch alfo as lie out of the wind; and fuch
as are on the funny fide of hills.* The fame
cover where you find one fox, when it has remained quiet any time, will probably produce
another.

It is to little purpofe to draw hazle coppices at
the time when nuts are gathered; furze covers,
or two or three years coppices, are then the only
quiet places that a fox can kennel in: *they* alfo
are difturbed when pheafant-fhooting begins, and
older covers are more likely. The feafon when
foxes are moft wild and ftrong is about Chriftmas; a huntfman, then, muft lofe no time in
drawing; he muft draw up the wind; unlefs the
cover be very large, in which cafe it may be better perhaps to crofs it; giving the hounds a fide
wind, left he fhould be obliged to turn down the
wind at laft:—in either cafe let him draw as
quietly as he can.

Young coppices, at this time of the year, are
quite bare; the moft likely places are four or five
years coppices, and fuch as are furzy at bottom.

* This muft of courfe vary in different countries, a huntfman who has been ufed to a country knows beft where to find
his game.

It is eafy to perceive, by the account you give
of your hounds, that they do not draw well;
your huntfman, therefore, muft be particularly
attentive to them after a wet night. The beft
drawing hounds are fhy of fearching a cover
when it is wet; your's, if care be not taken, will
not go into it at all: your huntfman fhould ride
into the likelieft part of the cover, and as it is
probable there will be no drag, the clofer he
draws the better: he muft not draw too much an
end, but fhould crofs the cover backwards and
forwards, taking care at the fame time to give
his hounds as much the wind as poffible.*

It is not often that you will fee a pack perfectly
fteady, where there is much riot, and yet draw
well: fome hounds will not exert themfelves, till
others challenge, and are encouraged.†

 I fear the many harriers that you have in your
neighbourhood will be hurtful to your fport. by
conftantly difturbing the covers, they will make

---

* Hounds that are hunted conftantly at an early hour,
feldom I think draw well; they depend too much upon a drag,
and it is not in the ftrongeft part of the cover that they are accuftomed to try for it.

† This relates to making hounds fteady only, which always
caufes confufion, and interrupts drawing. When once a pack
are become fteady, they will be more likely to draw well, than if
they were not.

z   the

the foxes fhy, and when the covers become thin, there will be but little chance of finding foxes in them: furze covers are then the moft likely places. Though I like not to fee a huntfman to a pack of fox-hounds ever off his horfe, yet, at a late hour, he fhould draw a furze cover as flowly as he were himfelf on foot. I am well convinced that huntfmen, by drawing in too great a hurry, leave foxes fometimes behind them. I once faw a remarkable inftance of it with my own hounds: we had drawn (as we thought) a cover, which in the whole, confifted of about ten acres; yet, whilft the huntfman was blowing his horn, to get his hounds off, one young fox was hallooed, and another was feen immediately after: it was a cover on the fide of a hill, and the foxes had ken-nelled clofe together at an extremity of it, where no hound had been. Some huntfmen draw too quick, fome too flow;—the time of day, the be-haviour of his hounds, and the covers they are drawing, will direct an obferving huntfman in the pace which he ought to go. When you try a furze brake, let me give you one caution;—never halloo a fox till you fee that he is quite clear of it. When a fox is found in fuch places, hounds are fure to go off well with him; and it muft be owing either to bad fcent, bad hounds, bad management, or bad luck, if they fail to kill him afterwards.

It

It is ufual in moft packs to rate, as foon as a young hound challenges. Though young hounds are often wrong, yet fince it is not impoffible that they may be fometimes right, is it not as well to have a little patience, in order to fee whether any of the old ones will join, before any thing is faid to them? *Have a care!* is fully fufficient, till you are more certain that the hound is on a wrong fcent. I mention this as a hint only—I am myfelf no enemy to a *rate*—I cannot think that a fox was ever loft, or pack fpoiled by it : it is *improper encouragement* that I am afraid of moft.

When a fox flinks from his kennel, gets a great way before the hounds, and you are obliged to hunt after him with a bad fcent; if it be a country where foxes are in plenty, and you know where to find another, you had better do it.*

While hounds are drawing for a fox, let your people place themfelves in fuch a manner that he cannot go off unfeen. I have known them lie in fheep's fcrapes on the fide of hills, and in fmall bufhes, where huntfmen never think of looking for them; yet, when they hear a hound, they generally fhift their quarters, and make for clofer

* Yet if this were practifed often, it might make the hounds indifferent when upon a cold fcent. Hounds fhould be made to believe they are to kill that game which they are firft encouraged to purfue.

covers.

covers.—Gentlemen fhould take this neceffary part of fox-hunting on themfelves, for the whipper-in has other bufinefs to attend on.*

I approve not of long drags in large covers; they give too great an advantage to the fox, they give him a hint to make the beft of his way, and he frequently will fet off a long while before you. This may be prevented by throwing your hounds into that part of the cover, in which he is moft likely to kennel: for want of this precaution, a fox fometimes gets fo far the ftart of hounds, that they are not able to do any thing with him afterwards. Alfo, when hounds firft touch on a drag, fome huntfmen are fo carelefs, that whilft they are going on with it the wrong way themfelves, a fingle hound the fox, and is not caught any more by the pack, till he has loft him again.

Foxes are faid to go down the wind to their kennel; but, I believe, they do not always obferve that rule.

Huntfmen, whilft their hounds, are drawing, or are at a fault, frequently make fo much noife themfelves, that they can hear nothing elfe: they

* Upon thefe occafions, when you fee two gentlemen *together*, you may reafonably conclude that one of them, at leaft, knows nothing of the matter.

fhould

fhould always have an ear to a halloo. I once faw an extraordinary inftance of the want of it in my own huntfman, who was making fo much noife with his hounds which were then at fault, that a man hallooed a long while before he heard him; and when he did hear him, fo little did he know whence the halloo came, that he rode two miles the wrong way, and loft the fox.

When hounds approach a cover which it is intended they fhould draw, and dafh away towards it, whippers-in ride after them to ftop them. It is too late, and they had better let them alone; it checks them in their drawing, and is of no kind of ufe; it will be foon enough to begin to rate when they have found, and hunt improper game: when a huntfman has his hounds under good command, and is attentive to them, they will not break off till he choofe that they fhould. When he goes by the fide of a cover which he does not intend to draw, his whippers-in muft be in their proper places; for if he fhould ride up to a cover with them unawed, uncontrouled; a cover where they have been ufed to find, they muft be flack indeed, if they do not dafh into it. It is for that reafon better, not to come into a cover always the fame way; hounds, by not knowing what is going forward will be lefs likely to break off, and will draw more quietly. I have feen hounds fo flafhy, that they would break away from the

huntfman

huntſman as ſoon as they ſaw a cover; and I have ſeen the ſame hounds ſtop when they got to the cover ſide, and not go into it. It is want of proper diſcipline which occaſions faults like theſe. Hounds that are under ſuch command as never to leave their huntſman till he encourage them to do it, will be then ſo confident, that they will not return to him again.

Were fox-hounds to ſtop, like ſtop-hounds, at the ſmack of a whip, they would not do their buſineſs the worſe for it, and it would give you many advantages very eſſential to your ſport;— ſuch, as when they have to wait under a cover ſide; when they run riot; when they change ſcents; when a ſingle hound is on before; and when a fox is headed back into a cover. Hounds that are not under good command ſubject you to many inconveniencies; and you may, at times, be obliged to go out of your way, or be made to draw a cover againſt your will. A famous pack of hounds in my neighbourhood, I mean the late Lord C——n's, had no fault but what had its riſe from bad management; nor is it poſſible to do any thing with a pack of fox-hounds unleſs they be obedient: they ſhould both love and fear the huntſman; they ſhould fear him much, yet they ſhould love him more. Without doubt hounds would do more for the huntſman if they loved him better. Dogs that are conſtantly with their

maſters

masters acquire a wonderful deal of penetration, and much may be done through the medium of their affections. I attribute the extraordinary sagacity of the buck-hound to the manner in which he is treated; he is the constant companion of his instructor and benefactor; the man whom he was first taught to fear, and has since learned to love: ought we to wonder that he should be obedient to him? Yet, who can view without surprise the hounds and the deer amusing themselves familiarly together upon the same lawn; living, as it were, in the most friendly intercourse; and know that a word from the keeper will dissolve the amity. The obedient dog, gentle when unprovoked, flies to the well-known summons; how changed from what he was! roused from his peaceful state, and cheered by his master's voice, he is now cheered on with a relentless fury that only death can satisfy—the death of the *very deer* he is encouraged to pursue; and which the various scents that cross him in his way cannot tempt him to forsake. The business of the day over, see him follow, careless and contented, his master's steps to repose upon the same lawn, where the frightened deer again return, and are again indebted to *his* courtesy for their wonted pasture. Wonderful proofs of obedience, sagacity, and penetration! The many learned dogs and learned horses that so frequently appear, and astonish the vulgar, sufficiently evince what education

cation

Earth Stopping.

cation is capable of; and it is to education I muſt chiefly attribute the ſuperior excellence of the buck-hound, ſince I have ſeen high-bred fox-hounds do the ſame under the ſame good maſ-ters. But to return to my ſubject.

Young foxes, that have been much diſturbed, will lie at ground. I once found ſeven or eight in a cover, where the next day I could not find one; nor were they to be found elſewhere: the earths, at ſuch time, ſhould be ſtopped three or four hours before day, or you will find no foxes.

The firſt day you hunt a cover that is full of foxes, and you want blood, let them not be checked back into the cover, which is the uſual practice at ſuch times, but let ſome of them get off: if you do not, what with continual changing, and ſometimes running the heel, it is probable that you will not kill any. Another precaution, I think, may be alſo neceſſary; that is, to ſtop ſuch earths only as you cannot dig. If ſome foxes ſhould go to ground it will be as well; and if you ſhould be in want of blood at laſt, you will then know where to get it.

It is uſual, when people are not certain of the ſteadineſs of their hounds from deer, to find a fox in an adjacent cover, that they may be on their right ſcent when they come where deer are.

R

I have

I have my doubts of the propriety of this proceeding: if hounds have not been well awed
from deer, it is not fit that they at any rate fhould
come among them; but if hounds be tolerably
fteady, I had rather find a fox with them amongft
deer, than bring them afterwards into covers
where deer are. By drawing amongft them, they
in fome degree will be awed from the fcent, and
poffibly may ftick to the fox when he is found;
but fhould unfteady hounds, when high on their
mettle, run into a cover where deer are in plenty,
there is no doubt, that the firft check they come
to they will all fall off. I always have found
hounds moft inclined to riot when moft upon
their mettle; fuch as are given to fheep will then
kill fheep; and fuch as are not quite fteady from
deer will then be moft likely to break off after
them. When hounds are encouraged on a fcent,
if they lofe that fcent, it is then an unfteady
hound is ready for any kind of mifchief.

I have already faid, that a huntfman ought
never to flog a hound. When a riotous hound,
confcious of his offence, may efcape from the
whipper-in, and fly to the huntfman, you will
fee him put his whole pack into confufion by en-
deavouring to chaftife him himfelf. This is the
height of abfurdity! Inftead of flogging the hound
he ought to encourage him, who fhould always
have fome place to fly to for protection. If the

offence

offence be a bad one, let him get off his horse
and couple up the dog, leaving him to be chaftifed by the whipper-in, after he himfelf is gone
on with the pack : the punifhment over, let
him again encourage the hound to come to him.
Hounds that are riotous in cover, and will not
come off readily to the huntfman's halloo, fhould
be flogged in the cover rather than out of it ;—
treated in this manner, you will not find any difficulty in getting your hounds off; otherwife, they
will foon find that the cover will fave them; from
whence they will have more fenfe, when they
have committed an offence, than to come to receive punifhment. A favourite hound, that has
acquired a habit of ftaying back in large covers,
had better not be taken into them.

I have been more particular than I otherwife
fhould have been, upon a fuppofition that your
hounds draw ill ; however, you need not obferve
all the cautions I have given, unlefs your hounds
require them.

Some art may be neceffary to make the moft of
the country that you hunt. I would advife you not
to draw the covers near your houfe, while you can
find elfewhere; it will make them certain places to
find in when you go out late, or may otherwife be
in want of them. For the fame reafon, I would
advife you not to hunt thofe covers late in the fea--

fon; they fhould not be much difturbed after Chriftmas: foxes will then refort to them, will breed there, and you can preferve them with little trouble. This relates to the good management of a pack of hounds, which is a bufinefs diftinct from hunting them.

Though a huntfman ought to be as filent as poffible at going into a cover, he cannot be too noify at coming out of it again; and if at any time he fhould turn back fuddenly, let him give as much notice of it as he can to his hounds, or he will leave many behind him; and fhould he turn down the wind, he may fee no more of them.

I fhould be forry that the filence of my huntfman fhould proceed from either of the following caufes.—A huntfman that I once knew, (who, by the bye, I believe, is at this time a drummer in a marching regiment) went out one morning fo very drunk, that he got off his horfe in the midft of a thick cover, laid himfelf down, and went to fleep: —he was loft, nobody knew what was become of him, and he was at laft found in the fituation I have juft defcribed. He had, however, great good luck on his fide, for at the very inftant he was found a fox was hallooed; upon which he mounted his horfe, rode defperately, killed his fox hand-fomely, and was forgiven.

I re-

I remember another huntfman filent from a different caufe; this was a fulky one. Things did not go on to pleafe him; he therefore alighted from his horfe in the middle of a wood, and, as quietly as he could, collected his hounds about him; he then took an opportunity, when the coaft was clear, to fet off filently, and by him-felf, for another cover: however his mafter, who knew his tricks, fent others after him to bring him back; they found him running a fox moft merrily, and, to his great aftonifhment, they ftopped the hounds, and made him go back along with them. This fellow had often been feverely beaten, but was ftubborn and fulky to the laft.

To give you an idea before I quit this fubject, how little fome people know of fox-hunting, I muft tell you, that not long ago a gentleman afked me if I did not fend people out *the day be-fore* to find where the foxes lay.

What relates to the cafting of hounds fhall be the fubject of my next letter.

R 3

LET.

LETTER XX.

IN my feventeenth letter I gave the opinion of my friend ****—" *that a pack of fox-hounds,* " *if left entirely to themfelves, would never lofe a* " *fox.*" I am always forry when I differ from that gentleman in any thing; yet I am fo far from thinking they never would lofe a fox, that I doubt much if they would ever kill one. There are times when hounds fhould be helped, and at all times they muft be kept forward; hounds will naturally tie on a cold fcent when ftopped by fheep or other impediments; and when they are no longer able to get forward, will oftentimes hunt the old fcent back again, if they find that they can hunt no other. It is the judicious encouraging of hounds to hunt when they cannot run, and the preventing them from lofing time by hunting too much when they might run, that diftinguifhes a good fportfman from a bad one.* Hounds that have been well taught will caft forward to a hedge of their own accord; but you may affure yourfelf, this excellence is never acquired by fuch as are

* In hunting a pack of hounds a proper medium fhould be obferved; for though too much help will make them flack, too little will make them tie on the fcent and hunt back the heel.

left

left entirely to themfelves. To fuffer a pack of fox-hounds to hunt through a flock of fheep, when it is eafy to make a regular caft round them, is, in my judgment, very unneceffary—it is wilfully lofing time to no purpofe. I have indeed been told, that hounds at no time fhould be taken off their nofes: I fhall only fay, in anfwer to this, that a fox-hound who will not bear lifting is not worth the keeping; and I will venture to fay, it fhould be made part of his education.

Though I like to fee fox-hounds caft wide and forward, and diflike to fee them pick a cold fcent through flocks of fheep to no purpofe, yet I muft beg leave to obferve, that I diflike ftill more to fee that unaccountable hurry which huntfmen will fometimes put themfelves into the moment their hounds are at fault: time ought always to be allowed them to make their own caft; and if a huntfman be judicious, he will take that opportunity to confider what part he himfelf has next to act; but, inftead of this, I have feen hounds hurried away the very inftant they came to a fault, a wide caft made, and the hounds at laft brought back again to the very place from whence they were fo abruptly taken; and where, if the huntfman could have had a minute's patience, they would have hit off the fcent themfelves. It is always great impertinence in a huntf-man to pretend to make *his* caft before the hounds

R 4

have

have made *their's*. Prudence fhould direct him to encourage, and I may fay, humour his hounds in the caft they feem inclined to make; and either to ftand ftill, or trot round with them, as circumftances may require.

I have feen huntfmen make their caft on bad ground when they might as eafily have made it on good: I have feen them fuffer their hounds to try in the midft of a flock of fheep, when there was a hedge near, where they might have been fure to take the fcent; and I have feen a caft made with every hound at their horfe's heels. When a hound tries for the fcent his nofe is to the ground; when a huntfman makes a caft his eye fhould be on his hounds; and when he fees them fpread wide, and try as they ought, his caft may then be quick.

When hounds are at fault, and the huntfman halloos them off the line of the fcent, the whippers-in fmacking their whips and rating them after him, if he fhould trot away with them, may they not think that the bufinefs of the day is over?— Hounds never, in my opinion, (unlefs in particular cafes, or when you go to a halloo) fhould be taken entirely off their nofes; but when lifted, fhould be conftantly made to try as they go. Some huntfmen have a dull, ftupid way of fpeaking to their hounds; at thefe times little fhould be faid,

and

and that fhould have both meaning and expreffion in it.

When your huntfman makes a caft, I hope he makes it perfect one way before he tries another, as much time is loft in going backwards and forwards. You will fee huntfmen, when a forward caft does not fucceed, come flowly back again—they fhould return as faft as they can.

When hounds are in fault, and it is probable that the fox has headed back, your caft forward fhould be fhort and quick, for the fcent is then likely to be behind you; too obftinate a perfeverance forward has been the lofs of many foxes. In heathy countries, if there be many roads, foxes will always run them in dry weather; when hounds, therefore, over-run the fcent, if your huntfman return to the firft crofs road, he, probably, will hit off the fcent again.

In large covers where there are feveral roads; in bad fcenting days when thefe roads are dry; or, after a thaw, when they carry; it is neceffary that your huntfman fhould be near to his hounds, to help them and hold them forward. Foxes will run the roads at thefe times, and hounds cannot always own the fcent. When they are at fault on a dry road, let not your huntfman turn back too foon, let him not ftop till he can be certain that

the

the fox is not gone on; the hounds fhould try on both fides the road at once: if he perceive that they try on one fide only, let him try the other, on his return.

When hounds are running in cover, if a huntf-man fhould fee a fox come into a road, and can-not fee which way he turns afterwards, let him ftand ftill, and fay nothing. If he ride on, he muft ride over the fcent; and if he encourage the hounds, they, moft probably, would run be-yond it.

Wide ridings, cut through large woods, render them lefs exceptionable to fportfmen than they otherwife might be; yet I do not think that they are of fervice to hounds:—they are taught to fhuffle; and, the fox being frequently headed back, they are put to many faults:—the roads are foiled by the horfes, and the hounds often inter-rupted by the horfemen:—fuch ridings only are advantageous, as enable the fervants belonging to the hounds to get to them.

If a fox fhould run up the wind, when firft found, and afterwards turn, he will feldom, if ever turn again. This obfervation may not only be of ufe to your huntfman in his caft, but may be of ufe to yourfelf, if you fhould lofe the hounds.

When

When you are purſuing a fox over a country, the ſcent being bad, and the fox a long way before, without ever having been preſſed, if his point ſhould be for ſtrong earths that are open, or for large covers, where game is in plenty, it may be acting wiſely to take off the hounds at the firſt fault; for the fox will go many miles to your one, and probably will run you out of all ſcent; and if he ſhould not, you will be likely to change at the firſt cover you come into:—when a fox has been hard preſſed, you have already my opinion, that he never ſhould be given up.

When you would recover a hunted fox, and have no longer ſcent to hunt him by, a long caſt to the firſt cover which he ſeems to point for, is the only reſource that you have left: get thither as faſt as you can, and then let your hounds try as ſlowly and as quietly as poſſible: if hunting after him be hopeleſs, and a long caſt do not ſucceed, you had better give him up—I need not remind you, when the ſcent lies badly, and you find it impoſſible for hounds to run, that you had better return home; ſince the next day may be more favourable. It ſurely is a great fault in a huntſman to perſevere in bad weather, when hounds cannot run; and when there is not a probability of killing a fox.*　Some there are, who,

* Though I would not go out on a very windy day, yet a bad ſcenting day is ſometimes of ſervice to a pack of fox-hounds— they acquire patience from it, and method of hunting.

after

after they have loft one fox for want of fcent to hunt him by, will find another; this makes their hounds flack, and fometimes vicious: it alfo difturbs the covers to no purpofe. Some fportf-men are more lucky in their days than others. If you hunt every other day, it is poffible they may be all bad, and the intermediate days all good; an indifferent pack, therefore, by hunting on good days, may kill foxes without any merit; and a good pack, notwithftanding all their ex-ertions, may lofe foxes which they deferve to kill. Had I a fufficiency of hounds I would hunt on every good day, and never on a bad one.*

A perfect knowledge of his country certainly is of great help to a huntfman : if your's, as yet, fhould have it not, great allowance ought to be made. The trotting away with hounds to make a long and knowing caft, is a privilege which a new huntfman cannot pretend to : an experienced one may fafely fay, a fox has made for fuch a cover, when he has known, perhaps, that nine

---

* On windy days, or fuch as are not likely to afford any fcent for hounds, it is better, I think, to fend them to be exercifed on the turnpike road; it will do them lefs harm than hunting with them might do, and more good than if they were to remain confined in their kennel; for though nothing makes hounds fo handy, as taking them out often; nothing inclines them fo much to riot, as taking them out *to hunt* when there is little or no fcent; and particularly on windy days, when they cannot hear one another.

out

out of ten, with the wind in the fame quarter, have conftantly gone thither.

In a country where there are large earths, a fox that knows the country, and tries any of them, feldom fails to try the reft. A huntfman may take advantage of this; they are certain cafts, and may help him to get nearer to his fox.

Great caution is neceffary when a fox runs into a village: if he be hallooed there, get forward as faft as you can. Foxes, when tired, will lie down any where, and are often loft by it.—A wide caft is not the beft to recover a tired fox with tired hounds;—they fhould hunt him out, inch by inch, though they are ever fo long about it; for the reafon I have juft given;—*that he will lie down any where.*

In chaces and forefts, where high fences are made to preferve the coppices, I like to fee a huntfman put only a few hounds over, enough to carry on the fcent, and get forward with the reft, it is a proof that he knows his bufinefs.

A huntfman muft take care, where foxes are in plenty, left he fhould run the heel; for it frequently happens, that hounds can run the wrong way of the fcent better than they can the right, when one is up the wind, and the other down.

Fox-

Fox-hunters, I think, are never guilty of the fault of trying up the wind, before they have tried down; I have known them lofe foxes rather than condefcend to try up the wind at all.

When a huntfman hears a halloo, and has five or fix couple of hounds along with him, the pack not running, let him get forward with thofe which he has; when they are on the fcent, the others will foon join them.

Let him lift his tail hounds, and get them for-ward *after the reft*; it can do no hurt; but let him be cautious in lifting any hounds to get them for-ward *before the reft*; it always is dangerous, and foxes are fometimes loft by it.

When a fox runs his foil in cover, if you fuf-fer all your hounds to hunt on the line of him, they will foil the ground, and tire themfelves to little purpofe. I have before told you, that your huntfman, at fuch a time, may ftop the tail hounds, and throw them in at head. I am almoft inclined to fay, it is the only time it fhould be done.—Whilft hounds run ftrait, it cannot be of any ufe, for they will get on fafter with the fcent, than they would without it.

When hounds are hunting a cold fcent, and point towards a cover, let a whipper-in get forward

ward to the oppofite fide of it: fhould the fox break before the hounds reach the cover, ftop them, and get them nearer to him.

When a fox perfifts in running in a ftrong cover, lies down often behind the hounds, and they are flack in hunting him, let the huntf-man get into the cover to them: it may make the fox break, it may keep him off his foil, or may prevent the hounds from giving him up.

It is not often that flow huntfmen kill many foxes; they are a check upon their hounds, which feldom kill a fox but with a high fcent, when it is out of their power to prevent it. What avails it to be told which way the fox is gone, when he is fo far before, that you cannot hunt him? A Newmarket boy, with a good underftanding and a good voice, might be preferable, perhaps, to an indifferent and flack huntfman; he would prefs on his hounds, while the fcent was good, and the foxes he killed he would kill handfomely.——— A perfect knowledge of the intricacies of hunting is chiefly of ufe to flow huntfmen and bad hounds; fince they more often ftand in need of it. Activity is the firft requifite in a huntfman to a pack of fox-hounds; a want of it no judgment can make amends for; while the moft difficult of all his undertakings is the diftinguifhing be-twixt different fcents, and knowing, with any

certainty,

certainty, the fcent of his hunted fox. Much
fpeculation is here required ;—the length of time
hounds remain at fault ;—difference of ground ;—
change of weather ;—all thefe contribute to increafe the difficulty; and require a nicety of
judgment, and a precifion, much above the com-
prehenfion of moft huntfmen.

When hounds are at fault, and cannot make
it out of themfelves, let the firft caft be quick ; the
fcent is then good, nor are the hounds likely to
go over it; as the fcent gets worfe, the caft
fhould be flower, and be more cautioufly made.
This is an effential part of hunting, and which,
I am forry to fay, few huntfmen attend to. I
wifh they would remember the following rules,
viz. that with a good fcent, their caft fhould be
quick ; with a bad fcent, *flow* ;—and that, when
their hounds are picking along a cold fcent,—
they are not to caft them at all.

When hounds are at fault, and ftaring about,
trufting entirely to their eyes, and to their cars ;
the making a caft with them, I apprehend, would
be to little purpofe. The likelieft place for them
to find the fcent, is where they left it ; and when
the fault is evidently in the dog, a forward caft is
leaft likely to recover the fcent.*

* Hounds know where they left the fcent, and if let alone
will try to recover it. Impatience in the huntfman, at fuch
times, feldom fails, in the end, to fpoil the hounds.

                          When

When hounds are making a regular caft, try-ing for the fcent as they go, fuffer not your huntf-man to fay a word to them; it cannot do any good, and probably may make them go over the fcent: nor fhould you fuffer either the voice or the whip of your whipper-in, to be now heard; his ufual roughnefs and feverity would ill fuit the ftillnefs and gentlenefs which are required at a time like this.

When hounds come to a check, a huntfman fhould obferve the tail hounds; they are leaft likely to over-run the fcent, and he may fee by them how far they brought it: in moft packs there are fome hounds that will fhew the point of the fox, and if attended to, will direct his caft: when fuch hounds follow flowly and unwillingly, he may be certain the reft of the pack are run-ning without a fcent.

When he cafts his hounds, let him not caft wide without reafon; for of courfe it will take more time. Huntfmen, in general, keep too for-ward in their cafts; or, as a failor would fay, keep too long *on one tack.* They fhould en-deavour to hit off the fcent by croffing the line of it.—*Two parallel lines, you know, can never meet.**

* By attending to this a huntfman cannot fail to make a good caft, for if he obferve the point of the fox, he may always crofs upon the fcent of him.

S

When

When he goes to a halloo, let him be careful left his hounds run the heel, as much time is loft by it. I once faw this miftake made by a famous huntfman:—after we had left a cover, which we had been drawing, a difturbed fox was feen to go into it; he was hallooed, and we returned. The huntfman, who never inquired *where* the fox was feen, or on *which fide* the cover he entered, threw his hounds in at random; and, as it happened, on the oppofite fide: they immediately took the heel of him, broke cover, and hunted the fcent back to his very kennel.

Different countries require different cafts: fuch huntfmen as have been ufed to a woodland, and inclofed country, I have feen lofe time in an open country, where wide cafts are always neceffary.

When you want to caft round a flock of fheep, the whipper-in ought to drive them the other way, left they fhould keep running on before you.

A fox feldom goes over or under a *gate* when he can avoid it.

Huntfmen are frequently very conceited, and very obftinate. Oftentimes have I feen them, when their hounds came to a check, turn directly back on feeing hounds at head which they had no opinion of. They *ſuppoſed* the fox was gone another way; in which caſe Mr. Bayes's remark in the Rehearſal always occurs to me, " *that, if* " *he ſhould not, what then becomes of their ſuppoſe?"* Better, ſurely, would it be, to make a ſhort caſt forward firſt; they then might be *certain* the hounds were wrong, and of courſe could make their own caſt with greater confidence:—the advantage, next to that of knowing whither the fox *is* gone, is that of knowing, with certainty, whither he is *not.*

Moſt huntſmen like to have all their hounds turned after them, when they make a caſt: I wonder not at them for it, but I am always ſorry when I ſee it done; for, till I find a huntſman that is infallible, I ſhall continue to think the more my hounds ſpread, the better; as long as they are within ſight or hearing, it is ſufficient.— Many a time have I ſeen an obſtinate hound hit off the ſcent, when an obſtinate huntſman, by caſting the wrong way, has done all in his power to prevent it. Two foxes I remember to have ſeen killed, in one day, by ſkirting hounds, whilſt the huntſman was making his caſt the contrary way.

When hounds, running in cover, come into a road, and horſes are on before, let the huntſman hold them quickly on beyond where the horſes

have

have been, trying the oppofite fide as he goes along: fhould the horfemen have been long enough there to have headed back the fox, let them then try back. Condemn me not for fuffering hounds *to try back* when the fox *has been headed back*; I recommend it at no other time.

When your hounds divide into many parts, you had better go off with the firft fox that breaks. The ground will foon get tainted, nor will hounds like a cover where they are often changing.

If a cover be very large, and you have many fcents, be not in a hurry to get your hounds together;—if your pack be numerous, let them run feparate, only taking care that none get away entirely from the reft; by this means many foxes will be equally diftreft, the hounds will get together at laft, and one fox, at the leaft, you may expect to kill.

The heading a fox back at firft, if the cover be not a large one, is oftentimes of fervice to hounds, as he will not ftop, and cannot go off unfeen.— When a fox has been hard run, I have known it turn out otherwife; and hounds, that would eafily have killed him out of the cover, have left him in it.

If

If it be not your intention that a fox should break, you should prevent him, I think, as much as you can from coming at all out of the cover; for though you should head him back afterwards, it moſt probably would put the hounds to a fault: when a pack of fox-hounds once leave a cover after their game, they do not readily return to it again.

When a fox has been often headed back on one ſide of a cover, and a huntſman knows there is not any body on the other ſide to halloo him, the firſt fault his hounds come to, let him caſt that way, leſt the fox ſhould be gone off; and if he be ſtill in the cover, he may ſtill recover him.

Suffer not your huntſman to take out a lame hound. If any be tender-footed, he will tell you, perhaps, that they will not mind it when they are out;—probably they may not; but how will they be on the next day? A hound, not in condition to run, cannot be of much ſervice to the pack; and the taking him out at that time may occaſion him a long confinement afterwards:—put it not to the trial. Should any fall lame while they are out, leave them at the firſt houſe that you come to.

I have

I have feen huntfmen hunt their young hounds in couples. 'Let me beg of you not to fuffer it. I know you would be forry to fee your hounds hanging acrofs a hedge, grinning at each other, perhaps in the very agonies of death : yet it is an accident that often has happened; and it is an accident fo likely to happen, that I am furprifed any man of common fenfe will run the rifk of it. If neceffary, I had much rather they fhould be held in couples at the cover fide, till the fox be found.

The two principal things which a huntfman has to attend to, are the keeping of his hounds *healthy* and *fteady*. The firft is attained by clean-linefs and proper food; the latter, by putting, as feldom as poffible, any unfteady ones amongft them.

At the beginning of the feafon let him be attentive to get his hounds well in blood. As the feafon advances, and foxes become ftout, attention then fhould be had to keep them as vigorous as poffible.—It is a great fault when hounds are fuffered to become too high in flefh at the beginning of the feafon, or too low afterwards.

When a fox is loft, the huntfman on his return home fhould examine into his *own conduct*, and endeavour to find in what he might have done better ;

ter; he may by this means make the very lofs of a fox of ufe to him.

Old tyeing hounds, and a hare-hunter turned fox-hunter, are both as contrary to the true fpirit of fox-hunting, as any thing can poffibly be.— One is continually bringing the pack back again; the other as conftantly does his beft to prevent them from getting forward. The natural prejudices of mankind are fuch, that a man feldom alters his ftyle of hunting, let him purfue what game he may; befides, it may be conftitutional, as he is himfelf flow or active, dull or lively, patient or impatient; it is for that reafon I object to a hare-hunter for a pack of fox-hounds; for the fame ideas of hunting will moft probably ftick by him as long as he lives.

Your huntfman is an old man; fhould he have been working hard all his life on wrong principles, he may be now incorrigible.

Sometimes you will meet with a good kennel huntfman, fometimes an active and judicious one in the field; fome are clever at finding a fox, others are better after he is found; whilft perfection in a huntfman, like perfection in any thing elfe, is fcarcely ever to be met with: there are not only good, bad, and indifferent huntfmen, but there are perhaps a few others, who being as

it

it were of a different fpecies, fhould be claffed apart;—I mean, fuch as have *real genius*. It is this peculiar excellence, which I told you in a former letter, I would rather wifh my firft whipper-in to be poffeffed of than my huntfman; and one reafon among others, is, that he, I think, would have more opportunities of exercifing it.

The keeping hounds clean and healthy, and bringing them into the field in their fulleft vigour, is the excellence of a good kennel huntfman:* if, befides this, he makes his hounds both love and fear him; if he be active, and prefs them on, whilft the fcent is good, always aiming to keep as near to the fox as he can; if, when his hounds are at fault, he make his caft with judgment, not cafting the wrong way firft, and only blundering upon the right at laft as many do; if, added

* To make the moft of a pack of hounds, and bring them into the field in their fulleft vigour, is an excellence that huntfmen are very deficient in.—To obtain a knowledge of the different conftitutions of fo many animals, requires more difcernment than moft huntfmen are endowed with.—To apply that knowledge, by making feparate drafts when they feed them, would alfo take up more time than they choofe to beftow; hence it is, that they generally are fed all together:—they may be well fed, but I much doubt if they are ever made the moft of—fuch as require to be fed *a little at a time*, and *often* muft, I believe, be contented with *a little only*.—Few huntfmen feem fond of their hounds;—one reafon of it, perhaps, may be, that they are paid for looking after them.

3

to

to this, he be patient and perfevering, never
giving up a fox, whilft there remains a chance of
killing him, he then is a perfect huntfman.

Did I not know your love of this diverfion,
I fhould think, by this time, that I muft have
tired you completely. You are not particular,
however, in your partiality to it; for to fhew you
the effect which fox-hunting has on thofe who
are really fond of it, I muft tell you what happened to me not long ago.——My hounds, in
running a fox, croffed the great weftern road,
where I met a gentleman travelling on horfeback,
his fervant, with a portmanteau, following him.
He no fooner faw the hounds than he rode up to
me, with the greateft eagernefs, " *Sir*," faid he,
" *are you after a fox?*"—When I told him, we
were, he immediately ftuck fpurs to his horfe,
took a monftrous leap, and never quitted us any
more, till the fox was killed.—I fuppofe, had I
faid, we were after a *hare*, my gentleman would
have purfued his journey.

LETTER XXI.

YOUR huntſman, you ſay, has hunted a pack of harriers. It might have been better, perhaps, had he never ſeen one, ſince fox-hunting and hare-hunting differ almoſt in every particular; ſo much, that I think it might not be an improper negative definition of fox-hunting to ſay it is of *all* hunting, *that* which reſembles hare-hunting the leaſt. A good huntſman to a pack of harriers ſeldom ſucceeds in fox-hunting; like old hounds they dwell upon the ſcent, and cannot get forward; nor do they ever make a bold caſt, ſo much are they afraid of leaving the ſcent behind them. Hence it is that they poke about and try the ſame place ten times over rather than they will leave it; and when they do, are totally at a loſs which way to go, for want of knowing the nature of the animal they are in purſuit of. As hare-hounds ſhould ſcarcely ever be caſt, hallooed, or taken off their noſes, hare-hunters are too apt to hunt their fox-hounds in the ſame manner; but it will not do, nor could it pleaſe you if it would. Take away the ſpirit of fox-hunting, and it is no longer fox-hunting; it is ſtale ſmall beer compared to briſk champain. You would alſo find in it more

fatigue

fatigue than pleafure. It is faid, *there is a pleafure in being mad which only madmen know*; and it
is the enthufiafm, I believe, of fox-hunting which
is its beft fupport : ftrip it of that, and you had
better leave it quite alone.

The hounds themfelves alfo differ in their manner of hunting : the beagle, who has always his
nofe to the ground, will puzzle an hour on one
fpot fooner than he will leave the fcent; while
the fox-hound, full of life and fpirit, is always
dafhing and trying forward. A high-bred fox-
hound, therefore, fhews himfelf to moft advantage when foxes are at their ftrongeft and run an
end. A pack of harriers will kill *a cub* better,
perhaps, than a pack of fox-hounds; but when
foxes are ftrong, they have not the method of getting on with the fcent which fox-hounds have,
and generally tire themfelves before the fox. To
kill foxes when they are ftrong, hounds muft run
as well as hunt; befides, catching a fox by hard
running is always preferred in the opinion of a
fox-hunter. Much depends, in my opinion, on
the ftyle in which it is done; and I think, without being fophiftical, a diftinction might be made
betwixt hunting a fox and fox-hunting. Two
hackneys become not racers by running round a
courfe, nor does the mere hunting of a fox change
the nature of the harrier. I have alfo feen a hare
hunted by high-bred fox-hounds; yet, I confefs

to you, it gave me not the leaſt idea of what hare-hunting ought to be. Certain ideas are neceſſarily annexed to certain words; this is the uſe of language; and when a fox-hound is mentioned, I ſhould expect not only a particular kind of hound, as to make, ſize, and ſtrength, by which the fox-hound is eaſy to be diſtinguiſhed: but I ſhould alſo expect by fox-hunting, a lively, animated, and eager purſuit, as the very eſſence of it.* Eagerneſs and impetuoſity are ſuch eſſential parts of this diverſion, that I am never more ſurpriſed than when I ſee a fox-hunter without them. One *hold hard*, or reproof *unneceſſarily* given, would chill me more than a north-eaſt wind; it would damp my ſpirits and ſend me home. The enthuſiaſm of a fox-hunter ſhould not be checked in its career, for it is the very life and ſoul of fox-hunting. If it be the eagerneſs with which you purſue your game that makes the chief pleaſure of the chace, fox-hunting ſurely ſhould afford the greateſt degree of it, ſince you purſue no animal with the ſame eagerneſs that you purſue a fox.

---

* The ſix following lines may have a dangerous tendency. Only a good ſportſman can know when a reproof is given *unneceſſarily*, and only a bad one will be deſerving of reproof. This paſſage, therefore, ſhould be compared with pages 149, 187, 189, 204, where the meaning of the author is very clearly expreſſed.

Knowing

Knowing your partiality to hounds that run in a good ftyle, I advife you to obferve ftrictly your own when a fox is finking in a ftrong cover; *that* is the time to fee the true fpirit of a fox-hound. If they fpread not the cover, but run tamely on the line of one another, I fhall fear it is a fort that will not pleafe you long. A fox-hound that has not fpirit and ambition to get forward at a time like this, is at no other likely to do much good.

You talked in your laft letter of pretty hounds; certainly I fhould not pretend to criticife others, who am fo incorrect myfelf; yet, with your leave, I think I can fet you right in that particular.— Pretty is an epithet improperly applied to a fox-hound: we call a fox-hound handfome when he is ftrong, bony, of a proper fize, and of exact fymmetry; and fitnefs is made effential to beauty. A beagle may be pretty, but, according to my idea of the word, a fox-hound cannot: but as it is not to be fuppofed that you will keep a pack of fox-hounds for the pleafure of looking at them, without doubt you will think goodnefs more ne-ceffary than beauty. Should you be ambitious to have a handfome pack of hounds, on no account ought you to enter an ugly dog, left you be tempted to keep him afterwards.

I once

I once heard an old fportfman fay, that he thought a fox, to fhew fport, fhould run four hours at leaft ; and, I fuppofe, he did not care how flow his hounds went after him. This idea, however, is not conceived in the true fpirit of fox-hunting, which is not to walk down a fox, or ftarve him to death, but to keep clofe at him, and kill him as foon as you can. I am convinced a fox-hound may hunt too much ; if tender-nofed, and not over-hurried, he will always hunt enough; whilft the higheft-bred hounds may be made to tye upon the fcent by improper management.*

It is youth and good fpirits which beft fuit with fox-hunting; flacknefs in the men occafions flacknefs in the hounds ; and one may fee by the manner in which hounds hunt what kind of men they have been accuftomed to. The fpeedieft hounds may, by degrees, be rendered flow ; and it is impoffible for the beft to do their bufinefs as they ought unlefs followed with life and fpirit. Men who are flack themfelves will be always afraid of hurrying their hounds too much ; and by carrying this humour too far, will commit a fault which has nothing to excufe it. The beft method to hunt a fox, they fay, is never upon

* It more frequently is owing, either to want of patience, or want of mettle, than to want of nofe, that a hound does not hunt well.

any

any account to caſt the hounds; but, on the contrary, to let them tye upon the ſcent as long as
they will, and that they will hit it off at laſt. I
agree with them partly;—it certainly muſt be the
beſt method *to hunt a fox*, for by this means you
may hunt him from morning till night; and, if you
have the luck to find him, may hunt him again
the next day—the likelieſt method, however, to
kill him, is to take every advantage of him that
you can.

All hounds go faſt enough with a good ſcent;
but it is the particular excellence of a fox-hound,
when rightly managed, to get on faſter with an
indifferent ſcent than any other hound:* it is the
buſineſs of a huntſman to encourage this; *and
here, moſt probably, the hare-hunter will fail.* He
has been uſed to take his time; he has enjoyed a
cold ſcent like a ſouthern hound; and has ſitten
patiently upon his horſe to ſee his hounds hunt.
It is, to be ſure, very pretty to ſee; and when
you conſider that the hare is all the time, perhaps, within a few yards of you, and may leap
up the next minute, you are perfectly contented
with what you are about; but it is not ſo in fox-
hunting: every minute that you loſe is precious,
and increaſes your difficulties; and while you

* It is a quick method of hunting that I moſtly value in
any hound; ſuch as are poſſeſſed of it are ſeldom long off the
ſcent; it is the reverſe of ſlackneſs.

Iare

are ftanding ftill the fox is running miles. It is a fatisfaction to a hare-hunter to be told where his game was feen, though a long while before; but it is melancholy news to a fox-hunter, whofe game is not likely to ftop. I believe I mentioned to you, in a former letter on hare hunting, a great fault which I had obferved in fome harriers from being let too much alone—that of *running back the heel.*—I have feen a pack of high-bred fox-hounds do the fame, for the fame reafons.

When hounds flag from frequent changes, and a long day, it is neceffary for a huntfman to animate them as much as he can; he muft keep them forward and prefs them on, for it is not likely, in this cafe, that they fhould over-run the fcent; at thefe times the whole work is generally done by a few hounds, and he fhould keep clofe to them: *here I alfo fear that the hare-hunter will fail:** if they come to a long fault it is over, and you had better then go home.

The

---

* It is at a time like this that good fportfmen may be of great fervice to hounds; it is the only time that they want encouragement, and it is (I am forry to fay) almoft the only time that they do not receive it. Thofe who ride too forward in the morning will in the evening, perhaps, be too far behind, and thereby lofe an opportunity that is offered them of making fome amends for the mifchiefs they have already done. When hounds flag from frequent changes, and the huntfman's horfe finks under the fatigue of a tirefome day, then it is that fportfmen may

affift

The many chances that are againſt you in fox-hunting; the changing frequently; the heading of the foxes; their being courſed by ſheep-dogs; long faults; cold hunting; and the dying away of the ſcent; make it neceſſary to keep always as near to the fox as you can; which ſhould be the firſt and invariable principle of fox-hunting. Long days do great hurt to a pack of fox-hounds. I ſat out one day laſt winter from the kennel at half paſt ſeven, .and returned home a quarter before eight at night, the hounds running hard the greateſt part of the time. The huntſman killed one horſe, and tired another, and the hounds did not recover for more than a week: we took them off at laſt when they were running with a better ſcent than they had had the whole day.*—I alſo remember, after it was dark, to have heard a better view halloo from *an owl*, than I ever heard from a ſportſman in my life, though I hope that I ſhall never hear ſuch another. A long

aſſiſt them; ſuch as know the hounds ſhould then ride up to them; they ſhould endeavour, by great encouragement, to keep them *running*, and get thoſe forward that may be behind; for ·when hounds that are tired once come to *hunting*, they tie upon the ſcent, and by loſing time loſe every chance they had of killing the fox—great encouragement, and proper and timely aſſiſtance only can prevent it.

* Hounds, after every hard day, ſhould have two clear days to reſt; it does them leſs hurt to hunt two days following when their work is eaſy, than to hunt before they may be perfectly recovered after having been hard run.

T

day,

day, neverthelefs, *once* or *twice* in a feafon, is of ufe to a huntfman; it fhews the real goodnefs and ftoutnefs of his hounds.

When long days happen to hounds that are low in flefh, nothing will get them up again fo effectually as reft; it is for this reafon hounds that are kept conftantly hunted ought always to be, as fportfmen call it, *above their work*. If your hounds, either from accident or inattention, fhould ever be in the low condition here alluded to, be not impatient to get them out of it; fhould you feed them high with *flefh*, the mange, moft probably, would be the immediate confequence of it: it is reft and wholefome meat that will recover them beft. It will furprife you to fee how foon a dog becomes either fat or lean; a little patience, therefore, and fome attention, will always enable you to get your hounds into proper condition; and I am certain, that you can receive no pleafure in hunting with them, if they be not.

I forgot, in my letter upon the feeding of hounds, to obferve that fuch hounds as have the mange actually upon them, or only a tendency towards it, fhould be fed feparately from the reft. They fhould have no flefh; their meat fhould be mixed up rather thin than thick; and they fhould

have

have vegetables in great plenty.* I muſt alſo add, that if my hounds return from hunting earlier than they were expeᶜted, I now order them to be ſhut up in the lodging room till their meat be made ready for them. Hounds never reſt contented till they have been fed; nor will they remain upon their benches unleſs they be confined; yet, without doubt, lying upon the pavement, or even ſtanding out in the cold, after violent exerciſe, muſt be prejudicial to them.

I am glad to hear that your huntſman knows the country which he is to hunt; nothing in fox-hunting is more eſſential than *that*; and it may make amends for many faults. Foxes are not capricious, they know very well what they are about; are quick, I believe, at determining, and reſolute in perſevering: they generally have a point to go to, and, though headed and turned di-reᶜtly from it, ſeldom fail to make it good at laſt; *this*, therefore, is a great help to an obſerving huntſman.

Suffer not your huntſman to encourage his hounds too much on a bad ſcenting day, particu-larly in covers where there is much riot. *Hark, Hark, Hark*, which injudicious huntſmen are ſo fond of

* Sulphur made into a ball with butter, or hog's lard, and given two or three mornings following, may alſo be neceſſary.

upon

upon every occasion, must often do mischief, and cannot do good; whilst hounds are near together, they will get sooner to the hound that challenges without that noise than with it: if it be a right scent, they will be ready enough to join; and if it be a wrong one, provided they be let alone, they will soon leave it. Injudicious encouragement, on a bad day, might make them run something or other, right or wrong.

I know of no fault so bad in a hound as that of running false; it should never be forgiven: such as are not stout, or are stiff nosed, or have other faults, may at times do good, and at their worst may do no harm; but such as run false most probably will spoil your sport. A hound capable of spoiling one day's sport is scarcely worth your keeping. Indifferent ones, such as I have above described, may be kept till you have better to supply their places.

A huntsman should know how to marshal every hound in his pack, giving to each his proper rank and precedence; for, without this knowledge, it is not possible he should make a large draft as he ought. There are, in most packs, some hounds that assist but little in killing the fox, and it is the judicious drafting off of such hounds that is a certain sign of a good huntsman.

My

My huntfman is very exact; he carries always a lift of his hounds in his pocket, and when in a diftant country, he looks it over to fee if any of them be miffing. He has alfo a book, in which he keeps a regular account where every fox is found, and where he is killed.

Your huntfman, you fay, knows perfectly the country he has to hunt; let him then acquire as perfect a knowledge of his hounds: good fenfe and obfervation will do the reft, at leaft will do as much as you feem to require of him; for I am glad to find that you had rather depend upon the goodnefs of your hounds for fport than the genius of your huntfman. It is, I believe, a much furer dependance.

LETTER XXII.

ARE not your expectations somewhat too sanguine, when you think that you shall have
no occasion for bag-foxes to keep your hounds in
blood the first season? It may be as well, perhaps, not to turn them all out till you can be
more certain that your young pack will keep good
and steady without them. When blood is much
wanted, and they are tired with a hard day, one
of these foxes will put them into spirits, and
give them, as it were, new strength and vigour.

You desire to know what I call *being out of
blood?* In answer to which, I must tell you,
that, in my judgment, no fox-hound can fail of
killing more than three or four times following,
without being visibly the worse for it. When
hounds are out of blood, there is a kind of evil
genius attending all they do; and though they
may seem to hunt as well as ever, they do not
get forward; whilst a pack of fox-hounds, well
in blood, like troops flushed with conquest, are
not easily withstood. What we call ill luck, day
after day, when hounds kill no foxes, may frequently, I think, be traced to another cause,

2   namely,

namely, *their being out of blood*; nor can there be any other reason assigned why hounds, which we know to be good, should remain so long as they sometimes do without killing a fox.*   Large packs are least subject to this inconvenience : hounds that are quite fresh, and in high spirits, least feel the want of blood.   The smallest packs therefore should be able to leave at least ten or twelve couple of hounds behind them, to be fresh against the next hunting day.   If your hounds be much out of blood, give them rest: take this opportunity to hunt with other hounds, to see how they are managed, to observe what stallion hounds they have, and to judge yourself, whether they be such as it is fit for you to breed from.   If what I have now recommended should not succeed, if a little rest and a fine morning do not put your hounds into blood again, I know of nothing else that will; and you must attribute your ill success, I fear, to another cause.

You say, you generally hunt at a late hour : after a tolerably good run, try not to find another fox.   Should you be long in finding, and should you not have success afterwards, it will hurt your hounds: should you try a long time, and

---

* A pack of hounds that had been a month without killing a fox, at last ran one to ground, which they dug, and killed upon the earth: the next seven days they hunted they killed a fox each day.

T 4

not

not find, *that* alfo will make them flack. Never try to find a fox after one o'clock; you had better return home, and hunt again on the next day. Not that I, in general, approve of hunting two days following with the fame hounds: the trying fo many hours in vain, and the being kept fo long off their food, both contribute to make them flack, and nothing furely is more contrary to the true fpirit of fox-hunting; for fox-hounds, I have already faid, ought always to be above their work. This is another particular, in which hare-hunting and fox-hunting totally differ; for harriers cannot be hunted too much, as long as they are able to hunt at all. The flower they go, the lefs likely they will be to over-run the fcent, and the fooner, in all probability, will they kill their game. I have a friend, who hunted his five days following, and affured me, that he had better fport with them the laft day than the firft.

I remember to have heard that a certain pack of fox-hounds, fince become famous, were many weeks, from a mixture of indifferent hounds, bad management, and worfe luck, without killing a fox. However, they killed one at laft, and tried to find another. They found him—and they loft him—and were then, as you may well fuppofe, a month without killing another fox. This

This was ill judged; they fhould have returned home immediately.

When hounds are much out of blood, fome men proceed in a method that muft neceffarily keep them fo: they hunt them every day; as if tiring them out were a means to give them ftrength and fpirit: this, however, proceeds more from ill-nature and refentment than found judgment.* As I know your temper to be the reverfe, without doubt you will adopt a different method; and, fhould your hounds ever be in the ftate here defcribed, you will keep them frefh for the firft fine day; when, fuppofing them to be all perfectly fteady, I do not queftion that they will kill their fox.

When hounds are in want of blood, give them every advantage: go out early; choofe a good quiet morning; and throw off your hounds where they are likely to find, and are leaft likely to change: if it be a fmall cover, or furze-brake, and you can keep the fox in, it is right to do it; for the fooner that you kill him, when you are in want of blood, the better for the hounds.

* It is not the want of blood only that is prejudicial to hounds, the trying long in vain to recover a loft fcent no lefs contributes to make them flack.

When

When hounds are in want of blood, and you get a fox into a fmall cover, it muſt be your own fault, if you do not kill him there: place your people properly, and he cannot get off again. You will hear, perhaps, that it is impoſſible to head back a fox. No animal is fo fhy, confe-quently, no animal is fo eafily headed back by thofe who underſtand it. When it is your inten-tion to check a fox, your people muſt keep at a little diſtance from the cover fide, nor fhould they be fparing of their voices; for, fince you cannot keep him in, if he be determined to come out, prevent him, if you can, from being fo in-clined. All kind of mobbing is allowable, when hounds are out of blood;* and you may keep the fox in cover, or let him out, as you think the hounds will manage him beſt.

Though I am fo great an advocate for blood as to judge it neceſſary to a pack of fox-hounds, yet I by no means approve of it, fo far as it is fometimes carried. I have known three young foxes chopped in a furze-brake in one day, with-out any fport; a wanton deſtruction of foxes fcarcely anfwering the purpofe of blood, fince that blood does hounds moſt good which is moſt dearly earned. Such fportfmen richly deferve

* Yet how many foxes owe their lives to the too great eager-nefs of their purfuers.

blank days; and, without doubt, they often meet with them. Mobbing a fox, indeed, is only allowable when hounds are not likely to be a match for him without it. One would almoſt be inclined to think blood as neceſſary to the men as to the hounds, ſince the beſt chace is flat, unleſs you kill the fox. When you aſk a fox-hunter what ſport he has had, and he replies, it was *good*, I think the next queſtion generally is, *Did your hounds kill?* If he ſhould ſay they did *not*, the converſation ends; but if, on the contrary, he tell you that they did, you then aſk a hundred queſtions, and ſeldom are ſatisfied, till he has related every particular of the chace.

When there is ſnow on the ground, foxes will lie at earth.* Should your hounds be in want of blood, it will at that time be eaſy to dig one to turn out before them, when the weather breaks; but I ſeem to have forgotten a new doctrine which I lately heard, that blood is not neceſſary to a pack of fox-hounds. If *you* alſo ſhould have taken up that opinion, I have only to wiſh, that the goodneſs of your hounds may prevent

* Earths ſhould be watched when there is ſnow upon the ground, for foxes then will lie at earth. Thoſe who are inclined to deſtroy them can track them in, and may dig them out.

you

you from changing it, or from knowing how far it may be erroneous.*

Before you have been long a fox-hunter, I expect to hear you talk of the ill luck which so frequently attends this diverfion. I can affure you it has provoked me often, and has made *even a parfon fwear*. It was but the other day we experienced an extraordinary inftance of it. We found, at the fame inftant, a brace of foxes in the fame cover, and they both broke at the oppofite ends of it; the hounds foon got together, and went off very well with one of them; yet, notwithftanding this, fuch was our ill luck, that, though the hunted fox took a circle of feveral miles, he, at laft, croffed the line of the other fox, the heel of which we hunted back to the cover from whence we came: it is true, we perceived that our fcent worfted, and were going to ftop the hounds; but the going off of a white froft deceived us alfo in that.

Many a fox have I known loft, by running into houfes and ftables. It is not long fince my hounds loft one, when hunting in the New Fo-

---

* Thofe who can fuppofe the killing of a fox to be of no fervice to a pack of fox-hounds, may fuppofe, perhaps, that it does them hurt. It is going but one ftep further.

reft :

reſt : after having tried the country round, they had given him up, and were gotten home ; when in rode a farmer, full gallop, with news of the fox : he had found him, he ſaid, in his ſtable, and had ſhut him in. The hounds returned ; the fox, however, ſtood but a little while, as he was quite *run up* before.

Some years ago, my hounds running a fox acroſs an open country, in a thick fog, the fox ſcarcely out of view, three of the leading hounds diſappeared all of a ſudden, and the whipper-in, luckily, was near enough to ſee it happen. They fell into a dry well, near an hundred feet deep : they and the fox remained there together till the next day ; when, with the greateſt difficulty, we got them all four out.

Another time, having run a fox a burſt of an hour and quarter, the ſevereſt I ever remember, the hounds, at laſt, got up to him by the ſide of a river, where he had ſtaid for them. One hound ſeized him as he was ſwimming acroſs, and they both went down together. The hound came up again, but the fox appeared no more. By means of a boat and a long pole we got the fox out. Had he not been ſeen to ſink, he would hardly have been tried for *under water*, and, without doubt, we ſhould have wondered what had become of him.

Now

Now we are in the chapter of accidents, I muſt mention another, that lately happened to me on croſſing a river, to draw a cover on the other ſide of it. The river Stower frequently overflows its banks, and is alſo very rapid and very dangerous. The flood that morning, tho' ſudden, was extenſive. The neighbouring meadows were all laid under water, and only the tops of the hedges appeared. There were poſts to direct us to the bridge, but we had a great length of water to paſs before we could get at it; it was, beſides, ſo deep that our horſes almoſt ſwam, and the ſhorteſt legged horſes and longeſt legged riders were worſt off. The hounds daſhed in as uſual, and were immediately carried by the rapidity of the current, a long way down the ſtream. The huntſman was far behind them; and as he could advance but ſlowly, he was conſtrained to ſee his hounds wear themſelves out in an uſeleſs contention with the current, from their efforts to get to him. It was a ſhocking ſcene! many of the hounds, when they reached the ſhore, had entirely loſt the uſe of their limbs, for it froze and the cold was intolerable. Some lay as if they were dead, and others reeled, as if they had been drinking wine. Our ill luck was not yet complete; the weakeſt hounds, or ſuch as were moſt affected by the cold, we now ſaw entangled in the tops of the hedges, and heard their lamentations. Well-known tongues! and ſuch as I

had

had never before heard without pleafure. It was
painful to fee their diftrefs, and not know how to
relieve it. A number of people, by this time,
were affembled near the river fide, but there was
not one amongft them that would venture in.
However, a guinea, at laft, tempted one man to
fetch out a hound that was entangled in a bufh,
and would otherwife have perifhed. Two hounds
remained upon a hedge all night, and though at
a confiderable diftance from each other when
we left them, yet they got together afterwards,
and the next morning, when the flood abated,
they were found clofely clafping each other:
without doubt, it was the friendly warmth they
afforded each other that kept both alive. We
loft but one hound by this unlucky expedition,
but could not fave any of our terriers. They
were feen to fink, their ftrength not being fufficient to refift the two enemies they had to en-
counter, powerful, when combined—the feverity
of the cold, and the rapidity of the ftream.

You afk, at what time you fhould leave off
hunting? It is a queftion which I know not
how to anfwer, as it depends as much on the
quantity of game that you have, as on the country that you hunt. However, in my opinion, no
good country fhould be hunted after February;
nor fhould there be any hunting at all after
March. Spring hunting is fad deftrudion of
foxes:

foxes: in one week you may deſtroy as many as would have ſhewn you ſport for a whole ſeaſon. We killed a bitch-fox one morning, with ſeven young ones, which were all alive: I can aſſure you we miſſed them very much the next year, and had many blank days, which we needed not to have had, but through our own fault. I ſhould tell you, this notable feat was performed, *lite-rally*, on the *firſt of April.* If you will hunt late in the ſeaſon, you ſhould, at leaſt, leave your terriers behind you. I hate to kill any ani-mal out of ſeaſon. A hen-pheaſant, with egg, I have heard, is famous eating; yet I can aſſure you I never mean to taſte it; and the hunting a bitch-fox, big with young, appears to me cruel and unnatural. A gentleman of my acquaint-ance, who killed moſt of his foxes at this ſeaſon, was humorouſly called, *midwife to the foxes.*

Are not the foxes heads, which are ſo pom-pouſly expoſed to view, often prejudicial to ſport in fox-hunting? How many foxes are wantonly deſtroyed, without the leaſt ſervice to the hounds or ſport to the maſter, that the huntſman may ſay he has killed ſo many brace! How many are digged out and killed, when blood is not wanted, for no better reaſon!—foxes that another day, perhaps, the earths well ſtopped, might have run hours, and died gallantly at laſt. I remember myſelf to have ſeen a pack of hounds kill three

in

in one day; and though the laſt ran to ground, and the hounds had killed two before, therefore could not be ſuppoſed to be in want of blood, the fox was digged out and killed upon the earth. However, it anſwered one purpoſe you would little expect—it put a clergyman preſent in mind that he had *a corpſe to bury*, which otherwiſe had been forgotten.

I ſhould have leſs objection to the number of foxes heads that are to be ſeen againſt every kennel door, did it aſcertain with more preciſion the goodneſs of the hounds; which may more juſtly be known from the few foxes they loſe than from the number that they kill. When you inquire after a pack of fox-hounds, whether they be good or not, and are told they ſeldom miſs a fox, your mind is perfectly ſatisfied about them, and you inquire no farther: it is not always ſo, when you are told the number of foxes they have killed. If you aſk a Frenchman what age he is of, he will tell you that he is *in good health.*—In like manner, when I am aſked how many brace of foxes my hounds have killed, I feel myſelf inclined to ſay the hounds *are good*; an anſwer which, in my opinion, goes more immediately to the ſpirit of the queſtion than any other that I could give; ſince the number of foxes heads is, at beſt, but a preſumptive proof of the goodneſs of the hounds. In a country neighbouring to

U

mine

mine foxes are difficult to be killed, and not eafy to be found; and the gentlemen who hunt that country are very well contented when they kill a dozen brace of foxes in a feafon. My hounds kill double that number ; ought it to be inferred from thence that they are twice as good ?

All countries are not equally favourable to hounds : I hunt in three, all as different as it is poffible to be ; and the fame hounds that behave well in one, fometimes appear to behave indifferently in another. Were the moft famous pack, therefore, to change their good country for the bad one I here allude to, though, without doubt, they would behave well, they certainly would meet with lefs fuccefs than they are at prefent ufed to : our cold flinty hills would foon convince them, that the difference of ftrength between one fox and another—the difference of goodnefs betwixt one hound and another — are yet but trifles, when compared with the more material difference of a good fcenting country and a bad one.*

I can

* Great inequality of fcent is very unfavourable to hounds. In heathy countries the fcent always lies, yet I have remarked that the many roads that crofs them, and the many inclofures of poor land that furround them, render hunting in fuch coun-tries at times very difficult to hounds ; the fudden change from a good fcent to a bad one puzzles their nofes and confufes their under-

I can hardly think you serious when you afk me, if the fame hounds can hunt both hare and fox; however, thus far you may affure yourfelf, that it cannot be done with any degree of confiftency. As to your other queftion of hunting the hounds yourfelf, *that* is an undertaking which, if you will follow my advice, you will let alone. It is your opinion, I find, that a gentleman might make the beft huntfman; I have no doubt that he would, if he chofe the trouble of it. I do not think there is any profeffion, trade, or occupation, to which a good education would not be of fervice; and hunting, notwithftanding it is at prefent exercifed by fuch as have not had an education, might, without doubt, be carried on much better by thofe that have. I will venture to fay, fewer faults would then be committed; nor would the fame faults be committed over and over again as they now are. Huntfmen never reafon by analogy, nor are they much benefited by experience.

Having told you, in a former letter, what a huntfman ought to be, the following, which I can affure you is a true copy, will fhew you, in fome inftances at leaft, what he ought not to be.

underftandings; and many of them, without doubt, follow the fcent unwillingly, owing to the little credit that they give to it. In my opinion, therefore, a fcent which is lefs good, but more equal, is more favourable to hounds.

SIR,

SIR,

YOUR's I received the 24th of this prefent Inftant June and at your requeft I will give you an impartial account of my man John G——'s Cha,acter. He is a Shoemaker or Cordwainer which you pleafe to call it by trade and now in our Town he is following the Carding Bufinefs for every one that wants him he ferved his Time at a Town called Brigftock in Northamptonfhire and from thence in great Addington Journeyman to this Occupation as before mentioned and ufed to come to my houfe and found by riding my horfes to water that he rode a horfe pretty well which was not at all miftaken for he rides a horfe well and he looks after a kennel of hounds very well and finds a hare very weil he hath no judgment in hunting a pack of hounds now tho he rides well he dont with difcretion for he dont know how to make the moft of a horfe but a very harey ftarey fellow will ride over a church if in his way tho may prevent the leap by having a gap within ten yards of him and if you are not in the field with him yourfelf when you are a hunting to tutor him about riding he will kill all the horfes you have in the ftable in one month for he hath killed downright and lamed fo that will never be fit for ufe no more than five horfes fince he hath hunted my hounds which is two years and upwards he can talk no dog language to a hound he hath no voice he fpeaks to a hound juft as if

his

his head were in a drum nor neither does he know
how to draw a hound when they are at a lofs no
more than a child of two years old as to his ho-
nefty I always found him honeft till about a week
ago and have found him difhoneft now for about
a week ago I fent my fervant that I have now to
fetch fome fheep's feet from Mr. Stanjan of
Higham Ferrers where G——— ufed to go for feet
and I always fend my money by my man that
brings the feet and Stanjan told my man that I
have now that I owed him money for feet and
when the boy came home he told me and I went
to Stanjan and when I found the truth of the matter G——— had kept my money in his hands and
had never paid Stanjan he had been along with
me once for a letter in order for his character to
give him one but I told him I could not give
him a good one fo I would not write at all G———
is a very great drunkard cant keep a penny in his
pocket a fad notorious lyar if you fend him upon
an errand a mile or two from Uppingham he will
get drunk ftay all day and never come home while
the middle of the night or fuch time as he knows
his mafter is in bed he can nor will not keep any
fecret neither hath he fo much wit as other people
for the fellow is half a fool for if you would have
bufinefs done with expedition if he once gets out
of the town or fight of you fhall fee him no more
while the next morning he ferves me fo and fo
you muft expect the fame if you hire him I ufe

U 3

you

you juft as I would be ufed myfelf if I defired a
character of you of a fervant that I had defigned
to hire of yours as to let you know the truth of
every thing about him.

I am Sir

Your moft humble fervant to command

**** ******

P. S.

He takes good care of his horfes with good
looking after him as to the dreffing 'em but if you
dont take care he will fill the manger full of corn
fo that he will cloy the horfes and ruin the whole
ftable of horfes.

  Great Addington

 June the 28th 1734.

LETTER XXIII.

I TOLD you, I believe, at the beginning of our correspondence, that I disliked bag-foxes; I shall now tell you what my objections to them are:—the scent of them is *different* from that of other foxes; it is *too good*, and makes hounds idle; besides, in the manner in which they generally are turned out, it makes hounds very wild. They seldom fail to know what you are going about before you begin; and, if often used to hunt bag-foxes, will become riotous enough to run any thing. A fox that has been confined long in a small place, and carried out afterwards in a sack, many miles perhaps, his own ordure hanging about him, must needs stink extravagantly. You are also to add to this account, that he most probably is weakened for want of his natural food and usual exercise; his spirit broken by despair, and his limbs stiffened by confinement; he then is turned out on open ground without any point to go to: he runs down the wind, it is true, but he is so much at a loss all the while, that he loses a deal of time in not knowing what to do; while the hounds, who have no occasion to hunt, pursue as closely as if they were tied to

 him.

him. I remember once to have hunted a bag-fox with a gentleman, who not thinking thefe advantages enough, poured a whole bottle of *anifeed* on the fox's back : I cannot fay that I could have hunted the fox, but I affure you I could very eafily have hunted the *anifeed*. Is it to be expected, that the fame hounds will have patience to hunt a cold fcent the next day o'er greafy fallows, through flocks of fheep, or on ftony roads? However capable they may be of doing it, I fhould much doubt their giving themfelves the trouble. If, notwithflanding thefe objections, you ftill chufe to turn one out, turn him into a *fmall* cover, give him what time you judge neceffary, and lay on your hounds as quietly as you can ; and, if it be poffible, let them think they find him.— If you turn out a fox for blood, I fhould, in that cafe, prefer the turning him into a *large* cover, firft drawing it well to prevent a change. The hounds fhould then find him themfelves, and the fooner he is killed the better. Fifteen or twenty minutes is as long as I fhould ever wifh a bag-fox to run that is defigned for blood—the hounds fhould then go home.

Bag-foxes always run down the wind; fuch fportfmen, therefore, as chufe to turn them out, may at the fame time chufe what country they fhall run. Foxes that are found do not follow this rule invariably. Strong earths and large

covers

covers are great inducements, and it is no incon-
fiderable wind that will keep foxes from them.
A gentleman, who never hunts, being on a vifit
to a friend of his in the country, who hunts a
great deal, heard him talk frequently of *bag-foxes*;
as he was unwilling to betray his ignorance, his
difcretion and curiofity kept him for fome time
in fufpenfe; till, at laft, he could not refrain from
afking " what kind of animal *a bag-fox* was ?—
and if it was not " *a fpecies of fox peculiar to that
country ?*

A pack of hounds having run a fox to ground
immediately after they had found him, he was
digged and turned out again; and that the operation of turning him out might be better performed, the mafter of the hounds undertook it
himfelf. You will hardly believe me when I tell
you, that he forgot the place where he turned
him out, and they never once hit upon the fcent.

If you breed up cubs, you will find a fox-
court neceffary: they fhould be kept there till
they are large enough to take care of themfelves.
It ought to be open at the top and walled in: I
need not tell you that it muft be every way well
fecured, and particularly the floor of it, which
muft be either bricked or paved. A few boards
fitted to the corners will alfo be of ufe to fhelter
and to hide them. Foxes ought to be kept very
clean,

clean, and have plenty of fresh water; birds and rabbits are their best food; horse-flesh might give them the mange, for they are subject to this disorder.—I remember a remarkable instance of it. Going out to course, I met the whipper-in returning from exercising his horses, and asked him if he had found any hares?—No, Sir, he replied, but I have caught a fox.—I saw him sunning himself under a hedge, and finding he could not run, I drove him up into a corner, got off my horse, and took him up, but he is since dead.—I found him at the place he directed me to, and he was indeed a curiosity; he had not a single hair on his brush, and very few on his body.

I have kept foxes too long; I also have turned them out too young: the safest way, I believe, will be to avoid either extreme. When cubs are bred in an earth near you, if you add two or three to the number, it is not improbable that the old fox will take care of them: of this you may be certain—that if they live they will be good foxes, for the others will shew them the country. Those which you turn into an earth should be regularly fed; if they should be once neglected, it is probable they will forsake the place, wander away, and die for want of food. When the cubs leave the earth, (which they may soon do) your gamekeeper should throw food for them in parts of the cover where it may be most easy for them

to find it; and when he knows their haunt, he
fhould continue to feed them there: nothing deftroys fo much the breed of foxes as buying them
to turn out, unlefs care be taken of them afterwards.

Your country being extenfive, probably it may
not be all equally good; it may be worth your
while, therefore, to remove fome of the cubs
from one part of it into the other; it is what I
frequently do myfelf, and find it anfwer.* A
fox-court is of great ufe; it fhould be airy, or I
cannot advife you to keep them long in it. I
turned out one year ten brace of cubs, moft of
which, by being kept till they were tainted before
they were turned out, were found dead in the
covers, with fcarcely any hair upon them; whilft
a brace, which had made their efcape by making
a hole in the fack in which they were brought,
lived and fhewed excellent fport. Should the

* Though turned out foxes may fometimes anfwer the purpofe of entering young hounds, yet they feldom fhew any diverfion; few of thofe I have turned into my woods have I
ever feen again: befides, the turning out of foxes, and alarming
the neighbourhood, may *haften* their deftruction. Foxes will
be plentiful enough where traps are not fet to deftroy them;
fhould they do any injury to the farmer, make fatisfaction for
it; encourage the neighbouring gamekeepers to preferve them
by paying them handfomely for every litter of cubs that they
take care of for you: if you act in this manner you may not
have occafion to turn any out.

cubs

cubs be large, you may turn them out immediately: a large earth will be beſt for that purpoſe,
where they ought to be regularly fed with rabbits, birds, or ſheeps henges, which ever you can
moſt conveniently get. I believe, when a fox is
once tainted, he never recovers. The weather
being remarkably hot, thoſe which I kept in my
fox-court (and it, at that time, was a very cloſe
one) all died, one after the other, of the ſame
diſorder.

Where rabbits are plentiful, nature will ſoon
teach your cubs how to catch the young ones;
and till that period of abundance arrives it may
be neceſſary to provide food for them.* Where
game is ſcarce wet weather will be moſt favourable to them; they can then live on beetles, chaffers, worms, &c. which they will find great plenty
of. I think the morning is the beſt time to turn
them out; if turned out in the evening they will
be likely to ramble, but if turned out early, and
fed on the earth, there is little doubt of their remaining there.† I alſo recommend to you, to

____

* If a ſheep die, let it be carried to the earth, and it will afford the cubs food for ſome time.

† A more certain method, perhaps, might be to pale in
part of a copſe which has an earth in it. It might be
well ſtocked with rabbits, the young ones of which the
cubs would ſoon learn to catch. You might have meuſes in
the pale, and let them out when capable of getting their own
food.

turn

turn them into large covers and ſtrong earths; out of ſmall earths they are more liable to be ſtolen, and from ſmall covers are more likely to ſtray. Your game-keeper, at this ſeaſon of the year, having little to do, may feed and take care of them. When you ſtop any of theſe earths, remember to have them opened again ; as, I have reaſon to think, I loſt ſome young foxes one year by not doing it. For your own ſatisfaction, put a private mark on every fox which you turn out, that you may know him again. Your cubs, though they may get off from the covers where they were bred, when hunted, will ſeldom fail to return to them.

Gentlemen who buy foxes, do great injury to fox-hunting : they encourage the robbing of neighbouring hunts; in which caſe, without doubt, the receiver is as bad as the thief.—It is the intereſt of every fox-hunter to be cautious how he behaves in this particular : indeed, I believe moſt gentlemen are; and it may be eaſy to retaliate on ſuch as are not.——I am told, that in ſome hunts it is the conſtant employment of one perſon to watch the earths at the breeding time, to prevent the cubs from being ſtolen. Furze-covers cannot be too much encouraged for that reaſon, for there they are ſafe. They have alſo other advantages attending them ;—they are certain places to find in ;—Foxes cannot break from them unſeen ;—

nor

nor are you fo liable to change as in other covers.*

Acquainted as I am with your fentiments, it would be needlefs to defire you to be cautious how you buy foxes. The price fome men pay for them might well encourage the robbing of every hunt in the kingdom, their own not accepted.—But you defpife the *foi difant* gentleman who receives them, more than the poor thief who takes them.—Some gentlemen afk no queftions, and flatter themfelves they have found out that convenient *mezzo termino* for the eafy accommodation of their confciences.

With refpect to the digging of foxes you run to ground; what I myfelf have obferved in that bufinefs, I will endeavour to recollect. My people ufually, I think, follow the hole, except when the earth is large, and the terriers have fixed the fox in an angle of it; for they then find it a more expeditious method to fink a pit as near to

* A fox, when preffed by hounds, will feldom go into a *furze-brake*. Rabbits, which are the fox's favourite food, may alfo be encouraged *there*, and yet do little damage. Were they fuffered to eftablifh themfelves in your woods, it would be difficult to deftroy them afterwards. Thus far I object to them as a farmer; I object to them, alfo, as a fox-hunter; fince nothing is more prejudicial to the breeding of foxes, than difturbing your woods, late in the feafon, to deftroy the rabbits.

him

him as they can. You fhould always keep a terrier
in at the fox, for if you do not, he not only may
move, but alfo, in loofe ground, may dig himfelf
further in. In digging, you fhould keep room
enough ; and care fhould be taken not to throw
the earth where you may have it to move again.
In following the hole, the fureft way not to lofe
it, is to keep below it.——When your hounds
are in want of blood, ftop all the holes, left the
fox fhould bolt out unfeen. It caufes no fmall
confufion, when this happens. The hounds are
difperfed about, and afleep in different places ;
the horfes are often at a confiderable diftance ;
and many a fox, by taking advantage of the moment, has faved his life.

If hounds want blood, and have had a long run,
it is the beft way, without doubt, to kill the fox
upon the earth; but if they have not run long; if it
be eafy to dig out the fox ; and the cover be fuch a
one as they are not likely to change in ; it is better
for the hounds to turn him out upon the earth, and
let them work for him. It is the blood that will do
them moft good, and may be ferviceable to the
hounds, to the horfes, and to yourfelf :—digging
a fox is cold work, and may require a gallop afterwards to warm you all again. Before you do
this, if there be any other earths in the cover, they
fhould be ftopped, left the fox fhould go to
ground again.

 Let

Let your huntfman try all around, and let him be perfectly fatisfied that the fox is not gone on, before you try an earth; for want of this precaution, I dug three hours to a terrier that lay all the time at a rabbit: there was another circumftance which I am not likely to forget,—" *that I had* " *twenty miles to ride home afterwards.*" A fox fometimes runs over an earth, and does not go into it; he fometimes goes in and does not ftay; he may find it too hot, and may not like the company that he meets with there: I make no doubt that he has good reafons for every thing he does, though we are not always acquainted with them.

Huntfmen, when they get near the fox, will fometimes put a hound in to draw him. This is however a cruel operation, and feldom anfwers any other purpofe than to occafion the dog a bad bite, the foxes head generally being towards him; befides, a few minutes digging will render it unneceffary. If you let the fox firft feize your whip, the hound will draw him more readily.*

You fhould not encourage badgers in your woods; they make ftrong earths, which will be ex-

---

* You may draw a fox by fixing a piece of whipcord made into a noofe to the end of a ftick; which, when the fox feizes, you may draw him out by.

penfive

penſive and troubleſome to you if you do ſtop; or fatal to your ſport if you do not. You, without doubt, remember an old Oxford toaſt,

> Hounds ſtout, and horſes healthy,
> Earths well ſtopp'd, and foxes plenty.

All certainly very deſirable to a fox-hunter; yet I apprehend the *earths ſtopped* to be the moſt neceſſary, for the others, without *that*, would be uſeleſs. Beſides, I am not certain that earths are the ſafeſt places for foxes to breed in; for frequently, when poachers cannot dig them, they will catch the young foxes in trenches, dug at the mouth of the hole, which I believe they call *turning* them. A few large earths near to your houſe are certainly deſirable, as they will draw the foxes thither, and, after a long day, will ſometimes bring you home.

If foxes ſhould have been bred in an earth which you think unſafe, you had better ſtink them out: *that*, or indeed any diſturbance at the mouth of the hole, will make the old one carry them off to another place.

In open countries, foxes, when they are much diſturbed, will lie at earth. If you have difficulty in finding, ſtinking the earths will ſometimes produce them again. The method which I uſe to

X

ſtink

ftink an earth is as follows:—three pounds of
fulphur, and one pound of aſſafœtida are boiled up
together ; matches are then made of brown pa-
per, and lighted in the holes, which are afterwards ſtopped very cloſe.—Earths, that are not
uſed by badgers, may be ſtopped early, which will
anſwer the fame purpoſe ; but where badgers frequent, it would be uſeleſs, for they would open
them again.

Badgers may be caught alive in facks, placed
at the mouth of the hole ; fetting traps for them
would be dangerous, as you might catch your
foxes alſo.   They may be caught by ftinking them
out of a great earth, and afterwards following them
to a fmaller one, and digging them.

Your country requires a good terrier ; I fhould
prefer the black or white terrier ; fome there are
fo like a fox, that awkward people frequently
miſtake one for the other.   If you like terriers to
run with your pack, large ones, at times, are uſeful ; but in an earth, they do but little good, as
they cannot always get up to a fox.   You had
better not enter a young terrier at a badger :—
young terriers have not the art of ſhifting like old
ones ; and, fhould they be good for any thing,
moſt probably will go up boldly to him at once,
and get themfelves moſt terribly bitten ; for this
reaſon you fhould enter them at young foxes,

2　　　when

when you can. Before I quit this fubject, I muft mention an extraordinary inftance of fagacity in a bitch-fox, that was digged out of an earth with four young ones, and brought in a fack upwards of twenty miles to a gentleman in my neighbour-hood, to be turned out the next day before his hounds. This fox, weak as fhe muft have been, ran in a ftrait line back again to her own country, croffed two rivers, and was at laft killed near to the earth fhe was digged out of the day before.— Foxes that are bred in cliffs near the fea, feldom are known to ramble any great diftance from them; and fportfmen, who know the country where this fox was turned out, will tell you, that there is not the leaft reafon to think that fhe could have any knowledge of it.

Befides the digging of foxes, by which method many young ones are taken, and old ones de-ftroyed; traps, &c. too often are fatal to them. Farmers for their lambs, (which, by the bye, few foxes ever kill) gentlemen for their game, and old women for their poultry, are their inveterate enemies. I muft, however, give an inftance of civility I once met with from a farmer.—The hounds had found, and were running hard; the farmer came up in high fpirits, and faid, " I hope, " Sir, you will kill him; he has done me much " damage lately; he carried away all my ducks " laft week :—I would not *gin* him though—too

" good

" good a fportfman for that."—So much for the honeft farmer.———

In the country where I live moft of the gentlemen are fportfmen; and even thofe who are not, fhew every kind of attention to thofe who are; I am forry it is otherwife with you : and that your old gouty neighbour fhould deftroy your foxes, I muft own, concerns me. I know fome gentlemen, who, when a neighbour had deftroyed all their foxes, and thereby prevented them from purfuing a favourite amufement, loaded a cart with fpaniels, and went all together and deftroyed his pheafants. I think they might have called this, very properly, *lex talionis*, and it had the defired effect ; for as the gentleman did not think it prudent to fight them *all*, he took the wifer method, he made peace with them. He gave an order that no more foxes fhould be deftroyed, and they never afterwards killed any of his pheafants.

LET-

LETTER XXIV.

I AM now, my friend, about to take leave of you; and at the fame time that I give repofe to you, let me intreat you to fhew the fame favour to your hounds and horfes. It is now the breeding feafon, a proper time, in my opinion, to leave off hunting; fince it is more likely to be your fervants amufement, than your's; and is always to the prejudice of two noble animals, which we fportfmen are bound in gratitude to take care of.

After a long and tirefome winter, furely the horfe deferves fome repofe. Let him then enjoy his fhort-lived liberty; and as his feet are the parts which fuffer moft, turn him out into a foft pafture. Some there are, who difapprove of grafs, faying, that when a horfe is in good order, the turning him out undoes it all again.—It certainly does.—Yet at the fame time, I believe, that no horfe can be frefh in his limbs, or will laft you long without it.—Can ftanding in a hot ftable do him any good?—and can hard exercife, particularly in the fummer, be of any advantage to him? Is it not foft ground and long reft that will beft

X 3

refrefh

refrefh his limbs, while the night air, and morning dews will invigorate his body ?—Some never
phyfic their hunters; only obferving, when they
firft take them up from grafs, to work them
gently: fome turn out their's all the year. It is
not unufual for fuch as follow the latter method,
to phyfic their horfes at grafs; they then are taken
up, well fed, and properly exercifed to get them
into order; this done, they are turned out for a
few hours every day when they are not ridden.
The pafture fhould be dry, and fhould have but
little grafs; there they will ftretch their limbs,
and cool their bodies, and will take as much exercife as is neceffary for them. I have remarked,
that thus treated they catch fewer colds, have the
ufe of their limbs more freely, and are lefs liable
to lamenefs than other horfes. Another advantage attends this method, which, in the horfes
you ride yourfelf, you will allow to be very material :—your horfe, when once he is in order, will
require lefs ftrong exercife than grooms generally
give their horfes; and his mouth, in all probability, will not be the worfe for it.

The Earl of Pembroke, in his Military Equi-
tation, is, I find, of the fame opinion; he tells
us,—" It is of the greateft confequence for horfes
" to be kept clean, regularly fed, and as regularly
" exercifed: but whoever choofes to ride in the
" way of eafe and pleafure, without any fatigue
" on

" on horfeback, or, in fhort, does not like to carry
" his horfe, inftead of his horfe's carrying him,
" muft not fuffer his horfe to be exercifed by a
" groom ; ftanding up on his ftirrups, holding
" himfelf on by means of the reins, and thereby
" hanging his whole dead weight on the horfe's
" mouth, to the entire deftruction of all that is
" good, fafe, or pleafant about the animal."——
And in another place he fays,—" Horfes fhould
" be turned loofe fomewhere, or walked about
" every day, when they do not work, particularly
" after hard exercife : fwelled legs, phyfic, &c.
" will be faved by thefe means, and many diftem-
" pers avoided." He alfo obferves that, " it is
" a matter of the greateft confequence, though
" few attend to it, to feed horfes according to
" their work. When the work is hard, food
" fhould be in plenty ; when it is otherwife, the
" food fhould be diminifhed immediately, the hay
" particularly."

I have no doubt that the noble author is perfectly right in thefe obfervations : I am alfo of
opinion that a handful or two of clean wheaten
ftraw, chopped fmall, and mixed with their corn,
would be of great fervice to your horfes, provided
that you have intereft enough with your groom
to prevail on him to give it them.

X 4

Such

Such of my horfes as are phyficked at grafs, have two dofes given them when they are turned out, and three more before they are taken up.— Grafs phyfic is of fo mild a kind, that you will not find this quantity too much; nor have I ever known an accident happen from it, although it has been given in very indifferent weather. I fhould tell you, that my horfes are always taken in, the firft night after their phyfic, though the printed directions, I believe, do not require it. Such horfes as are full of humours fhould be phyficked at houfe, fince they may require ftronger dofes than grafs phyfic will admit of, which, I think more proper to prevent humours, than to remove them. The only ufe I know in phyficking a horfe that does not appear to want it, is to prevent, if poffible, his requiring it at a time when you cannot fo well fpare him—I mean the hunting feafon: fhould an accident of this kind happen, Stibium's balls, of which I fend you the receipt, will be found of ufe :

Crocus Metallorum, levigated 2 ozs.
Stibium's ditto   -   -   2
Flour of brimftone   -   1
Caftile foap   -   -   1
Liquorice powder   -   1
Honey, q. f. to make it into a pafte.

A ball

A ball of one ounce weight is to be given for three mornings fucceffively.—The horfe muft be kept fafting for two hours after he has taken it : he then may have a feed of corn, and foon after that moderate exercife. The fame fhould be repeated four days afterwards.—Thefe balls purify the blood, and operate on the body by infenfible perfpiration.

I frequently give nitre to fuch of my hunters as are not turned out to grafs :—it cools their bodies, and is of fervice to them. It may be given either in their water, or in their corn ; I fometimes give an ounce in each.

To fuch of my horfes as are thick winded, and fuch as carry but little flefh, I give *carrots*. In many ftables they are given *at the time of feeding*, in the corn ; I prefer giving them at any other time—for it is a food which horfes are fo fond of, that if by any accident you fhould omit the *carrots*, I doubt if they would eat the *corn*, readily, without them.

I think you are perfectly in the right to mount your people well ; there is no good œconomy in giving them bad horfes ; they take no care of them, but wear them out as foon as they can, that they may have others.

The

The queſtion you aſk me about ſhoeing, I am unable to anſwer. Yet I am of opinion, that horſes ſhould be ſhod with more or leſs iron, according as the country where they hunt requires; but in this, a good farrier will beſt direct you. Nothing certainly is more neceſſary to a horſe than to be well ſhod. The ſhoe ſhould be a proper one, and it ſhould fit his foot. Farriers are but too apt to make the foot fit the ſhoe.* My groom carries a falſe ſhoe, which juſt ſerves to ſave a horſe's hoof, when he loſes a ſhoe, till it can be put on again. In ſome countries you ſee them loaded with ſaws, hatchets, &c. I am

---

* I venture to give the following rules on ſhoeing—in a ſhort and deciſive manner, as founded on the ſtricteſt anatomical and mechanical principles, laid down by the beſt maſters. The ſhoe ſhould be flat, and not turned up at the heel, or reach beyond *that*, or the *toe :* but the middle part ſhould extend rather beyond the outward edge of the hoof, that the hoof may not be contracted; the outward part of which may be pared to bring it down to an even ſurface, to fit it for the fixing on of the ſhoe.— If the foot be too long, the *toe* may be pared, or raſped down ; which, in many caſes, may even be neceſſary to preſerve the proper ſhape of the hoof, and bring the foot to a ſtroke, and bearing, the moſt natural and advantageous. Neither the horny-ſole, or frog, (meant by nature for the guard of the foot, and ſafety of the horſe) are, upon any account, to be pared or cut away. The ſmall, looſe, ragged parts, that at times appear, ſhould be cut off with a pen-knife ; but that deſtructive inſtrument called the *butteris*, which, in the hands of ſtubborn ignorance, has done more injury to the feet of horſes than all the chaces of the world, ſhould be baniſhed for ever.

glad

glad that the country in which I hunt does not require them. In the book I have juſt quoted, you will find the ſhoeing of horſes treated of very much at large. I beg leave, therefore, if you want further information on that head, to refer you to it.

Having declared my diſapprobation of ſummer hunting, on account of the horſes, I muſt add, that I am not leſs an enemy to it on account of the hounds alſo; *they*, I think, ſhould have ſome time allowed them to recover the ſtrains and bruiſes of many a painful chace; and their diet, in which the adding to their ſtrength has been, perhaps, too much conſidered, ſhould now be altered. No more fleſh ſhould they now eat; but in its ſtead, ſhould have their bodies cooled, with whey, greens, and thin meat: without this precaution, the mange, moſt probably, would be the immediate conſequence of hot weather, perhaps madneſs:—direful malady!

As a country life has been recommended in all ages, not leſs for the contentment of the mind, than the health of the body, it is no wonder that hunting ſhould be conſidered by ſo many as a neceſſary part of it, ſince nothing conduces more to both: a great genius has told us, that it is

Better to hunt in fields for health unbought,
Than fee the doctor for a nauſeous draught.

With

With regard to its peaceful ſtate, according to a modern poet :

No fierce unruly ſenate threatens here,
No axe, or ſcaffold to the view appear,
No envy, diſappointment, and deſpair.

And for the contentment which is ſuppoſed to accompany a country life, we have not only the beſt authority of our own time to ſupport it, but even that of the beſt poets of the Auguſtan age. Virgil ſurely felt what he wrote, when he ſaid, " *O fortuna nimium ſuati ſi bona norint, agricolæ* ;" and Horace's famous ode, " *Beatus ille qui procul* " *negotiis*," ſeems not leſs to come from the heart of a man, who is generally allowed to have had a perfect knowledge of mankind; and this, even at the time when he was the favourite of the greateſt emperor, and in the midſt of all the magnificence of the greateſt city in the world.

The elegant Pliny alſo, in his epiſtle to Minutius Fundanus, which is admirably tranſlated by the Earl of Orrery, whilſt he arraigns the life he leads at Rome, ſpeaks with a kind of rapture of a country life: " Welcome," ſays he, " thou " life of integrity and virtue! welcome ſweet " and innocent amuſement! Thou that art al " moſt preferable to buſineſs and employment of " every kind." And it was *here*, we are told,

that

that the great Bacon experienced his trueſt feli-
city. With regard to the *Otium cum dignitate*, ſo
much recommended, no one, I believe, under-
ſtands the true meaning of it better, or practiſes
it more ſuccefsfully than you do.

A rural life, I think, is better ſuited to this
kingdom than to any other ; becauſe the country
in England affords pleaſures and amuſements unknown in other countries; and becauſe its rival,
our Engliſh town (or ton) life, perhaps is a lefs
pleaſant one than may be found elſewhere. If
this, upon a nice inveſtigation of the matter,
ſhould appear to be ſtrictly true, the concluſion that
would neceſſarily reſult from it might prove more
than I mean it ſhould ; therefore we will drop the
ſubject. Should you, however, differ from me
in opinion of your town life, and diſapprove what
I have ſaid concerning it, you may excuſe me, if
you pleaſe, as you would a lawyer, who does the
beſt he can for the party for whom he is retained.
I think you will alſo excuſe any expreſſions I may
have uſed, which may not be current *here* ; if you
find, as I verily believe you may, that I have not
made uſe of a French word, but when I could not
have expreſſed my meaning ſo well by an Engliſh
one :—it is only an unneceſſary and affected application of a foreign language, that in my opinion, is deſerving of cenſure.

To

To thofe who may think the danger which attends upon hunting a great objection to the purfuit of it, I muft beg leave to obferve, that the accidents which are occafioned by it are very few. I will venture to fay, that more bad accidents happen to fhooters in one year than to thofe who follow hounds in feven. You will remind me, perhaps, of the death of T——k, and the fall of D——t; but do accidents never happen on the road? the moft famous huntfman and boldeft rider of his time, after having hunted a pack of hounds for feveral years unhurt, loft his life at laft by a fall from his horfe as he was returning home. A furgeon of my acquaintance has affured me, that in thirty years practice, in a fporting country, he had not once an opportunity of fetting a bone for a fportfman, though ten packs of hounds were kept in the neighbourhood. This gentleman furely muft have been much out of luck, or hunting cannot be fo dangerous as it is thought. Befides, they are all timid animals that we purfue, nor is there any danger in attacking them: they are not like the furious beaft of the *Gevaudan*, which, as a French author informs us, an army of 20,000 French chaffeurs went out in vain to kill.

If my time in writing to you fhould not have been fo well employed as it might have been, *you* at leaft will not find that fault with it; nor fhall
I repeat

I repent of having employed it in this manner,
unlefs it were more certain than it is, that it would
have been employed *better*. It is true, thefe letters are longer than I firft intended they fhould
be: they would have been *fhorter* could I have
beftowed *more time* upon them. Some technical
words have crept in imperceptibly, and with them
fome expreffions better fuited to the field than to
the clofet: nor is it neceffary, perhaps, that a
fportfman, when he is writing to a fportfman,
fhould make excufes for them. In fome of my
letters you have found great variety of matter;
the variety of queftions contained in *your's* made
it fometimes unavoidable. I know there muft be
fome tautology; it fcarcely is poffible to remember all that has been faid in former letters; let
that difficulty, if you pleafe, excufe the fault. I
fear there may be fome contradictions for the fame
reafon, and there may be many exceptions. I truft
them all to your candour, nor can they be in better hands. I hope you will not find that I have
at different times given different opinions; but
fhould that be the cafe, without doubt you will
follow the opinion which coincides moft with your
own. If on any points I have differed from great
authorities, I am forry for it; I have never hunted
with thofe who are looked up to as the great mafters of this fcience; and when I differ from them
it is without defign. Other methods, doubtlefs,
there are, to make the keeping of hounds much

more

more expensive, which, as I do not practise myself, I shall not recommend to you;—treated after
the manner here described they will kill foxes, and
shew you sport. I have answered all your questions as concisely as I was able, and it has been
my constant endeavour to say no more than I
thought the subject required. The time may
come, when more experienced sportsmen and
abler pens may do it greater justice; till then,
accept the observations that I have made: take
them, read them, try them. There was a time
when I should readily have received the information they give, imperfect as it may be; for experience is ever a slow teacher, and I have had no
other. With regard to books, Somervile is the
only author whom I have found of any use on
this subject; you will admire the poet and esteem
the man; yet I am not certain that you will be
always satisfied with the lessons of the huntsman.
Proud of the authority, I have quoted from him
as often as it would suit your purpose; and, for
your sake, have I braved the evident disadvantage
that attended it. I wish this elegant poet had
answered all your questions; you then would
have received but one letter from me—to refer
you to him. That no other writer should have
followed his steps may thus, I think, be accounted
for: those gentlemen who make a profession of
writing live chiefly in town, consequently cannot
be supposed to know much of hunting: and

those

thofe who do know any thing of it are either
fervants that cannot write, or country gentlemen
who will not give themfelves the trouble. However, I have met with fome curious remarks which
I cannot help communicating to you. One author
tells us, that " courfing is more agreeable than
" hunting, *becaufe it is fooner over :*"—" that a
" terrier *is a mungrel greyhound :*"—and " *that
" dogs have often coughs from eating fifh bones.*"

Another (a French author) advifes us to give a
horfe, after hunting, " a foup made of bread and
" wine, and an onion."—I fear an Englifh groom
would eat the onion and drink the wine.

The fame author has alfo a very particular
method of catching rabbits, which you will pleafe
to take in his own words. he calls it—*Chaffe du
lapin à l'ecreviffe.* " *Cette chaffe convient aux per-
" fonnes qui ne veulent employer ni furets ni armes à
" feu : on tend des poches d'une extrémité d'un ter-
" rier, et à l'autre on gliffe une ecreviffe ; cet animal
" arrive peu-a-peu au fond de la retraite du lapin,
" le pique, s'y attache avec tant de force, que le
" quadrupede eft obligé de fuir, emportant avec lui
" fon ennemi, et vient fe faire prendre dans le filet
" qu'on lui a tendu à l'ouverture du terrier. Cette
" chaffe demande beaucoup de patience : les opera-
" tions de l'ecreviffe font lentes, mais auffi elles font
" quelque fois plus fures que celles du furet.*"

Y

This

This gentleman's *fingular* method of hunting rabbits *with a lobfter*, reminds me of a method harlequin * has of killing hares, not lefs ingenious, with *Spanifh fnuff*. Brighella tells him, that the hares eat up all his mafter's green wheat, and that he knows not how to kill them; " no- " thing more eafy," replies harlequin—" I will " engage to kill them *all* with two pennyworth " of fnuff. They come in the night, you fay, " to feed on the green wheat; ftrew a little fnuff " over the field before they come, it will fet " them all a fneezing; nobody will be by to fay " *God blefs you*, and, of courfe, they will all die."

I believe, during our prefent correfpondence, that I have twice quoted the Encyclopedie with fome degree of ridicule; I muft, notwithftanding, beg leave to fay, in juftice to myfelf, that I have great efteem for that valuable work.

On opening a very large book called the *Gentleman's Recreation*, I met with the following remarkable paffage :—" Many have written of this " fubject, as well the antients as moderns, yet " but few of our countrymen to any purpofe; " and had one all the authors on this fubject, " (as indeed on any other) there would be more

* The harlequin of the Italian theatre, whofe *tongue* is at liberty as well as his *heels*.

" trouble

" trouble to pafs by than to retain; moft books
" being fuller of words than matter, and of that
" which is for the moft part very erroneous."—
All who have written on the fubject of hunting
feem to agree in this at leaft, to fpeak indifferently
of one another.

You have obferved in one of your letters, that
I do not always follow my own rules; and, as a
proof of it, you have remarked that many of my
hounds are oddly named:—I cannot deny the
charge. I leave a great deal to my huntfman;
but if you aim at perfection, leave as little as you
can help to your's. It is eafier, I believe, in
every inftance, to know what is right than it is to
follow it; but if the rules I have given be good,
what does it fignify to you whether I follow them
or not? A country fellow ufed to call every di-
recting poft he faw a *doctor*. He was afked, why
he called them fo? " Why, mafter," faid he, " I
" never fee them but they put me in mind of the
" parfon of our parifh, who conftantly points
" out a road to us he does not follow himfelf."

If I can add to the amufement of fuch as follow this diverfion, I fhall not think my time has
been ill employed; and if the rules which are
here given may any ways tend to preferve that
friendly animal the hound from one unneceffary
lafh, I fhall not think they have been written in

Y 2

vain.

vain.* It never was my expectation to be able to send you a complete treatise :—*Thoughts upon Hunting, in a series of familiar Letters,* were all I proposed to myself the pleasure of sending :—the trouble I have taken in writing them entitles me to some indulgence ; nor did I, therefore, whilst I endeavour to render them of use, stand in any fear of criticism. Yet if any man, as idle as I have already declared myself to be, should take the trouble to criticise these letters, tell him this :—An acquaintance of mine, who had bestowed much time in improving his place whenever he heard it found fault with, " asked where " the critic lived? whether he had any place of " his own? whether he had attempted any im- " provements? and concluded with promising *a* " *peep at it.*"—-The gentleman here alluded to had less humility than your humble servant.

* Strangely unfortunate should I think myself, if while I profess to be a friend to dogs, I should prove their bitterest enemy, and if those rules which were intended to lessen, should increase their sufferings; convinced as I am by experience, that a regular system of education is the surest means to render correction unnecessary. Hard is that heart (if any such there be) which can ill use a creature so affectionate and so good; who has renounced his native liberty to associate with man, to whose service his whole life is dedicated : who, sensible of every kindness, is grateful for the smallest favour; while the worst usage cannot estrange his affection, in which he is (beyond all example) constant, faithful, and disinterested; who guards him by night, and amuses him by day, and is, perhaps, the only companion who will not forsake him in adversity.

Take,

Take, therefore, my fentiments in the following
ines :

—————— *Si quid novifti rectius iftis,*
Candidus imperti ; fi non, his utere mecum.

Hor.

Farewell.*

* The fong which was at the end of the firft edition of thefe
letters having been already printed by its author, and thought
too local to be neceffary here, is now omitted.

————————

Note, Page 115, line 21, after *fervice*, add, I
now ufe, inftead of digeftive ointment, a poultice
made of Goulard, as recommended by Arnaud, in
his edition of that treatife, page 203.

AN

ACCOUNT

OF THE MOST CELEBRATED

DOG KENNELS

IN THE

KINGDOM.

Agreeable to the intimation given at the conclu-sion of the second Letter of this Work, the Editor presents the Readers of it with an account of the most celebrated DOG KEN-NELS, *beginning with—*

HIS MAJESTY's, AT ASCOT:

WITH AN EXACT REPRESENTATION OF THE SAME,
BEAUTIFULLY ENGRAVED.

THIS building is situated in the center of Af-cot Heath, just below the hill, about three quarters of a mile north-west of the starting post, and includes in its advantages one of the best situations for the purpose of any in the kingdom.

To

His MAJESTY's Dog Kennel at ASCOT.

Published by J. Wheble, Warwick Square, Dec.r 1 1793.

To the excellence and univerſally admitted ſuperiority of the eſtabliſhment, every inferior conſideration becomes ſubſervient, and the conſtant
ſuperintendance of his Majeſty contributes to the
promiſed attainment of every perfection. The
dwelling houſe of Johnſon, his Majeſty's huntſman, conſtitutes a part of the fabric, and of the
interior parts of this, his Majeſty condeſcends to
make a ſurvey, with the ſame congenial eaſe and
happy affability, as to ſuch parts of the ſtructure
as become more immediately appropriate to public purpoſe. We are well aware the world in general conſider his Majeſty's appearance in the
field as matter of *convenience* or *neceſſity*, and
adopted only as a preſervative of health or a preventative to ill; it becomes the peculiar province
however, of this article, to wipe away ſo ridiculous an idea, and to hold forth the moſt unequivocal aſſurance that there is no ſportſman in the
kingdom who enters more into the minutiæ of
the kennel, or the energy of the chace. His
Majeſty is not only familiar to the names of the
leading hounds in the pack, but frequently ſelects
them in the kennel, as peculiar objects of attention. The ſize of the hounds, the increaſe of
the packs, the diminution of ſtock, the entering
of puppies, or drafting old hounds, are equally
and rationally matters to which his Majeſty attends, though by no means dictatorially; but
once *well informed*, in reply to his inquiries, after·

Y 4

making

making his own obfervations, he moft happily and engagingly fubmits the final arrangements to thofe whofe official province it is to fuperintend the execution.

The hounds confift, in fact, of two packs, which pafs under the denomination of the " old" and the " young hounds," and are alternately brought into ufe in the following way: the great body of old and ftaunch hounds are always felected for fuch deer as are known to be good runners, and conftantly produced in the field when his Majefty meets: to thefe are frequently added three or four couple of young hounds, till the whole have been entered in rotation, and the two packs are, by fuch gradational introduction, enabled to conftitute a kind of confolidation in refpect to abilities, for whatever exigences may enfue or circumftances require.

The

Swinley Lodge, the residence of the Master of His Majesty's Stag Hounds.

Published March 1.st by W. Whible Warwick Square.

*The Refidence of the Mafter of his Majefty's Stag
Hounds being contiguous to the above Building, an
Engraving, equally defcriptive of its Situation,
is alfo annexed, and the following fhort Account,
it is hoped, will not be deemed uninterefting.*

SWINLEY LODGE,

IS fituated upon Afcot Heath, about a mile
fouth-weft of the ftarting poft, furrounded
by hills, and fheltered by lofty trees from fuch
feverity of the elements as is frequently experienced in fituations fo abftracted from rural affo-
ciation. Notwithftanding its fequeftered afpect
and remote erection in the middle of a dreary
heath, it has every internal convenience to render
it happily appropriate to the purpofe for which it
was originally intended. Exclufive of an excellent ruftic manfion, poffeffing the room and
requifites for which our buildings of former cen-
turies are fo eafily diftinguifhable, it has annexed
ranges of excellent ftabling, commodious yards,
domeftic gardens (lefs in the ftile of *ornament*
than *utility*); paddocks applied folely to pafture
for the reception of red deer, as well as various

parcels

parcels of land, diſtinctly divided into the required proportions of meadow and arable, for the
cultivation of ſuch hay and corn of every kind as
may be required upon the premiſes. To theſe
accumulated conveniences may be added the various fiſh ponds, which, with the live ſtock of
every kind produced upon the premiſes, may be
ſaid to conſtitute an aggregate of the moſt luxu-
rious gratification within a fenced circle of ferti-
lity, two miles in circumference, though ſur-
rounded by one of the moſt *barren* ſpots in the
univerſe, producing only *fuel* for the inhabitants
of that and diſtant pariſhes, and *heath* for *brooms,*
by manufacturing which moſt of the neighbouring indigents obtain a livelihood. To this dif-
trict, and its ſurrounding hills, his Majeſty's
herd of red deer appertain ; here they breed, and
being conſtantly fed (like the cattle more do-
meſticate) in the ſeverity of the winter ſeaſon,
they conſider it their home, and become (to thoſe
they are accuſtomed to ſee) much leſs ferocious,
and more aſſociate, than can well be ſuppoſed of
an animal ſo naturally wild, and ſo little ſubject
to a perſonal ſurvey from human viſitants.

The preſent reſident has given a life and ſpirit
to the ſcene that it never poſſeſſed during the official career of either of the two laſt of his prede-
ceſſors, and will ſecure to Lord Sandwich the re-
ſpect of every ſportſman in the kingdom.

DUKE

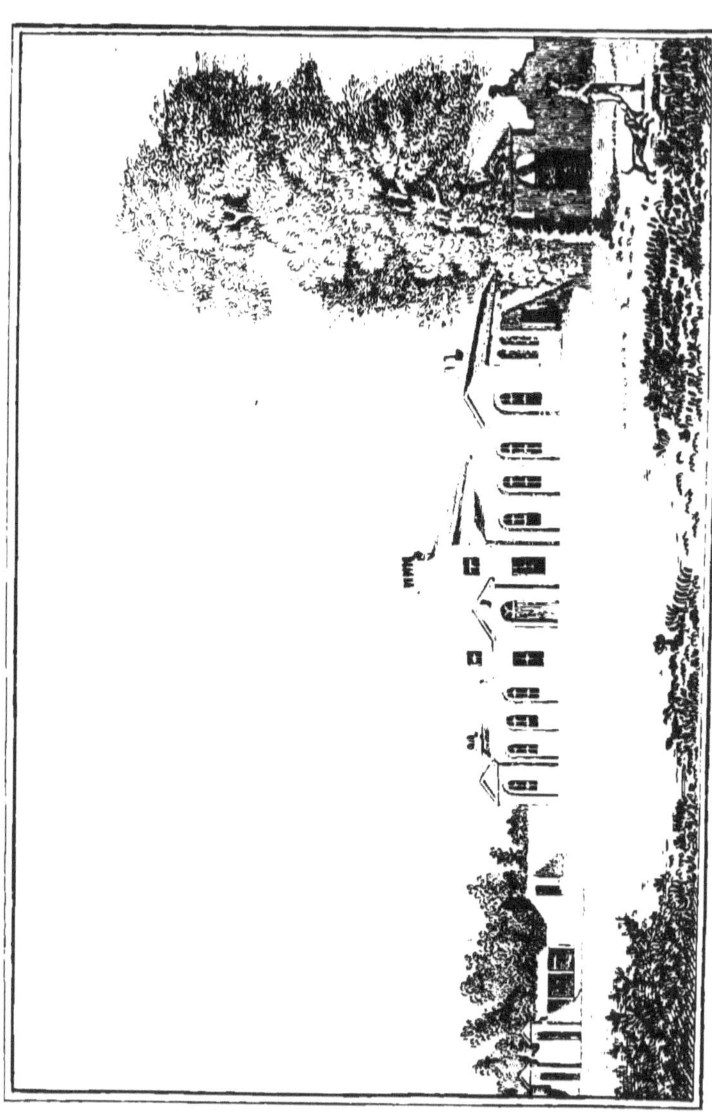

DUKE of RICHMOND's, at GOODWOOD.

THE next that claims attention is the kennel erected by his Grace of Richmond, at Goodwood, in Suffex, and which the engraving annexed is a perfect delineation. To a perfon unacquainted with his Grace, the expenditure of upwards of 10,000 _l._ on a dog kennel might appear a matter of furprize, but to the writer of this, who is no ftranger to his munificence, it appears no more than a common occurrence.

The duke was his own architect and builder: he dug his own flints, burnt his own lime, made his own bricks, and formed the wood-work in his own fhops.

THE DOG KENNEL

Is a place by itfelf in the park, and is a grand object to the beft rooms in the houfe. The front is handfome. The ground is well raifed about it, and turfed. The effect is good.

The dimenfions.—The length is 148 feet, the depth 30; the height, from the crown of the

arches

arches that fupport it, 18 feet on the fides; in the center 28 feet.

The materials are flints, finiſhed at all the angles by a light grey brick, like the Lymington white ſtock.

The diſtribution of the building is into five kennels; two of them 36 by 15—three more 30 by 15; two feeding rooms, 28 by 15. In each there are openings at the top for cold air, and ſtoves to warm the air when too cold. There are fupplies of water, and drains, into a ſtank, as it is called, a depth below, full of rain water. From the furface of this rain water to the rife of the arch, is 11 feet; fo that inconvenience from fmell there is none; and the whole at any time can be cleared off, by drains, to more dependent depths, dung-pits, &c. So that, as an aid to farming, it is not altogether ufclefs.

Round the whole building is a pavement five feet wide, airing yards, places for breeding, &c. &c. making part of each wing.

For the huntſman, and for the whipper-in, there is a parlour, a kitchen, and a ſleeping room for each.

It

It will contain two packs; but at prefent the duke has only fox-hounds. The dogs are reduced from 60 to 40 couple.

Before this building was finifhed, the dogs ufed to be kept at Hannaker and Charlton, and twelve hunters were farmed by an old huntfman, who is now dead. This part of the eftablifhment is farmed no more.

DUKE

DUKE of BEDFORD's, at WOBURN ABBEY.

BY way of introducing what is the more immediate object of our attention, it may be neceffary to flightly notice the other improvements of his Grace—particularly as the engraving which accompanies it, includes the whole of the buildings erected for his fporting. eftablifhment.

The tennis court and riding houfe (with apartments between to drefs in) forms a building 266 feet 8 inches long, and 49 feet 6 inches wide, the whole front of which is ftone: the roof is a flat one, and covered with a compofition of tar, chalk, &c. inftead of lead. There are flues run along the walls, and under the pavement of the tennis court, to keep off the damps: the walls of the infide of the riding houfe are painted in pannels, with high pilaflers, and the ceiling is painted to reprefent a clear fky.

There are two wings of ftables, one of which only is yet fitted up by Mr. Holland, and contains flalls for 36 hunters, with 11 hofpital apartments for fick and lame horfes: there is a

3

fad-

THE DUKE OF BEDFORD'S STABLES, WITH THE NEW TENNIS-COURT & RIDING-HOUSE AT WOBURN ABBEY.

faddle room with glafs-fronted preffes, and flues running along the walls, to keep the faddles dry; two cifterns with hot and cold water, one of which is heated by the fame fire that warms the flues, a pair of jockey fcales, &c.

The dog kennel (efteemed the completeft in England) is 405 feet long, in the center of which ftands the boiling-houfe, with feeding-houfes adjoining, and a granary behind: on the left are divifions for litter, ftraw, eleven apartments for bitches and puppies, with yards to each; eleven ditto for bitches in pup, with yards alfo, and a large divifion for bitches at heat. On the right of the center are apartments for two kennel keepers, two long lodging rooms for the hunting hounds, with flues running along the walls, fpacious yards to each, furnifhed with a fountain in the center for the hounds to drink at, and water cocks iffuing near the pavement, to cleanfe it: adjoining to thefe, are feven hofpitals for fick hounds, with yards to each.

In the front is a large pond, which fupplies the fountains and different cocks in the feveral yards within.

Behind is a large airing ground, flefh-houfe, &c.

The

The huntfman's houfe is a handfome building adjoining.

The forty and feventy couple of working hounds are kept in the kennel.

SIR WILLIAM ROWLEY's, AT TENDER-ING HALL, SUFFOLK.

With a beautiful Reprefentation of the Building, and a Ground Plan of the fame.

NEATNESS and convenience are moſt happily blended together in this compact kennel, and the whole gives no bad fpecimen of the taſte and judgment of the munificent proprietor, who planned it himfelf, without any reference to more fumptuous edifices.

The fituation is to the eaſtward of the noble manfion erected by the late Admiral Sir Joſhua Rowley, father to Sir William, at the diſtance of about half a mile. From near the kitchen garden it has a moſt picturefque and beautiful appearance: from this fpot the view is taken.

The

Perspective View of SIR WILLIAM ROWLEYS DOG KENNEL at Tendring Hall Suffolk

The kennel is placed in a deep valley in the park, a fituation admirably adapted for the purpofe, being equally defended from the cutting eafterly winds, and the heat of the fun in its meridian, by a thick fkirting of park and foreft trees. Not having the advantage of a rivulet to water the courts, that want is amply fupplied by a pump, which, by means of different cocks, turns the water to every part of the premifes.

The entrance to the building is at *a*.

a, Is a paffage, having on the right a coal-houfe, *b*, and on the left, *c*, the feeder's refidence, which is in the convenient cottage ftyle, with a neat bed-chamber over it.

d, Is the boiling houfe, with two coppers at *e*.

f, Is the furnace of a flue, which paffes under the adjoining room, viz.

g, The hunting kennel, or principal lodging room: this room is 20 feet by 18 in the clear, and 18 feet high, paved with flag-ftones. The beds, or benches, which cover almoft the whole area, are of an excellent and original contrivance, being lathed, like fome bedfteads, and all made to fold up with joints, for the convenience of wafhing the floor beneath them. By means of the flue

Z

at

at *f*, this room is heated to any temperature, and the hounds, after fevere chaces, and in wet weather, are rendered dry and comfortable in a much lefs time than they would be by any other means.

h, The kennel, or lodging room for the young hounds. This is of the fame dimenfions as the preceding, and enjoying all the fame conveniences, except the flue, which would here be ufelefs.

i, Several fmall kennels for bitches, previous to gefiation.

k, Several fmall kennels for bitches with young puppies.

l, Paved court to the hunting kennel.

m, Feeding houfe, one half of which is open, the reft under cover.

n, Paved court to the young hounds' kennel.

o, Pump: *p*, *q*, ftone water cifterns.

r, Great grafs yard, for airing the hounds belonging to the hunting kennel, containing about an acre and three quarters.

ſ, ſ, ſ,

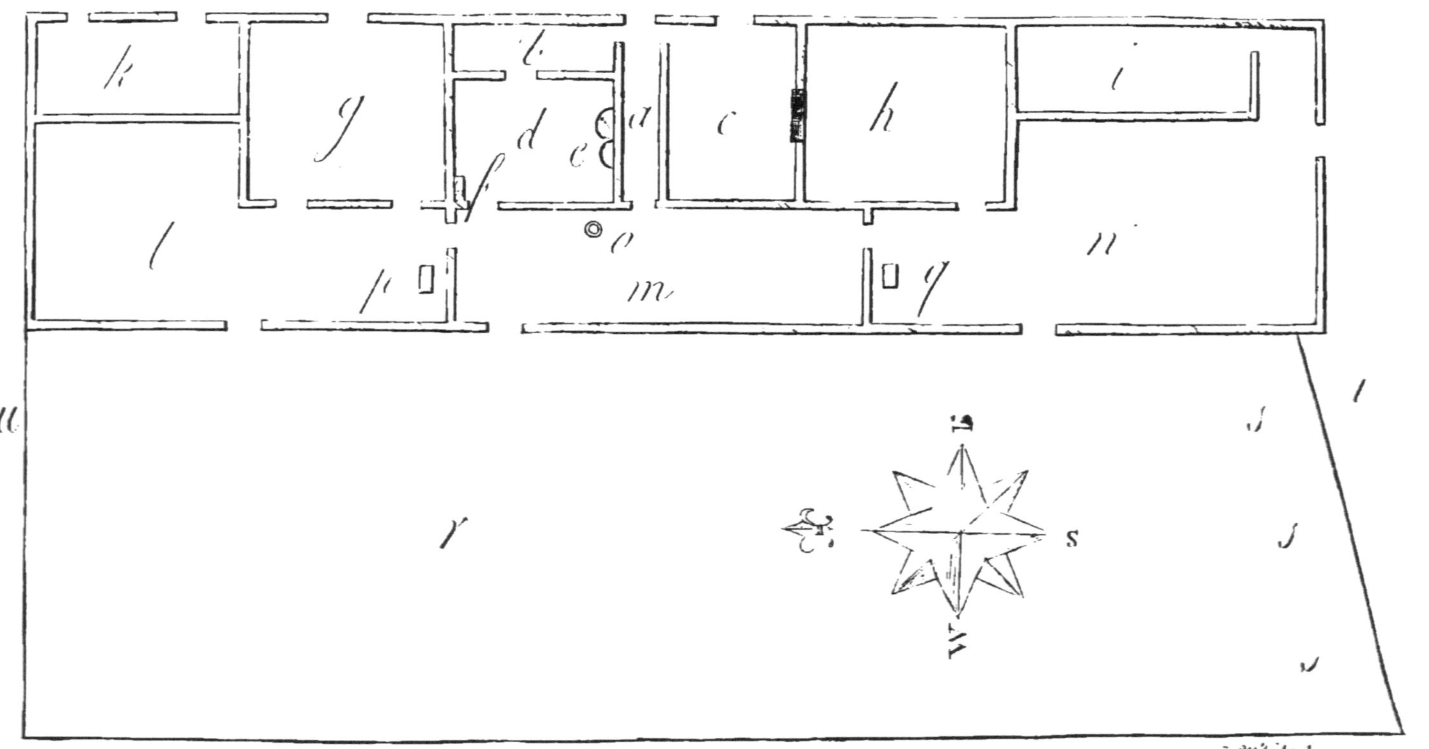

PLAN OF SIR WILLIAM ROWLEY'S DOG KENNEL.

f, f, f, Avenue of lime, chefnut, and other trees in the great grafs yard, forming a moft excellent fhade for the hounds.

t, Grafs yard for the young hounds, containing about one acre and a quarter, with lime, French afh, and other trees, for fhade.—N. B. The fize of the plate would not admit fhewing the boundaries of this yard, without diminifhing the fcale.

u, The park.

☞ To the puppy kennels, 12 in number, and admirably well adapted for the purpofe.

Tendering Hall is beautifully fituated in the parifh of Stoke-by-Nayland, in Suffolk, which is feparated from the county of Effex by the navigable river Stour, which runs from hence to Stratford, Dedham, Maningtree, and Miftley, where it receives veffels of confiderable burthen, and proceeding on about ten miles farther, difcharges itfelf into the ocean at Harwich.

The hunt has been eftablifhed about feven years, and we run no rifk of being contradicted when we fay, that, with regard to the excellence of the hounds, the regulations, and the management of the pack, which confifts of 36 couple,

it

it is inferior to none, of fimilar magnitude, in the kingdom.

Situated on the borders of two counties abounding with excellent covers, and every way well calculated for fox-hunting, the worthy baronet, greatly efteemed by the neighbouring gentry, and beloved by a numerous and refpectable tenantry, proves himfelf a true defcendant of Nimrod; while his lady, in the prime and bloom of life, adorned with every female virtue and accomplifhment, and not lefs efteemed and beloved by all ranks of people than her hufband, frequently enjoys with him the fports of the field, and convinces the world that the moft delicate habits of thinking and acting are not incompatible with being charmed with the mufic of the hounds, the delights of the chace, and the health-giving exercife of equeftrian diverfions.

F I N I S.